Creating Value in the Network Economy

The Harvard Business Review Book Series

Designing and Managing Your Career, Edited by Harry Levinson

Ethics in Practice, Edited with an Introduction by Kenneth R. Andrews

Managing Projects and Programs, With a Preface by Norman R. Augustine

Manage People, Not Personnel, With a Preface by Victor H. Vroom

Revolution in Real Time, With a Preface by William G. McGowan

Strategy, Edited with an Introduction by Cynthia A. Montgomery and Michael E. Porter

Leaders on Leadership, Edited with a Preface by Warren Bennis

Seeking Customers, Edited with an Introduction by Benson P. Shapiro and John J. Sviokla

Keeping Customers, Edited with an Introduction by John J. Sviokla and Benson P. Shapiro

The Learning Imperative, Edited with an Introduction by Robert Howard

The Articulate Executive, With a Preface by Fernando Bartolomé

Differences That Work, Edited with an Introduction by Mary C. Gentile

Reach for the Top, Edited with an Introduction by Nancy A. Nichols

Global Strategies, With a Preface by Percy Barnevik

Command Performance, With a Preface by John E. Martin

Manufacturing Renaissance, Edited with an Introduction by Gary P. Pisano and Robert H. Hayes

The Product Development Challenge, Edited with an Introduction by Kim B. Clark and Steven C. Wheelwright

The Evolving Global Economy, Edited with a Preface by Kenichi Ohmae

Managerial Excellence: McKinsey Award Winners from the *Harvard Business Review*, 1980–1994, Foreword by Rajat Gupta, Preface by Nan Stone

Fast Forward, Edited with an Introduction and Epilogue by James Champy and Nitin Nohria

First Person, Edited with an Introduction by Thomas Teal

The Quest for Loyalty, Edited with an Introduction by Frederick F. Reichheld, Foreword by Scott D. Cook

Seeing Differently, Edited with an Introduction by John Seely Brown

Ultimate Rewards, Edited with an Introduction by Stephen Kerr

Rosabeth Moss Kanter on the Frontiers of Management, by Rosabeth Moss Kanter

Peter Drucker on the Profession of Management, by Peter F. Drucker

On Competition, by Michael E. Porter

The Work of Teams, Edited with an Introduction by Jon R. Katzenbach

Delivering Results, Edited with an Introduction by Dave Ulrich

John P. Kotter on What Leaders Really Do, by John P. Kotter

Creating Value in the Network Economy, Edited with an Introduction by Don Tapscott

Creating Value in the Network Economy

Edited with an Introduction by
Don Tapscott

A Harvard Business Review Book

The *Harvard Business Review* articles in this collection are available as
individual reprints. Discounts apply to quantity purchases. For information
and ordering contact Customer Service, Harvard Business School Publishing,
Boston, MA 02163. Telephone: (617) 783-7500 or (800) 988-0886, 8 A.M.
to 6 P.M. Eastern Time, Monday through Friday. Fax: (617) 783-7555,
24 hours a day.

Library of Congress Cataloging-in-Publication Data

Creating value in the network economy / edited with an introduction by
Don Tapscott.
       p.   cm. — (The Harvard business review book series)
    Includes bibliographical references and index.
    ISBN 0-87584-911-3 (alk. paper)
    1. Information technology—Economic aspects. 2. Electronic
commerce. I. Tapscott, Don, 1947– II. Series.
    HC79.I55 C74 1999
    658.4'038—dc21   98-55293
                                                                  CIP

The paper used in this publication meets the requirements of the American
National Standard for Permanence of Paper for Printed Library Materials
Z39.48-1984.

Contents

Introduction

Don Tapscott

In 1994 Alan Webber, former editorial director of the *Harvard Business Review*, asked, "What's so new about the new economy?" A year later, I took a first crack at answering that question, with my book *The Digital Economy*. I described twelve themes of the new economy and noted that Webber's question is reminiscent of the time when Albert Einstein was monitoring an exam for graduate physics students. One student pointed out that the questions on the exam were the same as those on the previous year's test. "That's okay," Einstein replied. "The answers are different this year."

Over the last half-decade, many managers, academics, consultants, and entrepreneurs have given the same question considerable thought. *Creating Value in the Network Economy* collects recent articles I have chosen from the *Harvard Business Review* that tackle this question from the perspective of value creation. Together they provide a new set of guidelines for business. Managers who understand these guidelines will, I believe, be poised to create successful organizations in the network economy.

The articles are grouped in three categories. First are those having to do with the changing nature of value. The Net provides a new, function-rich, high-capacity, and nearly ubiquitous infrastructure for business. It enables firms to enrich products with information, knowledge, and services for unique competitive advantage. Value propositions and the value chains used to create products and deliver them to market can also become disaggregated, enabling value to be created in radically different ways. The second group of articles moves on, to describe new models of the firm, which appear to be as different from the integrated corporation of the industrial economy as it was from the penultimate, agrarian economy. The third describes how much of what is known about marketing is changing, as new interactive relationships with customers become possible.

1. The Changing Nature of Value

Increasingly the main assets of most companies are intellectual, not physical. Many business leaders and policymakers, including some in the SEC, have suggested that knowledge and other intellectual capital should be measured on balance sheets. They argue that current balance sheets, designed for the old economy, tell us little about the most important assets of companies. Although we can certainly expect a raging debate in the near future on the valuation of intangible assets, the experience of successful firms suggests that knowledge creation and knowledge sharing—on which innovation is dependent—lie at the center of the network economy. Twenty-five years ago, Microsoft had no capital. Today Microsoft is the most valuable corporation in America, with a market capitalization now exceeding GE's. Twenty-five years from now, Microsoft may have no capital, if it loses its capacity to innovate.

KNOWLEDGE-BASED VALUE

Knowledge permeates successful organizations. It resides in network digital documents and in the internetworked minds of knowledge workers. The Net is a new infrastructure for the sharing and management of knowledge within and between firms. It enables the networking of human intellect, know-how, and ingenuity.

Products and services also grow in information content, as they are embedded with technology that allows them to gather and codify knowledge about their creators' users and context. Davis and Botkin, in "The Coming of Knowledge-Based Business," explain this idea, giving the examples of "smart" products, such as a tire that notifies its driver of air pressure and a garment that heats or cools its wearer in response to temperature changes. Such products have new value by virtue of their increased intrinsic knowledge of customer needs and use, and their ability to sense and respond to customer needs.

Products don't need to be "smart"—that is, embedded with semiconductor technology that collects information about the environment and its use—to grow in knowledge content. "Dumb" products, which contain no embedded technology, can do this as well. Consider, for example, a product called "Don Tapscott's Eight-Grain Bread," available at a bakery in my city. The bread has a market of one: me. No one else buys this bread or even knows it exists. Because the bakery has created a system to monitor and customize requests, the bread, in a sense, grows in knowledge. The bread has knowledge about me—my tastes in bread and my diet—all of which I specified when I provided the bakery's computers with my recipe. It also knows when I want bread; I click the bread icon in my kitchen, and the bakery knows, through the Net, that I want bread.

When knowledge is the basis of value creation, work and learning are the same. Knowledge workers, whose "products" often don't exist in the physical world, have a different relationship to their work and their employers, and different expectations about their professional growth. Because knowledge is the crux of competitive advantage, companies need to provide lifelong learning opportunities to employees. Consequently, many progressive companies and private-sector organizations find themselves assuming more responsibility than ever before for employee training and lifelong learning. Motorola University grants degrees, and private-sector educational companies, such as the Virtual University or the PBS Business Channel, are spreading like wildfire. Davis and Botkin argue that education, once the purview of the church, then government, is increasingly falling to business, because having knowledgeable people is the foundation of competitiveness.

Factor in the demographic changes of the last few decades, specifically, the rise of the Net generation—the 80 million youngsters between the ages of two and twenty-two in the United States alone—entering the workforce over the next few years. Children of baby boomers, this generation is the first to come of age in the digital age. My research indicates that the interactive experience enabled by the Net is creating a new youth culture which values independence, innovation, knowledge sharing, and collaboration—all very different values from those of their TV generation parents, who grew up in the age of mass communications, mass production, mass marketing, and hierarchical organizations. Youth today are users, actors, shaping their world, read-ing, authenticating, debating, composing their thoughts. Through these activities this generation is developing the fluency and orientation required for effective innovation and value creation in the new economy.

Consider Michael Furdyk, age sixteen, Toronto. With a network of

colleagues around the world, Furdyk built mydesktop.com (http://
www.mydesktop.com). This Web site receives 20 million hits per
month, making this team of young people perhaps as influential on
the Web as many Fortune 500 companies, national governments, and
media empires. Michael, though talented, is pretty typical of the leaders of his generation. When Michael formally enters the workforce in
a few short years, will firms still try to treat him as a variable cost—the
way they treat labor today? Michael and the bulk of his generation
will no doubt expect to receive a share in the wealth they create.

Fortune magazine's Tom Stewart suggested to me that employees
should be viewed as "investors of intellectual capital." Already, the
majority of shares for many public new-economy companies (such as
Microsoft) were purchased with intellectual capital, not with money.
Employees gave their energy, knowledge, and capacity to innovate
and to create wealth. In exchange, they received stock options and
capital. In the emerging knowledge economy, employees, especially of
Michael's generation, will need to be treated as investors of knowledge, not as costs.

DISAGGREGATION AND REAGGREGATION OF VALUE

Every business or industry is based on a value proposition—value
that is proposed and consumed by customers. The value proposition
contains a number of elements that are aggregated from suppliers and
employees and delivered to customers. A newspaper, for example, is
an aggregated collection of content (news, listings, advertising); context (the physical newspaper, its format, its style); and infrastructure
(printing, physical distribution). These elements originate with employees and other individuals and organizations within the newspaper's value chain. Content comes from large advertisers, reporters,
photographers, people placing classified ads, wire services, editorial
writers, press releases, guest writers, external columnists, and other
syndicated papers. Format and style are developed by layout artists,
software packages, graphic arts suppliers, and others. Infrastructure is
provided by myriad companies and individuals ranging from massive
printing companies to the paper carrier. Publishers have traditionally
bundled these elements into a single, tightly integrated offering—a
value proposition consumed by customers.

However, in the digital economy, these elements can be
disaggregated into their constituent components, changing the value
network and the business model of everyone involved—from content

providers to suppliers to distributors—for the benefit of consumers. As Evans and Wurster explain, a firm's value chain consists of all the activities it performs to produce, design, market, deliver, and support its product. The value chain of companies that supply and buy from one another collectively make up an industry's value chain. At the heart of this chain is information. Having a relationship means that two companies have established certain channels of communication built around personal acquaintance, mutual understanding, trust, shared standards, and, increasingly, some kind of information systems and networking backbone. When this information is carried physically, it follows the linear flow of the value chain. But when unbundled from its physical carriers, the richness and the reach of the information are transformed. When information begins to move in a range of directions, companies can build much more intense, meaningful, and valuable relationships. In the broadcast, one-to-many world, information was communicated as a monologue—from producer to consumer with no interaction. In the network world, information is communicated as a dialogue.

The disaggregation of value means that newspaper readers are freed from having to subscribe to the entire newspaper. With the power of the Net, readers can mix and match content from many different sources, creating their own custom paper. Along the same lines, content providers are encouraged to interact directly with consumers, in effect usurping the newspaper's relationship with its subscribers. New "reintermediaries," as I have called them, can also emerge, packaging digital content in very personalized and customized ways. Reintermediaries create new value between producers and consumers using the Net. All the old functions are still performed, along with many new ones. In addition to altering the entire structure of an industry, disaggregation transforms the source of competitive advantage as well. In the case of newspapers, new value can be found in the transformation from the familiar, one-to-many broadcast model to an interactive model that values dialogue and personalization.

This example is, of course, not just a theory. Such transformation is occurring today in all sectors of the economy. Consequently, managers in all industries—from financial services to auto dealerships—need to examine their existing value propositions or spend time envisioning new proposals that would delight customers. Such proposals can then be disaggregated or deconstructed to determine how, by whom, and under what conditions value can be reaggregated or reconfigured through a new set of partners on the Net.

To take an extreme example, consider how laundry detergent might be enriched by knowledge and services. In the future, the molecular structure of Tide may remain unchanged, but new services may be bundled with Tide that create decisive value and enable Tide to "wash whiter." The Tide box may have a chip in it (costing mere pennies) that interacts with the washing machine, which in turn interacts with home computers and other appliances on the Net. Users of Tide may get access to a suite of services that provide both the user and the washing appliance with instructions for different fabric types, different levels of dirt, different kinds of stains, and so on. In this instance, Procter & Gamble changes from a soap company to a relationship company, delivering value-enriched products to those consumers interested in taking care of clothes, keeping the home clean, and keeping the family healthy. This will surely cause P&G to redefine what business it is in, who its partners should be, and how it markets to and relates to its customers.

In "Exploiting the Virtual Value Chain," Rayport and Sviokla explain how information and services can be added to products. They argue that every business competes in two worlds: a physical world of resources that managers can see and touch (marketplace) and a virtual world made of information (marketspace). The processes for creating value in the two worlds are different. Noting that traditional approaches to the value chain view information as a supporting element of the value-adding process, rather than a source of value itself, the authors argue that managers must focus on the marketspace. Creating value in any stage of a virtual value chain involves a sequence of five activities: gathering, organizing, selecting, synthesizing, and distributing information. Each extract from the flow of information along the virtual value chain can constitute a new product or service, as in the Tide case.

2. Whither the Firm?

Throughout most of the nineties, managers worked hard to flatten their organizations, both to control costs and because network structures perform better than hierarchies under most conditions. However, as the Net enables disaggregation of value and a new division of responsibilities among players, there is growing evidence that the integrated firm itself is being replaced as the most effective model of wealth creation.

Although this may sound like a radical statement, evidence is mounting that new forms of doing business, other than the traditional firm, are emerging—all based on the Internet. As I pointed out in *The Digital Economy*, it was over fifty years ago that economist Ronald Coase asked why firms exist. Why are there groups of people working together under one organizational framework? He wondered why there is no market within the firm. Why is it unprofitable to have each worker, each step in the production process, become an independent buyer and seller? Why doesn't the draftsperson auction his or her services to the engineer? Why is it that the engineer does not sell designs to the highest bidder?

Coase explained that the cost and challenges of information, communication, negotiation, and resolution of transactions among the many parties are prohibitive. He concluded that it makes sense to organize value creation into firms, based on a hierarchical management structure for decision making and the execution of work.

However, as the Internet grows in ubiquity, bandwidth, function, and robustness, a deep, rich information infrastructure is growing in the global economy that makes such negotiations, knowledge sharing, and transactions infinitely easier and faster. As a result, in many industries the traditional firm is being pushed aside by more effective and competitive Internet-based models of value creation. In each of these, the disaggregation of value leads not only to knowledge-rich or service-enhanced products but also to new organizational models which I call the "e-business community" (EBC).

These new organizational forms are networks of suppliers, distributors, commerce providers, and customers that execute substantial business communications and transactions via the Internet and other electronic media. They enable the creation and marketing of unique new value for customers in ways that dramatically reduce time, share risk, and reduce cost. It turns out that the main answer to the question, How do you make money on the Net? is the EBC.

Consider the stock brokerage industry. The old value proposition was that brokers provide clients with access to the stock market, real-time data, information, the ability to execute trades, a secure payments system, and advice on which stocks to buy and sell. The on-line broker E*Trade disaggregated that value proposition into its elements and then, through partners, reaggregated it on the Net. The result is that E*Trade can deliver the old value proposition of the industry at a fraction of the cost. More importantly, new value is created, because customers have direct access to a world of information that previously was the purview of the broker. And from the customer perspective, cost savings are just the beginning. E*Trade is creating a whole new class of customer—the empowered consumer who has cost-effective access to the resources required to control his or her own investment destiny.

EBCs are transforming the rules of competition, inventing new value propositions and mobilizing people and resources to unprecedented levels of performance. EBCs are already beginning to displace traditional firms in sectors ranging from financial services to manufacturing. Managers need to master and implement a new EBC strategy if they intend to compete effectively.

In "The Dawn of the E-Lance Economy," Thomas Malone and Robert Laubacher argue that, within a couple of decades, we will look back on the integrated firm of the twentieth century as a transitional structure that flourished for a relatively brief time in human history. They point to cases indicating that the fundamental unit of the economy is changing from the corporation to the individual. Work activities, rather than being conducted through a stable chain of management, are being conducted autonomously through independent contractors. Such network "e-lancers" join together in fluid and temporary webs to design, product, market, and service goods and services.

Today's merger and acquisition activity provides evidence that the large industrial corporation is still dominant, but Malone and Laubaucher point to other evidence that suggests the devolution of large permanent corporations into flexible temporary networks of individuals. Twenty-five years ago, one in five U.S. workers was employed by a Fortune 500 company. Today the ratio has plummeted to less than one in ten.

The Net is driving all this. The new coordination technologies are enabling us to return to a preindustrial organizational model comprised of tiny businesses—but with one crucial difference. These "microbusinesses," as Malone and Laubaucher define them, can tap into global, networked resources that were once available only to larger companies.

THE VIRTUAL FACTORY

So far I have emphasized the role of digital media in adding value to products through information, knowledge, and services. However, the Net is also becoming the new platform for the manufacturing of things. The illusive virtual factory appears finally to be coming of age with the e-business community. Manufacturing is at last becoming internetworked.

Many have marveled at how Cisco has, seemingly overnight, become a multibillion-dollar leader in the networking industry. Its success provides strong evidence that the EBC is an effective organizational form for product design and manufacturing. The company has created an elaborate web of partners on the Net, including manufacturers, assemblers, distributors, OEMs, strategic partners, standards groups, sales channels, and even competitors. Products are conceived, designed, developed, manufactured, sold, serviced, and enhanced from multiple locations—all on the Web. Cisco transfers its strategic knowledge (customer requirements and company strategy) and product knowledge assets to its EBC partners. In turn Cisco receives system design input and planning knowledge from these partners. With Cisco's active encouragement, participants lubricate the system by freely exchanging knowledge and opinions. On an hourly basis, the Net is the channel for these changes. This community enables dramatically lower cycle times, reduced costs, and fast innovation. Cisco's value network is drenched in intangible value exchanges which create its strategic advantage in the market.

David Upton and Andrew McAfee, in "The Real Virtual Factory," explain that the virtual factory has been a long time coming because traditional systems did not meet three basic requirements. An internetwork must be able to accommodate members whose I/T sophistication varies enormously. It must also cope with partners in both transient and long-term relationships, providing good security. Finally, it must provide a high level of functionality, including letting partners operate programs on one another's computers. Increasingly these requirements are being met through standards-based computing environments gathered in the Net—which is growing in function, security, bandwidth, and reliability. Upton and McAfee show convincingly how companies that cling to the old model of the manufacturing organization, with its closed proprietary systems, will find it increasingly difficult to survive.

DESIGN AND IMPLEMENTATION OF PRODUCTS CONVERGE

When value creation migrates to the Net, the process of product design and development changes as well.

In the old economy, a firm may have conducted market research to spark an innovation or test its viability. Typically a product concept was created, and often a specification was made. The specification led to the implementation of a product, which in turn was manufactured and sold to customers. Implementation began only after a product's concept had been specified in its entirety. For example, a typical road-block to software development projects occurred when the "system spec" was not complete. The time from concept to implementation was usually relatively long. Market needs were viewed as relatively stable. The technology contained in a product had at least a degree of maturity. Competition for the product was somewhat predictable, enabling companies to conduct a "competitive analysis" and to formulate strategies to defeat the competition.

In the digital economy, key aspects of product development and implementation converge. In "Developing Products on Internet Time," Marco Iansiti and Alan MacCormack investigate how product development on the Web is different and how these differences can be extrapolated to other product categories. They note that the market needs that a product is meant to satisfy and the technologies required to satisfy them can change radically—even as the product is under development. In response to such factors, companies have had to modify the traditional development process. For smart companies creating Web-based products, the development process allows designers to define and reshape products well after implementation has begun, incorporating rapidly evolving customer requirements and changing technologies into their designs until the last possible moment a product is introduced into the market.

The new approach has been most successful in the Net environment because of the turbulence and fast pace of change there, but Iansiti and MacCormack argue that the foundations for this approach exist in a wide range of industries where the need for responsiveness is paramount.

Let me add to their insights that most products—from cars to soap—will be infused with information, knowledge, and Net-based services. Most products and services will increasingly have some Net-based component for which merging development and implementation will be critical.

TRUST: THE SINE QUA NON OF THE NETWORK ECONOMY

A million sources for information. Thousands of new products and services weekly. New product categories every day, accompanied with boastful hyperbole. But whom are you going to trust? You purchase that antique book on-line. How do you know you'll receive it? When you're on-line, are you really chatting with a football star or with a mischievous nine-year-old or with a software robot? Knowledge management is critical to success, but how do you share knowledge with people you don't see and have never met? As new forms of retailing, such as on-line auction houses like eBay.com, take off, old mechanisms for authenticating and establishing trust and trustworthiness are proving woefully inadequate. If a physical store defrauds you, there are mechanisms for redress. In the traditional firm, if an employee committed fraud, he was fired. In physical communities, "everybody knows your name"—there is adequate density and interactivity for a sense of community to grow. People notice things that don't seem right. The shopkeeper takes responsibility for snow removal on the sidewalk or for breaking up a fight between a couple of children outside the store. People are unlikely to shoplift because it violates community values—these are consequences that go far beyond legalities. Moreover, the shop's survival is in everyone's interests.

But in the digital marketplace, how do you know you're talking to someone who actually has a Louis XIV chaise to sell? How do you know that when you make payment you'll receive the goods? At eBay, with hundreds of thousands of members buying and selling goods and millions of auctions taking place all the time, there has been only a handful of fraudulent events, violations of trust. Such high standards of trust have been maintained through the establishment of a new series of mechanisms and community norms. Each of these community standards taken alone is probably insufficient to deter criminals, but together they establish a trusting environment.

eBay has deliberately set out to manage trust by taking a number of initiatives to build a genuine community. Members must register and provide some information about themselves before they participate in an auction. People get to know each other, not unlike a physical community. Community values are conveyed loud and clear—that open markets provide fair prices to buyers and sellers, and benefits to all; that most people are fundamentally honest; and that individuals, not eBay, are ultimately responsible for protecting themselves and others against those who might be dishonest. There is also a feedback mechanism that accumulates the results of hundreds of thousands of individual interactions. This digital version of word of mouth means that virtually all sellers have ratings. All bidding histories are available for review. People can always leave some information about themselves behind, and the benefits of doing so outweigh the privacy concerns one might expect. For transactions with unknown parties, there are escrow provisions. Overall, a dozen mechanisms reinforce a culture of honesty and trust that seems to work.

New mechanisms are also emerging within EBCs to establish trusting relationships. In a recent speech, in a country thousands of miles from the Cisco headquarters, I discussed Cisco Systems as an EBC. Cisco develops and manufactures high-performance networking products that link geographically dispersed local and wide-area networks. After my talk, I was approached by a young entrepreneur who told me that his company was part of the Cisco EBC. He had just received a new multimillion-dollar contract to develop a component of a Cisco product. He told me that he really wasn't sure what he was building, yet as a member of the EBC, this young developer gained access to a network of community members, sharing knowledge to ensure that the right product was created and that in turn Cisco's trust in his little company was validated.

The story reminded me of my days developing products for Bell Northern Research in the late 1970s. My group would receive funding for a project with deliverables that were not entirely clear. But the mechanisms for collaboration, control, and shaping the effort existed—in this case, established within the framework of a traditional firm. The bandwidth for rich communication was created by the organization, which enabled trusting relationships between me as a project manager and management. In the case of the young entrepreneur, similar capabilities existed within the Cisco EBC, across many miles, time zones, currencies, and cultures.

In "Trust and the Virtual Organization," Charles Handy discusses this issue of establishing trusting relationships with employees and collaborators in the virtual world. With his hallmark eloquence, he explains how the digital world requires a rethinking of how trusting relationships can be established and maintained. Virtual organizations call for new forms of belonging and new mechanisms for building trust which go beyond conventional notions of control.

He proposes seven rules of trust. It is fascinating to see how most of these have been applied in the eBay example. (Perhaps they read Handy's article.)

Trust is not blind: it needs fairly small groupings in which people know each other well. Trust needs boundaries—define a goal, then leave the worker to get on with it. Trust demands learning and openness to change. Trust is tough—when it turns out to be misplaced, people have to go. Trust needs bonding—the goals of small units must gel with those of larger groups. Trust needs touch. Trust requires leaders.

THE COLLAPSE OF INDUSTRIES

In the old economy, value was created within the context of industrial "sectors," such as retail, financial services, manufacturing, and education. But these old sectors break down in the new economy as value generated in e-business communities transcends sectors. Consequently, many industries are beginning to implode as the walls between them disappear.

For example, what will it mean to be a "retail" company in five years, when there are a billion people on the Net, many of them media-savvy youngsters who have grown up digital? Perhaps every company becomes a retail company in the sense that companies will face considerable pressures to reach out directly to consumers.

What does it mean to be a "financial services" company in a world of digital cash and disaggregated financial services? Money is numbers, currently printed on paper. When money becomes digital, it will be issued in encrypted form onto disk drives, digital wallets, and smart cards. When your customer transfers numbers from her digital wallet to your firm's systems, there may be no bank or credit card company involved. Both of you become a financial services organization in the sense that you are both performing functions previously handled by banks.

What does it mean to be in the educational sector when work and learning become the same activity? Every company will become an "education" company, or it will fail, as Davis and Botkin illustrate. If your company doesn't have plans to establish its own "college," it is probably in trouble. Even the notion of government will blur as the social safety net is delivered through EBCs. Tax dollars go to private companies that perform government functions. Government agencies are involved in helping national companies compete. Parapublic and paraprivate NGOs (nongovernment organizations) do what many governments did in the past, increasingly through the Net. This will go way beyond outsourcing or the privatization of government services. Increasingly, government services and the social safety net will be delivered by various entities, public and private, cooperating in EBCs. What works for business will likely work well to cut costs and create new value propositions for citizens. The result is a blurring of government with other elements of the economy.

What does it mean to be a "manufacturing" company in the new economy? One-third of the cost of a Boeing 777 is software. So Boeing is clearly in the software business, and the new value leader in creating aircraft might be a company with leading-edge software development capabilities, such as Microsoft, EDS, Andersen Consulting, or IBM. A sophisticated aircraft will become, as they say, "a collection of parts flying in formation." The specifications will be shared on the Net with all relevant parties, and the plane will be constructed on a network by youthful knowledge workers of a new generation. Boeing will become a design, networking, project management, and marketing company, working with suppliers and customers to design aircraft in cyberspace.

Airbus Industries is the leader of an EBC that overlaps with traditional sectors such as aerospace, software development, entertainment, electronics, hospitality, and even government, as it is integrated with national governments and defense establishments in many countries. Similarly, Apple Computer is part of an ecosystem that includes hundreds of companies from a wide range of industries, including semiconductors (Motorola), consumer electronics (Sony), telecommunications (Farallon), storage media (IOMEGA), software (Claris), entertainment (Broderbund), photography (Kodak), graphic arts (Image Club), printers (Canon), and resellers (MacWarehouse), to name but a few. The business community also includes customers—for example, school boards that are deeply involved in the specification and testing of Apple products.

This business community is an ecosystem, not unlike ecosystems in the natural world. The notion of business ecosystems was first developed by James Moore in "Predators and Prey: A New Ecology of Competition." He explains how companies in an ecosystem coevolve capabilities around a new innovation: they work cooperatively and competitively to support new products, satisfy customer needs, and eventually incorporate the next round of innovations. It is competition among business ecosystems, not individual companies, that is fueling today's economic transformation and wealth creation. Ecosystems typically evolve through four stages: birth (around an innovation); expansion, in which ecosystem members scale up for maximum market coverage; leadership, in which a compelling vision for the future keeps the various organizations improving their value proposition; and self-renewal, in which continuous innovation brings new ideas to the ecosystem.

If you combine Moore's view of ecosystems with the network economy, the result is the EBC. Business ecosystems are becoming digital ecosystems. Increasingly, the main opportunities to exploit an innovation and bring a new value proposition to market will involve members of a business ecosystem collaborating on a digital infrastructure; that is, an EBC. In this light, Moore's insights are extremely pertinent for managers attempting to create new digital communities. Moore's four stages in the development of a business ecosystem, for example, are helpful in planning to launch, participate in, or change an EBC. Similarly, the notion of coevolution is helpful in planning and implementing an EBC. As Moore points out, managers whose horizons are bounded by traditional industry perspectives will find themselves missing the real challenges and opportunities facing their companies.

3. The Customer in a Network Economy

In the new economy, the gap between producers and consumers is blurring. As highly customized products and services replace mass production, producers must create specific products that are imbued with the knowledge, requirements, and tastes of individual customers. In the new economy, consumers become involved in the actual design process. They can, for example, enter a new car showroom and configure an automobile on the computer screen from a series of choices. Chrysler can produce special-order vehicles in sixteen days. The customer creates the specs and sets in motion the manufacture of a specific customized vehicle. In the old economy, viewers watched the evening network news. In the new economy, a "television viewer" will design a customized news broadcast by highlighting the top ten topics of interest and specifying preferred news sources, editorial commentators, and graphic styles. Moreover, that same viewer will be able to watch that broadcast whenever time permits or the need arises. Every day, and often throughout the day, I receive a publication called "Don Tapscott's Wall Street Journal." The publication is shaped to meet my news and information needs.

In *The Digital Economy* I called this "prosumption"—the production of goods and services by customers. I am the prosumer of "Don Tapscott's Wall Street Journal." I am not just the consumer; I am, in part, the publisher, because I define the end product.

Regis McKenna's article adds several important insights to the idea of prosumption and the convergence of design with development processes. McKenna argues that companies need to involve customers deeply in the product development process through initiating technology-facilitated dialogue. The concept of real-time marketing embraces a number of ideas. Most important to me is that the broadcast mentality that has long dominated marketing needs to be replaced with a dialogue mentality—a willingness to give consumers access to the company and to view their actions and feedback as integral to developing and improving products. Through such interaction, companies can cut through market chaos and establish binding relationships with their customers.

It is clear that power is shifting to customers—not simply because customers have more choice, better information about products and services, and better access to suppliers. It is shifting not even because marketplace friction is disappearing and customers can switch suppliers of say, financial services, with little effort and cost. Instead, consumers of the network world expect relationships that are two-way, one-to-one, and many-to-many; distributed; and highly malleable. The three dynamics discussed above regarding the changing nature of value also shift power to consumers. Customers, not just suppliers, increasingly create value by drenching products with their knowledge; customers can disaggregate value and reaggregate it from multiple suppliers, as in the example of newspapers, enhancing their power; and through infomediation, customers ultimately become markets of one, requiring highly differentiated service and in turn moving the locus of power closer to themselves.

Moreover, consumers are acquiring powerful new shopping and purchasing tools, which likely outweigh the data-mining and database-marketing tools of suppliers. Sometimes called "softbots," "knowbots," or just "bots," software agents are personal assistants owned and controlled by you. They will get to know you, your preferences, and your sense of style. These tireless little workers surf the Net for you day and night, looking for information you've requested; evaluating the veracity of a vendor's marketing message; finding that perfect chocolate chip cookie; evaluating new movies based on your preferences and the opinions of others you trust; comparing sport utility vehicles; organizing your personalized daily newspaper; communicating for you; trying on different types of jeans; and doing other jobs. As Alliance collaborators John MacDonald and Jim Tobin say, "New technologies equip the hunted with better camouflage—perhaps turning the tables completely. The hunter becomes the hunted."[1]

John Hagel and Jeffrey Rayport tackle an interesting side of this shift: the coming battle for customer information. They argue that consumers are going to take ownership of information about themselves and start demanding value in exchange for it. As a result, companies will have to manage their relationships with customers to ensure cost-effective access to this information.

THE END OF THE BRAND IMAGE

All of this emphasizes customer relationships, as opposed to brand images. In addition to the interactive media, there is another powerful force to change the brand: the Net generation.

As consumers, N-geners already have greater disposable income than previous generations of youth. They influence family purchasing like never before. They have greater power in households because of their command of the new media, and they typically have better access to comparative product information on the Net. As they enter the workforce as a massive wave—the largest ever—they will affect consumption and marketing even more profoundly than their boomer parents did.

Because N-geners are used to highly flexible, custom environments which they can influence, they want highly customized services and products. They are as used to having options as they are to breathing. As the song says, they want to "change their minds a thousand times." They want to try everything out for free, meaning that companies will have to give products and services away and find new models for retrieving revenue. They will also want the option to purchase any commodity, such as grocery staples, on-line. The Net is becoming a new medium for sales, support, and service of virtually anything, as tens of millions of Net-savvy purchasers are coming of age.[2]

All this spells trouble for the brand as an image. N-geners will send their smart software agents—which are brand blind—onto the Net to select everything from cookies to cars.

A brand is something that exists in the minds and actions of customers in the market. A trademark is something owned by a company. Brands were established in part as a result of mass communications. Using the one-way broadcast and print media, marketers could convince people through relentless one-way communications to "Just do it!" If you said, "Things go better with Coke" enough times, you could establish the Coca-Cola brand in the market.

The Net generation and the digital media will cause a change in thinking among marketers—away from focusing on brand image and brand equity to thinking about relationships with customers. The Net provides new opportunities to evidence the true value of products and services as well as to create meaningful relationships between providers and customers based on trust. As the power of mass communications declines, replaced by the power of the interactive media and therefore the consumer, brand loyalties will make sense for informed and value-conscious purchasers.

For example, Tide can say that it washes whiter 'til the cows come home, but if it doesn't, media-savvy youthful shoppers will find out. They will go on the Net to examine third-party evaluations or participate in discussion groups to determine who really washes whitest.

It is network information that is bringing value and real benefits to the fore. Grocery shoppers using the Peapod network can ask for all the products in a certain category sorted by different criteria, such as calorie count or nutritional value. The most frequently used sort criteria are cost followed by fat content. Determining the healthiest peanut butter takes seconds. And Kraft's mass-marketing has little impact on the purchasing decision. Good brands will correspond closer to good products. A free market for value is enabled by unmediated access to information. In this environment, products that are undifferentiated in value quickly become commodities.

Even smarter software on the horizon—software agents—will extend this weakening of branding. Rather than trusting the brand, kids may begin to trust their agents. In many areas, trusting your agent will become synonymous with trusting your own experience.

The brand image appears important for now, and mass media will no doubt have some effectiveness for some time to come. The digital world still lacks the superpowerful smart software agents required to bring value and services to the fore. But the axis of belonging is shifting. In marketing, interactivity equals increased power to the consumer to make informed choices and to buy products that deliver real benefits and value over those that do not. The brand will be stronger than ever, but it will be a relationship, not an image.

To stimulate your thinking on this issue, I have chosen two articles. (For some strong insights on the brand, also look at the articles by Evans and Wurster, Rayport and Sviolka, and McKenna.)

Armstrong and Hagel, in "The Real Value of On-Line Communities," point out that businesses have used the Net primarily to showcase their companies, products, and services. Few have gone beyond that to develop communities that directly involve and communicate with customers. They argue that companies that create on-line communities with customers will create loyalty hitherto undreamed of.

In "Making Business Sense of the Internet," Shikhar Ghosh adds helpful insights regarding customer relationships. Companies may decide to master their Internet channel to decrease costs, deliver new value, and build customer loyalty through highly personalized interactions. For example, Staples is creating customized supply catalogs that can run on its customers' intranets. Each catalog contains lists of previously ordered items. Over time, Staples can learn much about its customers, deliver new services based on information that would be hard to deliver in the physical world, and suggest new items based on the customer's purchasing behavior. It could also make recommendations based on the purchasing behaviors of others, like Amazon.com recommends similar books to you after you've made a purchase.

Conventional wisdom says that the Net is a "friction-free" environment where customers can more easily change loyalties to, say, their bank than when switching banks in the physical world. But Ghosh shows that loyalty can be enhanced (and a strong brand established) in the interactive world. When customers choose a company on-line, they may make an investment of their time and attention. It takes time to figure out a site and to personalize it to your needs. A company may change its computer systems to deal effectively with a supplier. The supplier also makes an investment in you, getting to know your behaviors, your interests, your preferences—all of which strengthen loyalty. Trust is developed when sensitive information, such as a credit card number, is protected. Reluctance to abandon what works grows.

Ultimately, Ghosh says, companies can create a customer magnet on-line. Examples include product magnets (like Amazon.com for books); service magnets (Yahoo!); customer segment magnets (Auto-By-Tel); or business model magnets which create a whole new model (eBay). Overall, he argues, most companies need to move beyond having a Web presence to having a Web-based business model for success in a new economy.

Four years ago, when I completed *The Digital Economy,* Netscape was just arriving on the scene to change the Net from an arcane environment for technologists to a tool for the masses. There was much excitement but also much cynicism regarding how important this new medium would be to business and society. Over the last year, the cynics have become fewer, as new companies using new business models have created almost instant value for customers and, in doing so, instant wealth.

The new e-businesses have come to dominate many new and traditional sectors as sectors themselves implode. The market capitalization of Amazon.com is now greater than the combined market caps of competitors Borders and Barnes & Noble. Microsoft is the most valuable corporation in America. Auto-By-Tel and its on-line competitors have overnight captured 20 percent of auto sales. The on-line grocery business will be almost $85 billion by 2005, according to my research. On-line brokers have now captured one-third of retail stock trades. *Forbes'* list of the most wealthy Americans is beginning to read like a who's who of the Net. The top three billionaires are from one company—Microsoft—and Amazon.com's Jeff Bezos and Yahoo!'s Tim Koogle have taken their place in the network economy like the silk-hatted tycoons of the industrial age.

When it comes to creating value in the network economy, questions still outnumber answers. But the evidence is growing. Firms that don't reinvent their business models around the Net will be bypassed and fail. In the year 2020, we are likely to look back and see that companies fell into the categories of those that "got it" and those that didn't.

Notes

1. John MacDonald and Jim Tobin, "Customer Empowerment in the Digital Economy" in *Blueprint to the Digital Economy,* ed. Don Tapscott, Alex Lowy, and David Ticoll (New York: McGraw Hill, 1998).

2. Don Tapscott, *Growing Up Digital: The Rise of the Net Generation* (New York: McGraw Hill, 1998).

PART

I

The Changing Nature of Value

1

The Coming of Knowledge-Based Business

Stan Davis and Jim Botkin

The next wave of economic growth is going to come from knowledge-based businesses. What will those businesses and their products look like?

A tire that notifies the driver of its air pressure and a garment that heats or cools in response to temperature changes are early versions of knowledge-based, or "smart," products already on the market. Diapers that change color when wet and tennis rackets that glow where they strike the ball would be smart versions of other common products.

These products are smart because they filter and interpret information to enable the user to act more effectively. Smart products, created by knowledge-based businesses, can be identified by a variety of characteristics: they are interactive, they become smarter the more you use them, and they can be customized. We will discuss these and other characteristics, but we are sure that many more will become apparent as the knowledge era generates more such products.

Consumers become learners when they use smart products, which both oblige and help them to learn. Businesses will move toward making their offerings smarter because they will profit from doing so. When their customers use those products, they will be engaging in an educational process.

Seeing customers as learners requires a major change in thinking. But over the next two decades, businesses will come to think of their customers as learners and of themselves as educators. They will promote the learning experience for profit, and their customers will profit from that experience.

In the years ahead, people's use of knowledge-based products both as consumers and on the job will be critical to their economic success. The value of a business will be similarly determined: businesses that are based on providing information to customers will do better than those that are not, and businesses that know how to convert information into knowledge will be the most successful.

From Data to Information to Knowledge

Changing technology is driving the next wave of economic growth. To take advantage of that growth, we will have to apply not only new technology but also new thinking. First and foremost will be our ability to understand the shift in the economy from data to information to knowledge.

Data are the basic building blocks of the information economy and of a knowledge-based business. Or, as Robert Lucky, a former director of AT&T Bell Laboratories, says, they are the "unorganized sludge" of the information age. In the early years of this economy, we focused on data that came to us in four particular forms: numbers, words, sounds, and images. What we did with those data—how we processed, stored, or otherwise manipulated them—determined their value.

Information is data that have been arranged into meaningful patterns. Numbers are data; a random number table is information. Similarly, sounds (converted into notes) are data that can be arranged in an infinite number of systems to produce the information we call music. Whether a piece of music becomes the stuff of *knowledge*—whether, that is, it enables those who hear it to learn—depends not only on the composition but also on the skill and purpose of the performer. For a beginning pianist, a halting rendition of a waltz can be a learning experience. The same waltz performed by a virtuoso can be a source of knowledge for his or her audience.

The importance of data as an economic factor first became apparent in the 1950s and 1960s, when room-sized computers made it possible to collect, sort, and store vast amounts of data, which then had to be programmed by users to produce information. With the advent of electronic computers, including the microprocessor and standard software, that process became more sophisticated and more useful, to the point where the information a business produced often became more valuable than the business itself. Computer-generated airline guides and reservation systems such as American Airlines' SABRE are well-known examples of information that often is more profitable than the businesses it was created to serve.

Yield management is another example of how information can enhance or even transform a business. In the airline industry, yield management allows carriers to maximize revenue on a fixed asset by varying prices—which is why there can be 20 different prices for the coach seats on a single flight. In agriculture, yield management can provide benefits for the farmer—and it created a new business for tractor manufacturer Massey Ferguson.

Farmers used to guesstimate the average yield of an entire field, but with Massey Ferguson's yield mapping system they can practice small-scale farming on a large scale and maximize the yield of each square yard in every field. The system links the farmer's tractor to a satellite-based Global Positioning System, which records the latitude, longitude, and yield of every square yard. The traditional harvesting operation does not have to change in any way. The data are automatically sent to the farmer's desktop computer, which generates yield maps showing where variations are above or below target. Armed with this specific information, the farmer can investigate selected areas and pinpoint the reasons for the variations (soil compaction or nutrient imbalance, for example), quantify them in financial terms, and find out if it is economical to implement remedies. Soil sampling, for example, can be much more selective than it is using traditional random methods. Today this knowledge-based system is being used to provide a competitive edge. In the future, it may be worth more than Massey Ferguson's primary business.

As these examples suggest, businesses that generate information often begin as adjuncts to the "real" work of the company, and the information seems nothing more than a by-product of the core business. Over time, however, the importance of the information increases, until the value added by its content outweighs the value of the original business itself.

Now the process of change is about to take place again. As an economy, we are on the cusp of the transition from information to knowledge, with *knowledge* meaning the application and productive use of information.

An intuitive way to appreciate the difference between information and knowledge is to substitute the word *data* every time you see or hear the word *information*. Chances are it won't feel right. A chief information officer, for example, has a very different role and set of responsibilities than a data processor has. Data today are commodities, neither as powerful nor as valuable as the information derived from them. Within a decade, we will feel the same kind of resistance if we try to substitute *information* for *knowledge*, because knowledge will have superseded information just as information has now super-seded data.

The shift from a data to an information economy involved two sequential developments, one technological and the other behavioral. AMR Corporation (the holding company of American Airlines) used its technological expertise to diversify into myriad information activities ranging from handling medical and insurance claims for the Travelers Corporation and Blue Cross Blue Shield to managing the Warsaw airport for the Polish government. Only after technology had led the company into new lines of business did the people involved realize that those businesses would call for different ways of managing and organizing.

The shift from information to knowledge, however, is giving rise to a different phenomenon: awareness of the value of knowledge is exceeding the ability of many businesses to extract it from the goods and services in which it is embedded. How can businesses, for example, extract the knowledge value from a pair of socks, a home mortgage, an electric bill, or a foreign exchange credit? Those that can figure it out will derive as much power and profit as data and information brought in their turn. But to do so, they will have to understand the basic elements of knowledge-based business.

Six Elements of Knowledge-Based Business

We have identified six characteristics of knowledge-based business. Although they are interrelated, not all of them are necessarily present in any one smart product or service. Nevertheless, they provide guidelines on how a mature business can become a knowledge-based business by upgrading its offerings in a way that puts information to productive use.

1. THE MORE YOU USE KNOWLEDGE-BASED OFFERINGS, THE SMARTER THEY GET

The Ritz-Carlton hotel chain is installing a knowledge-based system that tracks customers' preferences and needs and automatically transmits the information worldwide. If a customer in Boston asks for six hypoallergenic pillows, for example, she will find them in her room the next time she checks in to a Ritz-Carlton, whether it is in Boston or Hawaii or Hong Kong. Thus the system has learned more about the customer and can put the new information to productive use. Similarly, credit-card transactions are sources of data, and each customer's monthly bills are information; but when Citibank AAdvantage calls up to inquire about unusual activity on your account, it's putting what it has learned about you to work for both you and the card provider. The system has gotten so smart that it can recognize buying patterns that are out of character for a particular cardholder and may be a sign of fraud.

2. THE MORE YOU USE KNOWLEDGE-BASED OFFERINGS, THE SMARTER *YOU* GET

Some knowledge-based goods and services not only get smarter themselves but also enable their users to learn. Consider CAMS, General Motors' Computer Aided Maintenance System. Designed as a tutor to help novice mechanics diagnose and repair cars, it has evolved into an even more sophisticated system that allows expert mechanics to refine their skills. Now every mechanic can benefit from the combined expertise of all the mechanics on the system.

As recently as 1965, a mechanic who had absorbed 500 pages of repair manuals could fix just about any car on the road. Today that same mechanic would need to have read nearly 500,000 pages of manuals, equivalent to some 300 Manhattan telephone books. Access to CAMS makes mechanics smarter without manuals. While one could claim that the increased knowledge resides in the system and not in any particular person, the fact is that many mechanics are smarter because they now have the experience of all the other mechanics. The system itself continually improves because it is always learning new techniques from the best mechanics. The result, of course, is better service for the customer.

3. KNOWLEDGE-BASED PRODUCTS AND SERVICES ADJUST TO CHANGING CIRCUMSTANCES

A fixed offering is simply not as valuable as one that assesses new situations and modifies itself accordingly. We have long been accustomed to refrigerators that "know" when to defrost. The simple home thermostat that senses a room's temperature and then calls for heating or cooling is another pre-computer-age smart product. When knowledge is built into a tangible product, it might even be built in at the atomic or molecular level, as in chemicals that are engineered to biodegrade when they reach a noxious or dangerous stage. Phase-change materials, or micro-PCMs, are more recent developments that are also independent of computers yet have the ability to adjust. When the cloth of a micro-PCM ski jacket senses cold, it turns warm. The same micro-PCMs can be embedded in car seats, curtains, insulation materials, and wallpaper.

Another new material that adjusts to changing conditions is designed to be applied to glass windows. Cloud Gel, developed by Suntek in Albuquerque, New Mexico, can reflect—or transmit—90% of the sun's rays depending on the temperature or the intensity of the sun. When it's 68 degrees Fahrenheit, for example, a treated window or skylight will let in more warmth, but when it's 71 it will start to bounce radiant heat back into the atmosphere. Each year, some 6 billion square feet of new glass are installed worldwide. If all that glass were coated with this substance, Suntek claims, energy consumption would drop by 17% and more than 1 billion tons of air pollution would be eliminated.

Today, computer chips are routinely built into products, such as the chip in an oven that buzzes when the turkey is done and turns off the heat if the cook doesn't. Other smart products and services tell you how to act. For example, automobile tires tend to lose air, reducing performance and gobbling gas. Goodyear has developed a "smart tire," which contains a microchip that collects and analyzes data about air pressure. Eventually it may be able to flash a message to the dashboard that says, "Low Tire Pressure—Time for a Pit Stop." The first part of the message conveys information; the second, the knowledge component, will tell you what to do. It will be up to you to make the wise move.

4. KNOWLEDGE-BASED BUSINESSES CAN CUSTOMIZE THEIR OFFERINGS

Knowledge-based products and services can determine customers' changing patterns, idiosyncrasies, and specific needs. For example, the telephone companies are working intensively to produce phones with knowledge-based features. Your telephone credit card will soon know which language you want to use when you call a long-distance operator. It will also allow you to create your own distinctive ring so that your best friend knows it's you calling. This new smart service can also recognize your most frequently called numbers not just by number but also by name, so when you pick up the phone and say, "Call my travel agent," the system will know who that is. Voiceprint recognition will soon be a major step in customizing many products and services such as telephone credit cards and may even replace the card itself.

5. KNOWLEDGE-BASED PRODUCTS AND SERVICES HAVE RELATIVELY SHORT LIFE CYCLES

Patent protections on intellectual property are still not nearly as developed as they are on "hard" technologies, so the half-life of proprietary information is short. Consider the foreign exchange advisory services offered by commercial and investment banks. This knowledge is highly specialized, and the products are often customized for corporate clients. Because those products depend on the existence of certain market conditions, their viability is short-lived. Yet because information about the markets is widely disseminated, proprietary products can be copied quickly by competitors. Therefore, to maintain their profits—and their proprietary edge—the banks must constantly upgrade their products. The managerial challenge for those running foreign exchange advisory services is getting their professionals in New York, London, and Tokyo to cooperate so that they can develop the next generation of offerings faster than their competitors can.

6. KNOWLEDGE-BASED BUSINESSES ENABLE CUSTOMERS TO ACT IN REAL TIME

Information becomes more valuable when it can be acted on instantly. AAA Triptiks and TourBooks have long given drivers information about highways, hotels, and hot spots. Automakers are preparing to deliver such information into vehicles electronically, in real time. Not only will drivers be provided with routing services, but the information will also be continually updated with traffic reports displayed on a dashboard screen. It will be up to the driver, of course, to apply the information wisely by taking a suggested detour, waiting out a traffic jam, or stopping at the "best" place for dinner. If the service can be made interactive so that it responds to a motorist's questions, its value will be even greater.

Knowledge-based products can also act in real time. This is what happens when the Otis service agent shows up to fix elevator 8 in a skyscraper and the building manager says nothing is wrong with it: "Yes, but there's going to be," says the service agent, who has just received a call from the elevator, "and I'm here to prevent that." Xerox also provides preventive maintenance for some of its large machines with a built-in modem and a telephone that automatically calls for field service.

Knowledgeburgers and Other Smart Products

Any product or service has the potential to become knowledge based. How, for example, could you turn a hamburger business into a knowledge-based business? Start with some basic hamburger data, including its ingredients and its benefits, such as nutrition, convenience, low price, and tastiness. When the company puts those data into a meaningful pattern, it knows both the menu and the target market. In short, it knows what business it is in.

If this business is truly to become a knowledge-based business, however, in addition to serving tasty, inexpensive food, it must give customers a way to use the nutritional information. Perhaps the calorie and fat content could be calculated and printed out alongside the items on the bill—or even presented before the order is placed—so that customers could make more informed judgments about their meals. One result might be market pressure for more nutritious offerings—in other words, the beginning of a business transformation.

Selecting television programs, to use another example, will likely become a knowledge-based experience, incorporating several of the characteristics we described above. With more than 100 channels to choose from, and 500 to 1,500 on the way, viewers will have to be able to filter and select more effectively than present systems allow. Flipping channels is simply selecting among data. When these choices are organized into lists, whether in a printed version like *TV Guide* or in electronic form on a special channel, they become an information-based product.

If an electronic program guide were interactive, however, with the viewer and the guide getting smarter about each other with use, it would have the potential to become a smart product. But nothing ensures that it will be used as such. If viewers do nothing more than control the speed at which the choices scroll past, then they will be using the guide only to get information. But if they ask the guide for all the comedies televised that week, or all the programs on pollution or cooking fish, they will be elevating the information to knowledge.

The Federal Communications Commission's 1992 decision to allow telephone companies to transmit television programming is making electronic program selection a reality. The fiber optic or wireless digital networks on which this programming will run will not be in place until the end of the century. But when they are, schools and businesses, students and consumers will be able to browse through electronic libraries that offer everything from soap operas and movies to scientific texts and medical files. Using that information wisely will be up to the viewer. The FCC decision will ultimately mean interactive multimedia programming on demand—spawning knowledge-based businesses that we cannot yet imagine.

Billing summaries for credit cards, telephone calls, and the like provide another instance of the opportunities a knowledge-based mindset can open up. American Express was the first to distinguish itself from its competitors by sorting a year's worth of transactions into categories that are useful for tax and business purposes. The individual charges are the data, and the monthly bill is the information; but the billing summary becomes a knowledge tool when it helps the user control travel expenses and prepare tax forms.

Some credit-card companies now provide this summary at year-end for a nominal fee. But why not extend the service with monthly and year-to-date displays as well? Why not offer a menu of alternate variables for displaying the data or, for a one-time fee, organize charges by category instead of by date? New knowledge-based businesses can be built around fee-based services that give customers choices about how they can put information to the most productive use.

Business as Educator

The development of knowledge-based business is a reflection of an even larger transformation occurring in our society. The market for learning is being redefined dramatically to encompass not just formal students but also lifelong learners. A new meaning of education and learning is bursting on the scene.

Learning in agricultural economies is often church led, focuses on children between 7 and 14 years of age, and is sufficient to last all the years of a working life. In industrial economies, learning has been government led, and the age range of students is between 5 and 22. In knowledge economies, the rapid pace of technological change means that learning must be constant and that education must be updated throughout one's working life. People have to increase their learning power to sustain their earning power.

Knowledge is doubling about every seven years, and in technical fields in particular, half of what students learn in their first year of college is obsolete by the time they graduate. In the labor force, the need to keep pace with technological change is felt even more acutely. For companies to remain competitive, and for workers to stay employable, they must continue to learn. This shadow education market is underestimated.

Consumers as a learning segment are also underestimated: they will be the newest and largest learning segment in the twenty-first-century marketplace. As information technologies become so much friendlier and smarter, and as they become intrinsic to more and more products and services, learning will become a by-product (and by-service) of the customers' world. Never before have customers considered themselves learners, and businesses considered themselves educators.

Business, more than government, is instituting the changes in education that are required for the emerging knowledge-based economy. School systems, public and private, are lagging behind the transformation in learning that is evolving outside them, in the private sector at both work and play, with people of all ages. Over the next few decades, the private sector will eclipse the public sector as our predominant educational institution.

2
Strategy and the New Economics of Information

Philip B. Evans and Thomas S. Wurster

A fundamental shift in the economics of information is under way—a shift that is less about any specific new technology than about the fact that a new behavior is reaching critical mass. Millions of people at home and at work are communicating electronically using universal, open standards. This explosion in connectivity is the latest—and, for business strategists, the most important—wave in the information revolution.

Over the past decade, managers have focused on adapting their operating processes to new information technologies. Dramatic as those *operating* changes have been, a more profound transformation of the business landscape lies ahead. Executives—and not just those in high-tech or information companies—will be forced to rethink the *strategic* fundamentals of their businesses. Over the next decade, the new economics of information will precipitate changes in the structure of entire industries and in the ways companies compete.

Early signs of this change are not hard to find. Consider the recent near-demise of Encyclopædia Britannica, one of the strongest and best-known brand names in the world. Since 1990, sales of Britannica's multivolume sets have plummeted by more than 50%. CD-ROMs came from nowhere and devastated the printed encyclopedia business as we traditionally understand it.

How was that possible? The *Encyclopædia Britannica* sells for somewhere in the region of $1,500 to $2,200. An encyclopedia on CD-ROM, such as Microsoft Encarta, sells for around $50. And many people get Encarta for free because it comes with their personal computers or CD-ROM drives. The cost of producing a set of encyclopedias—

printing, binding, and physical distribution—is about $200 to $300. The cost of producing a CD-ROM is about $1.50. This is a spectacular, if small, example of the way information technologies and new competition can disrupt the conventional value proposition of an established business.

Imagine what the people at *Britannica* thought was happening. The editors probably viewed CD-ROMs as nothing more than electronic versions of inferior products. Encarta's content is licensed from the Funk & Wagnalls encyclopedia, which was historically sold in supermarkets. Microsoft merely spruced up that content with public-domain illustrations and movie clips. The way *Britannica's* editors must have seen it, Encarta was not an encyclopedia at all. It was a toy.

Judging from their initial inaction, *Britannica's* executives failed to understand what their customers were really buying. Parents had been buying *Britannica* less for its intellectual content than out of a desire to do the right thing for their children. Today when parents want to "do the right thing," they buy their kids a computer.

The computer, then, is *Britannica's* real competitor. And along with the computer come a dozen CD-ROMs, one of which happens to be—as far as the customer is concerned—a more-or-less perfect substitute for the *Britannica*.

When the threat became obvious, *Britannica* did create a CD-ROM version—but to avoid undercutting the sales force, the company included it free with the printed version and charged $1,000 to anyone buying the CD-ROM by itself. Revenues continued to decline. The best salespeople left. And *Britannica's* owner, a trust controlled by the University of Chicago, finally sold out. Under new management, the company is now trying to rebuild the business around the Internet.

Britannica's downfall is more than a parable about the dangers of complacency. It demonstrates how quickly and drastically the new economics of information can change the rules of competition, allowing new players and substitute products to render obsolete such traditional sources of competitive advantage as a sales force, a supreme brand, and even the world's best content.

When managers hear this story, many respond, "Interesting, but it has nothing to do with *my* business. *Britannica* is in an information business. Thank goodness I'm not." They feel less secure, however, when they learn that the largest chunk of *Britannica's* cost structure was not the editorial content—which constituted only about 5% of costs—but the direct sales force. *Britannica's* vulnerability was due mainly to its dependence on the economics of a different kind of information: the economics of intensive personal selling. Many businesses fit that description, among them automobiles, insurance, real estate, and travel.

Every Business Is an Information Business

In many industries not widely considered information businesses, information actually represents a large percentage of the cost structure. About one-third of the cost of health care in the United States— some $300 billion—is the cost of capturing, storing, and processing such information as patients' records, physicians' notes, test results, and insurance claims.

More fundamentally, information is the glue that holds together the structure of all businesses. A company's value chain consists of all the activities it performs to design, produce, market, deliver, and support its product. The value chains of companies that supply and buy from one another collectively make up an industry's value chain, its particular configuration of competitors, suppliers, distribution channels, and customers.[1]

When we think about a value chain, we tend to visualize a linear flow of physical activities. But the value chain also includes all the information that flows within a company and between a company and its suppliers, its distributors, and its existing or potential customers. Supplier relationships, brand identity, process coordination, customer loyalty, employee loyalty, and switching costs all depend on various kinds of information.

When managers talk about the value of customer relationships, for example, what they really mean is the proprietary information that they have about their customers and that their customers have about the company and its products. Brands, after all, are nothing but the information—real or imagined, intellectual or emotional—that consumers have in their heads about a product. And the tools used to build brands—advertising, promotion, and even shelf space—are themselves information or ways of delivering information.

Similarly, information defines supplier relationships. Having a relationship means that two companies have established certain channels of communication built around personal acquaintance, mutual understanding, shared standards, electronic data interchange (EDI) systems, or synchronized production systems.

In any buyer-seller relationship, information can determine the relative bargaining power of the players. Auto dealers, for example, know the best local prices for a given model. Customers—unless they invest a lot of time shopping around—generally do not. Much of the dealer's margin depends on that *asymmetry* of information.

Not only does information define and constrain the relationship among the various players in a value chain, but in many businesses it also forms the basis for competitive advantage—even when the cost of that information is trivial and the product or service is thoroughly physical. To cite some of the best-known examples, American Airlines for a long time used its control of the SABRE reservation system to achieve higher levels of capacity utilization than its competitors. Wal-Mart has exploited its EDI links with suppliers to increase its inventory turns dramatically. And Nike has masterfully employed advertising, endorsements, and the microsegmentation of its market to transform sneakers into high-priced fashion goods. All three companies compete as much on information as they do on their physical product.

In many ways, then, information and the mechanisms for delivering it stabilize corporate and industry structures and underlie competitive advantage. But the informational components of value are so deeply embedded in the physical value chain that, in some cases, we are just beginning to acknowledge their separate existence.

When information is carried by things—by a salesperson or by a piece of direct mail, for example—it goes where the things go and no further. It is constrained to follow the linear flow of the physical value chain. But once everyone is connected electronically, information can travel by itself. The traditional link between the flow of product-related information and the flow of the product itself, between the economics of information and the economics of things, can be broken. What is truly revolutionary about the explosion in connectivity is the possibility it offers to unbundle information from its physical carrier.

The Trade-Off Between Richness and Reach

Let's back up for a minute to consider why this is such a revolutionary proposition. To the extent that information is embedded in physical modes of delivery, its economics are governed by a basic law: the trade-off between richness and reach. *Reach* simply means the number of people, at home or at work, exchanging information. *Richness* is defined by three aspects of the information itself. The first is *bandwidth*, or the amount of information that can be moved from sender to

Exhibit 2-1   The Traditional Economics of Information

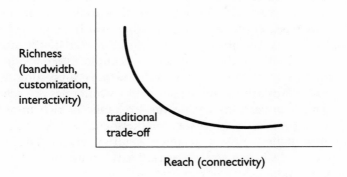

receiver in a given time. Stock quotes are narrowband; a film is broadband. The second aspect is the degree to which the information can be *customized.* For example, an advertisement on television is far less customized than a personal sales pitch but reaches far more people. The third aspect is *interactivity.* Dialogue is possible for a small group, but to reach millions of people the message must be a monologue.

In general, the communication of rich information has required proximity and dedicated channels whose costs or physical constraints have limited the size of the audience to which the information could be sent. Conversely, the communication of information to a large audience has required compromises in bandwidth, customization, and interactivity. (See Exhibit 2-1.) This pervasive trade-off has shaped how companies communicate, collaborate, and conduct transactions internally and with customers, suppliers, and distributors.

A company's marketing mix, for example, is determined by apportioning resources according to this trade-off. A company can embed its message in an advertisement, a piece of customized direct mail, or a personal sales pitch—alternatives increasing in richness but diminishing in reach.

When companies conduct business with one another, the number of parties they deal with is inversely proportional to the richness of the information they need to exchange: Citibank can trade currencies with hundreds of other banks each minute because the data exchange requires little richness; conversely, Wal-Mart has narrowed its reach by moving to fewer and larger long-term supplier contracts to allow a richer coordination of marketing and logistical systems.

Within a corporation, traditional concepts of span of control and hierarchical reporting are predicated on the belief that communication cannot be rich and broad simultaneously. Jobs are structured to channel rich communication among a few people standing in a hierarchical relationship to one another (upward or downward), and broader communication is effected through the indirect routes of the organizational pyramid. Indeed, there is an entire economic theory (pioneered by Ronald H. Coase and Oliver E. Williamson[2]) suggesting that the boundaries of the corporation are set by the economics of exchanging information: organizations enable the exchange of rich information among a narrow, internal group; markets enable the exchange of thinner information among a larger, external group. The point at which one mode becomes less cost-effective than the other determines the boundaries of the corporation.

The trade-off between richness and reach, then, not only governs the old economics of information but also is fundamental to a whole set of premises about how the business world works. And it is precisely this trade-off that is now being blown up.

The rapid emergence of universal technical standards for communication, allowing everybody to communicate with everybody else at essentially zero cost, is a sea change. And it is as much the agreement on standards as the technology itself that is making this change possible. It's easy to get lost in the technical jargon, but the important principle here is that the *same* technical standards underlie all the so-called Net technologies: the *Internet,* which connects everyone; *extranets,* which connect companies to one another; and *intranets,* which connect individuals within companies.

Those emerging open standards and the explosion in the number of people and organizations connected by networks are freeing information from the channels that have been required to exchange it, making those channels unnecessary or uneconomical. Although the standards may not be ideal for any individual application, users are finding that they are good enough for most purposes today. And they are improving exponentially. Over time, organizations and individuals will be able to extend their reach by many orders of magnitude, often with a negligible sacrifice of richness.

Where once a sales force, a system of branches, a printing press, a chain of stores, or a delivery fleet served as formidable barriers to entry because they took years and heavy investment to build, in this new world, they could suddenly become expensive liabilities. New competitors on the Internet will be able to come from nowhere to steal customers. Similarly, the replacement of expensive, proprietary, legacy systems with inexpensive, open extranets will make it easier and cheaper for companies to, for example, bid for supply contracts, join a virtual factory, or form a competing supply chain.

Inside large corporations, the emergence of universal, open standards for exchanging information over intranets fosters cross-functional teams and accelerates the demise of hierarchical structures and their proprietary information systems. (See Exhibit 2-2.)

The Deconstruction of the Value Chain

The changing economics of information threaten to undermine established value chains in many sectors of the economy, requiring virtually every company to rethink its strategy—not incrementally, but fundamentally. What will happen, for instance, to category killers such as Toys "R" Us and Home Depot when a search engine on the Internet gives consumers more choice than any store? What will be the point of having a supplier relationship with General Electric when it posts its purchasing requirements on an Internet bulletin board and entertains bids from anybody inclined to respond? What will happen to health care providers and insurers if a uniform electronic format for patient records eliminates a major barrier that today discourages patients from switching hospitals or doctors?

Consider the future of newspapers, which like most businesses are built on a vertically integrated value chain. Journalists and advertisers supply copy, editors lay it out, presses create the physical product, and an elaborate distribution system delivers it to readers each morning.

Newspaper companies exist as intermediaries between the journalist and the reader because there are enormous economies of scale in printing and distribution. But when high-resolution electronic tablets advance to the point where readers consider them a viable alternative to newsprint, those traditional economies of scale will become irrelevant. Editors—or even journalists—will be able to E-mail content directly to readers.

Freed from the necessity of subscribing to entire physical newspapers, readers will be able to mix and match content from a virtually unlimited number of sources. News could be downloaded daily from different electronic-news services. Movie reviews, recipes, and travel features could come just as easily from magazine or book publishers. Star columnists, cartoonists, or the U.S. Weather Service could

Exhibit 2-2   The End of Channels and Hierarchies

In today's world, rich content passes through media, which we call channels, that can reach only a limited audience. The existence of channels creates hierarchy, both of choice (people have to gather rich information in an order dictated by the structure of the channels) and of power (some people have better access to rich information than others do). Hierarchy of choice is illustrated by the decision tree along

(continued at top of facing page)

Hierarchical Decision Tree

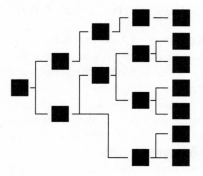

Hierarchy of power is illustrated by the traditional organization chart, in which senior executives have a wider span of knowledge than do their subordinates.

Hierarchical Organization

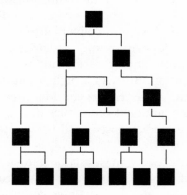

Hierarchy enables richness but constrains choice and creates asymmetries in information. The alternative to hierarchy is *markets,* which are symmetrical and open to the extent that they are *perfect.* But traditional markets trade only in less rich information.

(continued from top of previous page)
which consumers are compelled to do their shopping in the physical world: they must choose a street, then a shop, then a department, then a shelf, then a product. They cannot select in any other sequence. They can return to the street and search along a different path, of course, but only by expending time and effort.

When the trade-off between richness and reach is eliminated, channels are no longer necessary: everyone communicates richly with everyone else on the basis of shared standards. This might be termed *hyperarchy* after the hyperlinks of the World Wide Web.

Hyperarchy

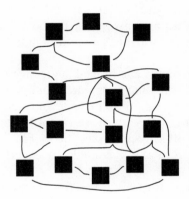

The World Wide Web is a hyperarchy. So are a deconstructed value chain within a business and a deconstructed supply chain within an industry. So are intranets. So are structures allowing fluid, team-based collaboration at work. So, too, is the pattern of amorphous and permeable corporate boundaries characteristic of the companies in Silicon Valley. (So, too, incidentally, are the architectures of object-oriented programming in software and of packet switching in telecommunications.)

Hyperarchy challenges *all* hierarchies, whether of logic or of power, with the possibility (or the threat) of random access and information symmetry. It challenges all markets with the possibility that far richer information can be exchanged than that involved in trading products and certificates of ownership. When the principles of hyperarchy are thoroughly understood, they will provide a way to understand not only positioning strategies within businesses and industries but also more fundamental questions of corporate organization and identity.

send their work directly to subscribers. Intermediaries—search engines, alert services, formatting software, or editorial teams—could format and package the content to meet readers' individual interests. It does not follow that all readers will choose to unbundle all the current content of the physical newspaper, but the principal logic for that bundle—the economics of printing—will be gone.

This transformation is probably inevitable but distant. As newspaper executives correctly point out, the broadsheet is still an extraordinarily cheap and user-friendly way to distribute information. Little electronic tablets are not going to replace it very soon.

However, the timing of total deconstruction is not really the issue. *Pieces* of the newspaper can be unbundled today. Classified advertising is a natural on-line product. Think how much easier it would be to submit, pay for, update, search through, and respond to classified ads electronically. Stripping away classifieds, however, would remove 25% of the typical newspaper's revenues but less than 10% of its costs.

Newspaper companies have moved aggressively into the electronic-classifieds business. They have exploited their advantage as makers of the original print marketplace to provide an integrated print and electronic offering that reaches the widest population of buyers and sellers. This electronic offering preserves the margins of 60% to 80% that newspapers need from the classifieds to cover their fixed printing costs.

But as more and more people use the electronic medium, companies focused on targeted segments of the electronic-classifieds market (operating on, say, 15% margins) will gain share. The greater their share, by definition, the more attractive they will become to buyers and sellers. Eventually, the newspapers will either lose business or (more likely) retain it by settling for much lower margins.

Either way, the subsidy that supports the fixed costs of the print product will be gone. So newspapers will cut content or raise prices for readers and advertisers, accelerating their defection. That, in turn, will create opportunities for another focused competitor to pick off a different part of the value chain. Thus the greatest vulnerability for newspapers is not the total substitution of a new business model but a steady erosion through a sequence of partial substitutions that will make the current business model unsustainable.

Retail banking is ripe for a similar upheaval. The current business model depends on a vertically integrated value chain through which multiple products are originated, packaged, sold, and cross-sold through proprietary distribution channels. The high costs of distribution drive economies of utilization and scale and thus govern strategy in retail banking as it works today.

Home electronic banking looks at first glance like another, but cheaper, distribution channel. Many banks see it that way, hoping that its wide-spread adoption might enable them to scale down their higher-cost physical channels. Some banks are even offering proprietary software and electronic transactions for free. But something much deeper has happened than the emergence of a new distribution channel. Customers now can access information and make transactions in a variety of new ways.

Some 10 million people in the United States regularly use personal-financial-management software such as Intuit's Quicken or Microsoft Money to manage their checkbooks and integrate their personal financial affairs. Current versions of these programs can use modems to access electronic switches operated by CheckFree or VISA Interactive, which in turn route instructions or queries to the customers' banks. Such a system lets customers pay bills, make transfers, receive electronic statements, and seamlessly integrate account data into their personal financial plans. In addition, almost all financial institutions supply information at their Web sites, which anybody on-line can access using a browser.

No single software program can achieve both richness and reach, yet. Quicken, Money, and proprietary bank software permit *rich* exchanges but only with the customer's own bank. Web browsers do much less but *reach* the entire universe of financial institutions. However, the software vendors and switch providers have the resources, and ultimately will be motivated, to form alliances with financial institutions to eliminate this artificial trade-off. Bridges between financial management software and the Web, combined with advances in reliability, security, digital signatures, and legally binding electronic contracts, will enable financial Web sites to provide the full range of banking services.

If that happens, the trade-off between richness and reach will be broken. Customers will be able to contact any financial institution for any kind of service or information. They will be able to maintain a balance sheet on their desktop, drawing on data from multiple institutions. They will be able to compare alternative product offerings and to sweep funds automatically between accounts at different institutions. Bulletin boards or auctioning software will allow customers to announce their product requirements and accept bids. Chat rooms will permit customers to share information with each other or get advice from experts.

The sheer breadth of choice available to potential customers will create the need for third parties to play the role of navigator or facilitating agent. For example, some companies will have an incentive to create (or simply make available) databases on interest rates, risk ratings, and service histories. Others will create insurance and mortgage calculators or intelligent-agent software that can search for and evaluate products. Still other companies will authenticate the identity of counterparties or serve as guarantors of performance, confidentiality, or creditworthiness. (See Exhibit 2-3.)

As it becomes easier for customers to switch from one supplier to another, the competitive value of one-stop shopping and established relationships will drop. Cross-selling will become more difficult. Information about customers' needs or behavior will be harder for companies to obtain. Competitive advantage will be determined product by product, and therefore providers with broad product lines will lose ground to focused specialists.

In this new world, distribution will be done by the phone company, statements by financial management software, facilitation by different kinds of agent software, and origination by any number of different kinds of product specialists. The integrated value chain of retail banking will have been deconstructed.

Deconstructed but not destroyed. All the old functions will still be performed, as well as some new ones. Banks will not become obsolete, but their current business definition will—specifically, the concept that a bank is an integrated business where multiple products are originated, packaged, sold, and cross-sold through proprietary distribution channels.

Many bankers—like encyclopedia executives—deny all this. They argue that most customers do not have personal computers and that many who do are not choosing to use them for banking. They point out that people worry about the security of on-line transactions and that consumers trust banks more than they trust software companies. All true. However, on-line technology is advancing inexorably. And because they generate a disproportionate share of deposits and fees, the 10% of the population that currently use personal-financial-management software probably account for 75% of the profits of the banking system.

Market research suggests that Quicken users are more likely to be loyal to their software than to their banks. In one study, half of them said that if they were changing banks *anyway*, they would require their new bank to support the software—that is, allow them to transact their business on-line using Quicken. Now, bank accounts churn at the rate of about *10%* per year. If a bank that doesn't support Quicken loses half of the new Quicken-using customers it might otherwise attract every year, and if such customers churn at the average rate, then it follows that the bank will lose 3% to 5% of its retail-customer margin per year. Refusal to support Quicken (or provide an acceptable alternative) could undermine the entire value of a franchise within just a few years.

The deconstruction of the value chain in banking is not unprecedented. Fifteen years ago, *corporate* banking was a spread business—that is, banks made money by charging a higher interest rate for loans than they paid for deposits. Their business model required them to form deep relationships with their corporate customers so that they could pump their own products through that distribution system. But then, thanks to technology, corporate customers gained access to the same financial markets that the banks used. Today, corporate banking consists of small businesses that largely stand alone (even when they function under the umbrella of a big bank) and compete product by product. Credit flows directly from the ultimate lender to the ultimate borrower, facilitated by bankers who rate the risk, give advice, make markets, and serve as custodians. The bankers make money through the fees they charge for those individual services. Clients no longer bundle their purchases, and relationships are more volatile. Once critical, an advantage in distribution today counts for little.

Newspapers and banking are not special cases. The value chains of scores of other industries will become ripe for unbundling. The logic is most compelling—and therefore likely to strike soonest—in information businesses where the cost of physical distribution is high: newspapers, ticket sales, insurance, financial information, scientific publishing, software, and of course encyclopedias. But in any business whose physical value chain has been compromised for the sake of delivering information, there is an opportunity to unbundle the two, creating a separate information business and allowing (or compelling) the physical one to be streamlined. All it will take to deconstruct a business is a competitor that focuses on the vulnerable sliver of information in its value chain. (See "What Will Happen to Your Business?")

Exhibit 2-3   The Transformation of Retail Banking

In today's integrated business model, the retail bank stands between the customer and the full range of financial services. But soon, through Internet technologies, customers will have direct access to product providers. As choices proliferate, totally new businesses will arise to help customers navigate through the expanded range of banking options.

Integrated Business Model

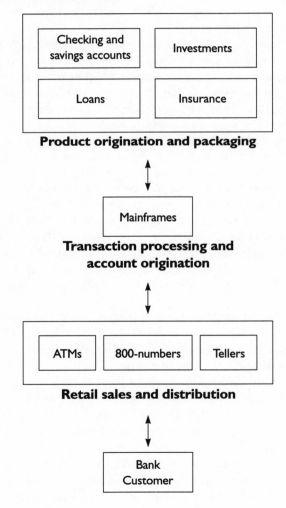

Exhibit 2-3   (continued)

Reconfigured Business Model

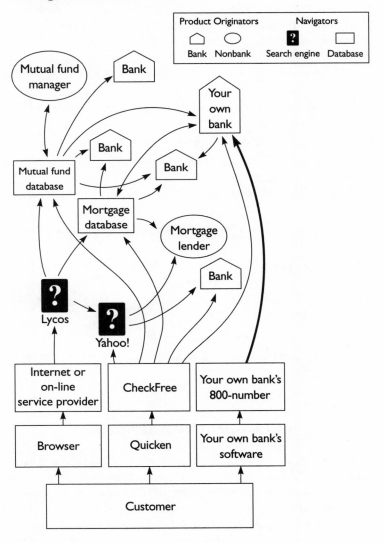

What Will Happen to Your Business?

All businesses will eventually be affected by the shifting economics of information, but not all at the same rate or in the same way. Answers to the following questions are a first step in determining how a business could be restructured:

1. How and where in the current value chain of this business is information a component of value?

2. Where are trade-offs currently being made between richness and reach in this business?

3. In what situations will these trade-offs be eliminated?

4. Which critical activities—especially informational activities—could be peeled off as stand-alone businesses?

5. Could the underlying physical business be run more efficiently if the information functions were stripped away?

6. What new activities—especially facilitating-agent roles—might be required?

7. Among the successor businesses, how would risks and rewards be distributed?

8. How would losing control over key activities affect the profitability of the current business model?

9. Which current strategic assets could become liabilities?

10. What new capabilities are needed to dominate the new businesses that will emerge?

Implications for Competitive Advantage

Deconstructing a vertically integrated value chain does more than transform the structure of a business or an industry—it alters the sources of competitive advantage. The new economics of information therefore not only present threats to established businesses but also represent a new set of opportunities. Every industry will shift according to its own dynamics, and those shifts will occur at different speeds and with varying intensity. No single set of predictions can be applied across the board, but some fundamental strategic implications of the changing economics of information can be drawn:

EXISTING VALUE CHAINS WILL FRAGMENT INTO MULTIPLE BUSI-NESSES, EACH OF WHICH WILL HAVE ITS OWN SOURCES OF COM-PETITIVE ADVANTAGE. When individual functions having different economies of scale or scope are bundled together, the result is a compromise of each—an averaging of the effects. When the bundles of functions are free to re-form as separate businesses, however, each can exploit its own sources of competitive advantage to the fullest.

Take, for example, car retailing in the United States. Dealerships provide information about products in showrooms and through test-drives. They hold inventory and distribute cars. They broker financing. They make a market in secondhand cars. They operate maintenance and repair services. Although most of these activities are physical, the bundle of functions is held together by the classic *informational* logic of one-stop shopping. A dealer's competitive advantage is therefore based on a mixture of location, scale, cost, sales force management, quality of service, and affiliations with car manufacturers and banks.

Bundling these functions creates compromises. Each step in the value chain has different economies of scale. If the functions were unbundled, specialty companies that offer test-drives could take cars to prospective buyers' homes. Distributors of new cars could have fewer and larger sites in order to minimize inventory and transportation costs. Providers of after-sales service would be free to operate more and smaller local facilities to furnish better service. Auto manufacturers could deliver product information over the Internet. And car purchasers could obtain financing by putting their business out for bid via an electronic broker. Eliminate the informational glue that combines all these functions in a single, compromised business model, and the multiple businesses that emerge will evolve in radically different directions.

SOME NEW BUSINESSES WILL BENEFIT FROM NETWORK ECONOMIES OF SCALE, WHICH CAN GIVE RISE TO MONOPOLIES. In a networked market, the greater the number of people connected, the greater the value of being connected, thus creating *network economies of scale*. There is no point, for example, in being the only person in the world who owns a telephone. As the number of people who own telephones rises, the value to any one individual of hooking up increases progressively.

This self-reinforcing dynamic builds powerful monopolies. Businesses that broker information, make markets, or set standards are all taking advantage of this dynamic. The implication: the first company to achieve critical mass will often take all, or nearly all—although the continuing battle between first-mover Netscape and Microsoft in the market for network browsers illustrates that the lead of the first mover is not always definitive.

Reaching critical mass can be an enormous challenge. General Electric may have solved the problem by using its own huge purchasing power. GE has opened its internal electronic-procurement system to other buyers of industrial goods, turning its own sourcing system into a market-making business.

AS VALUE CHAINS FRAGMENT AND RECONFIGURE, NEW OPPORTU-NITIES WILL ARISE FOR PURELY PHYSICAL BUSINESSES. In many businesses today, the efficiency of the physical value chain is compromised for the purpose of delivering information. Shops, for example, try to be efficient warehouses and effective merchandisers simultaneously and are often really neither. The new economics of information will create opportunities to rationalize the physical value chain, often leading to businesses whose physically based sources of competitive advantage will be more sustainable.

Consider the current battle in bookselling. Amazon.com, an electronic retailer on the Web, has no physical stores and very little inventory. It offers an electronic list of 2.5 million books, ten times larger than that of the largest chain store, and customers can search through that list by just about any criterion. Amazon orders most of its books from two industry wholesalers in response to customers' requests. It then repacks and mails them from a central facility.

Amazon cannot offer instant delivery; nor can customers physically browse the shelves the way they can in a traditional bookstore. Its advantages are based on superior information and lower physical costs. Customers can, for example, access book reviews. They have greater choice and better searching capabilities. And Amazon saves money on inventory and retail space.

But Amazon's success is not a given. The discount chains are aggressively launching their own Web businesses. There is nothing defensible about Amazon's wide selection since it really comes from publishers' and wholesalers' databases. By double-handling the books, Amazon still incurs unnecessary costs.

In fact, the wholesalers in the book industry could probably create the lowest-cost distribution system by filling customers' orders directly. If competition pushes the industry in that direction, electronic retailers would become mere search engines connected to somebody else's database—and that would not add much value or confer on them much of a competitive advantage. The wholesalers could be the big winners.

WHEN A COMPANY FOCUSES ON DIFFERENT ACTIVITIES, THE VALUE PROPOSITION UNDERLYING ITS BRAND IDENTITY WILL CHANGE. Because a brand reflects its company's value chain, deconstruction will require new brand strategies. For instance, the importance of branches and automated teller machines today leads many banks to emphasize *ubiquity* in their brand image (Citibank, for example). However, the reconfiguration of financial services might lead a company to focus on being a product provider. For such a strategy, *performance* becomes the key message, as it is for Fidelity. Another brand strategy might focus on helping customers navigate the universe of third-party products. The key message would be *trust*, as it is for Charles Schwab.

NEW BRANDING OPPORTUNITIES WILL EMERGE FOR THIRD PARTIES THAT NEITHER PRODUCE A PRODUCT NOR DELIVER A PRIMARY SERVICE. Navigator or agent brands have been around for a long time. The Zagat guide to restaurants and *Consumer Reports* are two obvious examples. It's Zagat's own brand—its credibility in restaurant reviewing—that steers its readers toward a particular establishment. A more recent example is the Platform for Internet Content Selection (PICS), a programming standard that allows browsers to interpret third-party rating labels on Web sites. With it a parent might search for sites that have been labeled "safe for children" by EvaluWeb. PICS enables anybody to rate anything, and it makes those ratings ubiquitous, searchable, sortable, and costless. The dramatic proliferation of networked markets increases the need for such navigators and other facilitating agents, those that guarantee a product's performance or assume risk, for example. Thus there will be many new opportunities to develop brands. (See "Where the New Businesses Will Emerge.")

BARGAINING POWER WILL SHIFT AS A RESULT OF A RADICAL REDUCTION IN THE ABILITY TO MONOPOLIZE THE CONTROL OF INFORMATION. Market power often comes from controlling a choke point in an information channel and extracting tolls from those dependent on the flow of information through it. For example, sellers to retail customers today use their control over the information available to those customers to minimize comparison shopping and maximize cross-selling. But when richness and reach extend to the point where such channels are unnecessary, that game will stop. Any choke point could then be circumvented. Buyers will know their alternatives as well as the seller does. Some new intermediaries—organizers of virtual markets—may even evolve into aggregators of buying power, playing suppliers off against one another for the benefit of the purchasers they represent.

CUSTOMERS' SWITCHING COSTS WILL DROP, AND COMPANIES WILL HAVE TO DEVELOP NEW WAYS OF GENERATING CUSTOMER LOYALTY. Common standards for exchanging and processing information and the growing numbers of individuals accessing networks will drastically reduce switching costs.

Proprietary EDI systems, for example, lock companies into supply relationships. But extranets linking companies with their suppliers using the Internet's standard protocols make switching almost costless. The U.S. auto industry is creating such an extranet called the Automotive Network eXchange (ANX). Linking together auto manufacturers with several thousand automotive suppliers, the system is expected to save its participants around a billion dollars a year, dramatically reduce ordering and billing errors, and speed the flow of information to second- and third-tier suppliers. By reducing switching costs and creating greater symmetry of information, ANX will intensify competition at every level of the supply chain.

INCUMBENTS COULD EASILY BECOME VICTIMS OF THEIR OBSOLETE PHYSICAL INFRASTRUCTURES AND THEIR OWN PSYCHOLOGY. Assets that traditionally offered competitive advantages and served as barriers to entry will become liabilities. The most vulnerable companies are those currently providing information that could be delivered more effectively and inexpensively electronically—for example, the physical parts of sales and distribution systems, such as branches, shops, and sales forces. As with newspapers, the loss of even a small portion of customers to new distribution channels or the migration of a high-margin product to the electronic domain can throw a business with high fixed costs into a downward spiral.

It may be easy to grasp this point intellectually, but it is much harder for managers to act on its implications. In many businesses, the assets in question are integral to a company's core competence. It is not easy psychologically to withdraw from assets so central to a company's identity. It is not easy strategically to downsize assets that have high fixed costs when so many customers still prefer the current business model. It is not easy financially to cannibalize current profits. And it is certainly not easy to squeeze the profits of distributors to whom one is tied by long-standing customer relationships or by franchise laws.

Newcomers suffer from none of these inhibitions. They are unconstrained by management traditions, organizational structures, customer relationships, or fixed assets. Recall the cautionary tale of *Encyclopædia Britannica*. Executives must mentally deconstruct their own businesses. If they don't, someone else will.

Where the New Businesses Will Emerge

In a world of limited connectivity, choices at each point in the value chain are, by definition, finite. In contrast, broadband connectivity means infinite choice. But infinite choice also means infinite bewilderment. This navigation problem can be solved in all sorts of ways, and each solution is a potential business.

The navigator could be a database. The navigator could be a search engine. The navigator could be intelligent-agent software. The navigator could be somebody giving advice. The navigator could be a brand providing recommendations or endorsements.

The logic of navigation can be observed in a number of businesses in which choice has proliferated. People often react to clutter by going back to the tried and true. Customer research indicates that people faced with complex choices either gravitate toward dominant brands or confine their search to narrow formats, each offering a presorted set of alternatives. In the grocery store, for example, where the number of products has quadrupled over the last 15 years, hundreds of segmented specialty brands have gained market share in almost every category. But so have the one or two leading brands. The proliferation of choice has led to the fragmentation of the small brands and the simultaneous concentration of the large ones. The losers are the brands in the middle.

Similarly, television viewers seem to flock to the hit shows without caring which network those shows are on. But they select specialty programming, such as nature documentaries or music videos, by tuning in to a cable channel offering that format. In essence, the viewer selects the channel, and the channel selects the content. In the first case, the product's brand pulls volume through the channel; in the second, the channel's brand pushes content toward receptive viewers.

Those two approaches by the consumer yield different patterns of competitive advantage and profitability. Networks need hit shows more than the hit shows need any network: the producers have the bargaining power and therefore receive the higher return. Conversely, producers of low-budget nature documentaries need a distributor more than the distributor needs any program, and the profit pattern is, therefore, the reverse. In one year, the popular comedian Bill Cosby earned more than the entire CBS network; the Discovery Channel probably earns more than all of its content providers put together. Despite the fact that CBS's 1996 revenues were about six times those of the Discovery Channel, Discovery's 52% profit margin dwarfed CBS's 4%.

The economics playing out in the television industry are a model for what will likely emerge in the world of universal connectivity. Think of it as two different value propositions: one is a focus on popular content; the other, a focus on navigation.

Navigation might have been the right strategy for *Encyclopædia Britannica* in responding to the threat from CD-ROMs. Its greatest competitive asset, after all, was a brand that certified high-quality, objective information. Given the clutter of cyberspace, what could be more compelling than a Britannica-branded guide to valuable information on the Internet?

If *Britannica*'s executives had written off their sales force, if they had built alliances with libraries and scientific journals, if they had built a Web site that had hot links directly to original sources, if they had created a universal navigator to valuable and definitive information validated by the *Encyclopædia Britannica* brand, they would have been heroes. They might have established a monopoly, following the example of Bill Gates. In fact, he might have been forced to acquire them.

Notes

1. For a complete discussion of the value chain concept, see Michael Porter's *Competitive Advantage* (New York: The Free Press, 1985). Differences in value chains—that is, differences in how competitors perform strategic activities or differences in which activities they choose to perform—are the basis for competitive advantage.

2. Ronald H. Coase, "The Nature of the Firm," *Economica*, vol. 4, no. 4, 1937, p. 386; Oliver E. Williamson, *Markets and Hierarchies: Analysis and Antitrust Implications* (New York: Free Press, 1975).

3
Exploiting the Virtual Value Chain

Jeffrey F. Rayport and John J. Sviokla

Every business today competes in two worlds: a physical world of resources that managers can see and touch and a virtual world made of information. The latter has given rise to the world of electronic commerce, a new locus of value creation. We have referred to this new information world as the *marketspace* to distinguish it from the physical world of the *marketplace*. (See "Managing in the Marketspace," *Harvard Business Review* November–December 1994.) A few examples illustrate the distinction. When consumers use answering machines to store their phone messages, they are using objects made and sold in the physical world, but when they purchase electronic answering services from their local phone companies, they are utilizing the *marketspace*—a virtual realm where products and services exist as digital information and can be delivered through information-based channels. Banks provide services to customers at branch offices in the marketplace as well as electronic on-line services to customers in the marketspace; airlines sell passenger tickets in both the "place" and the "space"; and fast-food outlets take orders over the counter at restaurants and increasingly through touch screens connected to computers.

Executives must pay attention to how their companies create value in both the physical world and the virtual world. But the processes for creating value are not the same in the two worlds. By understanding the differences and the interplay between the value-adding processes of the physical world and those of the information world, senior managers can see more clearly and comprehensively the strategic issues facing their organizations. Managing two interacting value-adding processes in the two mutually dependent realms poses new conceptual and tactical challenges. Those who understand how to master both can create and extract value in the most efficient and effective manner.

Academics, consultants, and managers have long described the process of creating value in the physical world, often referring to the stages involved as links in a "value chain." The value chain is a model that describes a series of value-adding activities connecting a company's supply side (raw materials, inbound logistics, and production processes) with its demand side (outbound logistics, marketing, and sales). By analyzing the stages of a value chain, managers have been able to redesign their internal and external processes to improve efficiency and effectiveness.

The value chain model treats information as a supporting element of the value-adding process, not as a source of value itself. For instance, managers often use information that they capture on inventory, production, or logistics to help monitor or control those processes, but they rarely use information itself to create new value for the customer. However, Federal Express Corporation recently did just that by allowing customers to track packages through the company's World Wide Web site on the Internet. Now customers can locate a package in transit by connecting on-line to the FedEx site and entering the airbill number. After the package has been delivered, they can even identify the name of the person who signed for it. Although FedEx provides this service for free, it has created added value for the customer—and thus increased loyalty—in a fiercely competitive market.

To create value with information, managers must look to the marketspace. Although the value chain of the space can mirror that of the place—buyers and sellers can transfer funds over electronic networks just as they might exchange cold, hard cash—the value-adding processes that companies must employ to turn raw information into new marketspace services and products are unique to the information world. In other words, the value-adding steps are *virtual* in that they are performed through and with information. Creating value in any stage of a virtual value chain involves a sequence of five activities: gathering, organizing, selecting, synthesizing, and distributing information. Just as someone takes raw material and refines it into something useful—as in the sequence of tasks involved in assembling an automobile on a production line—so a manager today collects raw information and adds value through these steps.

Adapting to a Virtual World

An examination of Geffen Records, a unit of MCA's music division, illustrates the use of information to create value. The traditional product of a major record label such as Geffen is a package of prerecorded music captured on an audiocassette or compact disc. The product is the end point of a set of value-adding processes that occur in the physical world. Those processes include discovering new musicians, screening them for potential marketability, recording their work in a studio, editing and selecting their music, creating master tapes, producing CDs or cassettes, and finally packaging, promoting, and distributing the products.

Increasingly, new competitors for Geffen's business are emerging in the marketspace. These entrants are viable because of the new economics of doing business in the world of information. For example, groups such as the Internet Underground Music Archive (IUMA) are posting digital audio tracks from unknown artists on the network, potentially subverting the role that record labels play. Today's technology allows musicians to record and edit material inexpensively themselves, and to distribute and promote it over networks such as the World Wide Web or commercial on-line services. They also can test consumers' reactions to their music, build an audience for their recorded performances, and distribute their products entirely in the marketspace.

The point here is simple: Bringing music to market can sometimes be done faster, better, and less expensively in the marketspace. Hence the challenge for Geffen. The company has a site on the World Wide Web devoted to the label's bands and uses it to distribute digital audio and video samples and to provide information about the bands' tours. The Web page has become Geffen's showroom in the marketspace and a potential new retail channel. It is also an information mirror of an activity that traditionally has occurred in the physical world—a stage in a virtual value chain that parallels a stage in a physical value chain.

In addition to using its own Web page, Geffen could search for new talent at IUMA's home site rather than audition bands in a studio, or edit and modify music on a computer rather than record take after take with a band to create one suitable version for the master tape. Each activity is a stage in a virtual value chain that occurs through and with information and mirrors a stage in the physical world.

To truly exploit the virtual value chain, however, Geffen's managers might go further by applying the generic value-adding steps of the marketspace to the information the company collects at every stage of the physical chain, thereby creating new value for customers. For example, they might utilize the digital information captured during a band's practice sessions by inviting fans to sit in the studio on the Internet. They might also allow fans to listen as engineers edit the material or to electronically download interviews with a band's members before they are published or distributed more widely. In the physical value chain, information collected in the studio or during editing has value to the extent that it enables Geffen to produce and sell CDs more efficiently; in the virtual world, it is a potential source of new revenue. Moreover, that information presents opportunities to develop new relationships with customers at very low cost—for instance, a customer not interested in a new compact disc by the Rolling Stones may nevertheless pay to sit in on a chat session with them in the Internet's Voodoo Lounge.

Like most companies, Geffen must play both in the place and in the space. The company's managers must continue to oversee a physical value chain—making and selling CDs—but they must also build and exploit a virtual value chain. We have studied scores of companies in a variety of industries attempting to do business in both the place and the space and have found that organizations making money in the information realm successfully exploit both of their value chains. Rather than managing one series of value-adding processes, they are actually managing two. The economic logic of the two chains is different: A conventional understanding of the economies of scale and scope does not apply to the virtual value chain (VVC) in the same way as it does to the physical value chain (PVC). Moreover, the two chains must be managed distinctly but also in concert.

We have observed that companies adopt value-adding information processes in three stages. In the first stage, *visibility*, companies acquire an ability to "see" physical operations more effectively through information. (See Exhibit 3-1.) At this stage, managers use large-scale information technology systems to coordinate activities in their physical value chains and in the process lay the foundation for a virtual value chain. In the second stage, *mirroring capability*, companies substitute virtual activities for physical ones; they begin to create a parallel value chain in the marketspace. Finally, businesses use information to establish *new customer relationships*. At this third stage, managers draw on the flow of information in their virtual value chain to deliver value to customers in new ways. In effect, they apply the generic value-adding

Exhibit 3-1   Building the Virtual Value Chain

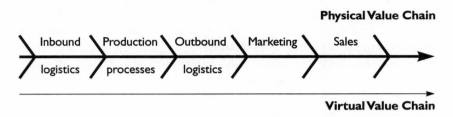

Physical Value Chain

| Inbound logistics | Production processes | Outbound logistics | Marketing | Sales |

Virtual Value Chain

When companies integrate the information they capture during stages of the value chain—from inbound logistics and production through sales and marketing—they construct an information underlay of the business. This integrated information provides manager with the ability to "see" their value chains from end to end.

activities to their virtual value chain and thereby exploit what we call the *value matrix.*

As companies move into the information world to perform value-adding steps, the potential for top-line growth increases. Each of the three stages represents considerable opportunity for managers.

Visibility

During the last 30 years, many companies have invested in technology systems to enable managers to coordinate, measure, and sometimes control business processes. The information collected by these systems about steps in the value chain has helped managers to plan, execute, and evaluate results with greater precision and speed. In other words, information technology has allowed managers to see their operations more effectively through the information world. In recent years, managers have been able to gain access to the information generated in the course of traditional operating activities, and that information helps them see their physical value chains as an integrated system rather than as a set of discrete though related activities. In this way, they can gain new insight into managing the value chain as a whole rather than as a collection of parts.

Companies such as FedEx, Wal-Mart, and Frito-Lay have transformed this kind of visibility into competitive advantage. The successful use of world-class information systems by each of these companies is now common knowledge, but consider one example—Frito-Lay— from the perspective of the marketspace. Frito's achievement with its widely publicized "information revolution" initiative illustrates the necessary first steps companies must take if they are to establish and then exploit their virtual value chains.

Underlying the manufacture and distribution of a variety of Frito-brand snack foods is an efficient information system that gives managers the ability to visualize nearly every element of the company's value chain as part of an integrated whole. It is a central nervous system within the business that integrates marketing, sales, manufacturing, logistics, and finance; it also provides managers with information on suppliers, customers, and competitors.

Frito's employees in the field collect information on the sales of products daily, store by store across the nation, and feed it electronically to the company. The employees also collect information about the sales and promotions of competing products or about new products launched by competitors in select locations. By combining this field data with information from each stage of the value chain, Frito's managers can better determine levels of inbound supplies of raw materials, allocate the company's manufacturing activity across available production capacity, and plan truck routing for the most efficient coverage of market areas. The company's ability to target local demand patterns with just the right sales promotion means that it can continuously optimize margin in the face of inventory risk. In short, Frito can use information to see and react to activities along its physical value chain. The company executes actions in the marketplace while it monitors and coordinates those actions in the marketspace.

Mirroring Capability

Once companies have established the necessary infrastructure for visibility, they can do more than just monitor value-adding steps. They can begin to manage operations or even to implement value-adding steps in the marketspace—faster, better, with more flexibility, and at lower cost. In other words, managers can begin to ask, What are we doing now in the place, and what could we do more efficiently or more effectively in the space? What value-adding steps currently performed in the physical value chain might be shifted to the mirror world of the virtual value chain? When companies move activities

Exhibit 3-2   Exploiting the Virtual Value Chain

Physical Value Chain

Virtual Value Chain

With an integrated information underlay in place, companies can begin to perform value-adding activities more efficiently and effectively through and with information. In other words, these information-based activities mirror steps in the physical value chain. When companies move a number of value-adding activities from the marketplace to the marketspace, they exploit a virtual value chain.

from the place to the space, they begin to create a virtual value chain that parallels but improves on the physical value chain. (See Exhibit 3-2.)

Executives at Ford Motor Company engaged in such work during the past decade as the company aggressively adopted video-conferencing and CAD/CAM technologies. When Ford developed its "global car" (marketed in North America as the Contour sedan), the automaker moved one key element of its physical value chain—product development—into the marketspace. Ford intended to create a car that would incorporate its best engineering, design, and marketing talent worldwide while also bringing to bear a vision of how a single car design could appeal at once to all major world markets. To gain leverage from its substantial investments in marketspace-enabling technology systems, Ford brought managerial talent from around the world together in the marketspace. Rather than creating national product teams or convening elaborate design summits, Ford established a *virtual* work team to develop the car. In this way, it extracted the best talent and the broadest vision it could muster.

By moving product development from the place to the space, Ford's managers did more than perform tasks in an information-defined world that were traditionally accomplished through physical actions. In the virtual world, the design team could transcend the limitations of time and space that characterize management in the physical world. They built and tested prototypes in a simulated computer environment and shared the designs and data with colleagues over a computer network, 24 hours a day, around the world. In the virtual world of information, they established common global specifications for manufacturing, integrated component systems centrally, and even drew suppliers into the design process. Ford thus performed critical value-adding steps not on the PVC but on the VVC—in other words, in a world that mirrored traditional managerial realities.

With such a complete information-based representation of the product, everyone on the team could see the project holistically in the mirror world. The goal: a global car with global appeal. The virtual value chain made a much more integrated process possible. The marketing challenge of getting customers to buy the Contour remains.

Managers at the Boeing Company took their exploitation of the mirror world one step further. A few years ago, they redesigned the engine housing for a new model of the 737 airplane. Previously, Boeing and other airplane manufacturers would design airframes by developing physical prototypes, testing them in wind tunnels to gauge the flow of air over their contours, and then repeating the process through multiple iterations. When Boeing addressed the question of how to create a new engine to improve the performance of its existing 737 airframe design, it turned not to wind tunnels but to a synthetic environment—a mirror world made of information. Boeing engineers developed the prototype as a virtual product that incorporated relevant laws of physics and materials sciences and enabled the company to test an evolving computer-simulated model in a virtual wind tunnel. As a result, engineers could test many more designs at dramatically lower costs and with much greater speed. The outcome was a teardrop shape for the engine housing that stunned the aerospace world. Why? Because only a process that could endlessly test different possibilities at near-zero incremental cost per synthetic prototype could give rise to a product concept that was outside the bounds of conventional thinking. By moving elements of the PVC—R&D, product design, prototyping, and product testing—to the mirror world of the VVC, Boeing succeeded in shattering a dominant paradigm of engine design and delivered a product that easily outperformed the competition, a feat that had proved impossible in 20 years of wind-tunnel testing.

Every manager knows that staying competitive today depends on achieving higher levels of performance for customers while incurring lower costs in R&D and production. Traditionally, companies have gotten more for less by exploiting vast economies of scale in production while focusing on raising levels of quality. Japanese automakers such as Toyota have successfully pursued that strategy, delivering highly differentiated products at the lowest possible costs. When scale economies do not apply, as in many service-sector businesses, managers seeking better performance at lower cost can tap the mirror world, in which the economics are altogether different. On the VVC, companies may find dramatic low-cost approaches to delivering extraordinarily high-value results to customers.

New Customer Relationships

Ultimately, however, companies must do more than create value in the space: They also must extract value from it. They can often do so by establishing space-based relationships with customers.

Once companies become adept at managing their value-adding activities across the parallel value chains, they are ready to develop these new relationships. In the world of high technology, examples of building customer relationships on the VVC abound. Today thousands of companies have established sites on the World Wide Web to advertise products or elicit comments from customers. Some companies have gone further and have actually automated the interface with the customer, thus identifying and fulfilling customers' desires at lower cost. Digital Equipment Corporation, making a comeback from its slump in the late 1980s, has developed a new channel for serving customers on the Internet. DEC's World Wide Web site allows prospective customers to use a personal computer to contact sales representatives, search for products and services, review the specifications of DEC equipment, and actually take a DEC machine for a "test drive." Similarly, Oracle Corporation, a data-base software maker, now distributes a new product over the Internet as well as through physical channels. These companies are joining the burgeoning ranks of major high-tech firms in the business-to-business sector that have become Internet marketers; the group includes GE Plastics, Sun Microsystems, and Silicon Graphics, all of which use the Web to establish and maintain relationships with selected accounts.

Other companies view their challenge as that of managing each individual customer relationship in both the marketspace and the marketplace. Those that succeed have an opportunity to reinvent the core value proposition of a business, even an entire industry. One extraordinary example of success in this regard is United Services Automobile Association, which has truly maximized its opportunities to deliver value to customers in both the space and the place and has thereby become a world-class competitor.

USAA began as an insurance company. Over time, it has used its information systems—installed to automate its core business, insurance sales and underwriting—to capture significant amounts of information about customers, both individually and in aggregate. USAA integrated information about customers and distributed it throughout the company so that employees are ready to provide products, services, and advice anytime a customer contacts the company. Having made this investment in visibility, USAA found that among other things it could prepare customer risk profiles and customize policies on the VVC. Looking at the flow of information harvested along its VVC, USAA's managers invented business lines targeted to specific customers' needs, such as insurance for boat owners.

But USAA also used its growing expertise with information to create new value for customers in ways that had little or nothing to do with insurance. For example, the company went one step further for the boat owners: It designed financing packages for purchasing boats. In fact, USAA now offers a wide range of financial products as well as shopping services for everything from jewelry to cars. Further, when a customer calls in with a theft claim, the company can offer to send a check or to replace the stolen item. (Many customers opt for the latter because it involves less work and solves their problem.)

By aggregating demand statistics and likely loss ratios, USAA has become a smart buyer for its loyal customer base, getting discount prices through high-volume purchases and passing some *or* all of the savings along to the customer. Today USAA is one of the largest direct merchandisers in the country, shipping real goods along its PVC as directed by the sensing capabilities of its VVC. USAA does not actually manufacture anything. Rather, it is a trusted intermediary between the demand it senses and the supply it sources.

Although USAA's "product line" is eclectic, it represents a logical, cost-effective, and profitable progression of new business ventures, all of which are underwritten by the information about customers captured in the company's virtual value chain. (Management of that information has become USAA's central activity.) Through clever integration of the information harvested along the VVC and through a PVC that delivers goods and services, USAA creates new value for customers by serving a broader set of their needs.

The Value Matrix

The new relationships that companies such as USAA are developing with customers spring from a matrix of value opportunities. Each stage of the virtual value chain—as a mirror of the physical value chain—allows for many new extracts from the flow of information, and each extract could constitute a new product or service. If managers want to pursue any of these opportunities, they need to put into place processes to gather the information, organize it for the customer, select what's valuable, package (or synthesize) it, and distribute it—the five value-adding steps unique to the information world. In effect, these value-adding steps, in conjunction with the virtual value chain, make up a value matrix that allows companies to identify customers' desires more effectively and fulfill them more efficiently. (See Exhibit 3-3.) For instance, when an automobile manufacturer can shift its R&D activities from the PVC to the VVC, it becomes possible for the company to exploit the matrix by engaging customers in the new-product-development process even if they are located around the world. The company could gather, organize, select, synthesize, and distribute design information drawn from the R&D process to create a computer simulation for customers, who could then enter the virtual design space and give feedback—which in turn could be used to add value in the unfolding design of the vehicle.

Moreover, the information can be turned into new spin-off products: Digitally captured product designs can become the basis for personal-computer-based or television-based multimedia software, such as the Lamborghini driving game, a software package now on the market. While the information used in such products also aids physical processes and feeds into a physical end point—an automobile, a compact disc, an insurance policy—it is also the raw material for new kinds of value.

The newspaper industry is another example of how such processes can be shifted from the place to the space. Executives can apply the five value-adding steps to each link of the virtual value chain to envision a matrix of opportunities for creating value. For instance, drawing from the information used to support reporting and editing, newspapers could provide information packets to readers with audio files of reporters' interviews, images from their notebooks, photos that did not make it into the paper, and even editors' comments about early drafts of stories. The value matrix guides managers as they consider how to establish the processes necessary to exploit new opportunities.

Exhibit 3-3   Value Matrix: Building Relationships

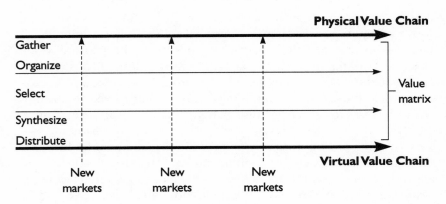

Companies create new markets and new relationships with existing markets by applying the five generic value-adding steps of the information world to each activity in the virtual value chain. They create a value matrix.

By thinking boldly about the integration of place and space, executives may be able to create valuable digital assets that, in turn, could change the competitive dynamics of industries. Consider Image Technology International (recently acquired by MCI Communications Corporation), a company that has entered the imaging market with an entirely digital approach to the capture, organization, selection, manipulation, and distribution of photographic images.

By using digital code as its raw material rather than chemicals as in traditional photography, Image can offer higher value to its customers in a number of ways. First, the company offers lower-cost prepress services. The cost of a high-quality industrial photo for a catalog is $150 to $250 or more when captured on photographic film. The output of a chemical-based photo is limited: The incremental costs of using the image captured for the catalog in an additional product—such as a follow-on brochure—start at $15 and go up from there. In the world of digital code, the image (captured on a digital camera) costs half as much to create because of the photographer's increased productivity, the avoidance of chemical processing, improved image quality, and efficiencies of storage and manipulation.

Second, Image Technology can manipulate and reuse a digital photo in several different ways to allow businesses to communicate with their customers in either the marketplace or the marketspace. For in-stance, using specially designed software, the company can incor-porate an image on acetate film or a digital press; both are used in printing promotional flyers. The same image can be directed to a pho-tocopier to create a black-and-white or color copy of the same image for distribution of handbills announcing a sale. Image can manipulate a digital photo (which the company can organize in a database with other relevant data, such as the price of the object photographed and a text description of it) so that customers can use it in CD-ROM catalogs, videos, or on-line services. In short, by exploiting a virtual value chain the company can capture an image more efficiently and transform that image so that it can be used in many different physical pro-cesses—from dye transfer to photocopier to video—and virtual pro-cesses. Image can create an asset that has tremendous economies of scale and scope.

For example, consider one of the vertical markets Image competes in: the hardlines industry—the industry that makes, distributes, and sells hardware. Any business in the industry can use Image's pre-production technology to publish product images and data less ex-pensively. A local hardware store can draw on Image's database of hammers, screwdrivers, and other products to create a newspaper flyer conventionally with pictures, halftones, and pasteup—or digi-tally, using Image's picture-processing software. A large distributor that wants to create a major catalog of product lines can do so less expensively, faster, and more flexibly using information-based ser-vices and products from Image. Whereas once the process of creating a catalog required tens of thousands of photos and months of layout work, Image can create a database of images and text for a customer far more quickly. Subsequent catalogs, drawing from the same digital asset, can be prepared for publication in just days, even if the distribu-tor drops several items from the list and changes the price of many others or adds a broad range of hammers with different handle colors. Image can manipulate the size of images, reshuffle their order, and change text or even colors far more easily in the space than in the place.

In the process of helping hardline industry businesses to reduce the cost of communicating with their customers, Image is amassing a huge database of photos that will provide it with a dominant position in the industry. If Image's database can contain an industrial-grade picture of almost every piece of hardware in existence, why would any player in the hardlines channel—manufacturer, distributor, or retailer—go to another source or shoot a picture that was already available in physical and virtual form? (Pursuing the same logic, Bill Gates and other pioneers of electronic commerce are quickly buying up electronic rights to works of art and many other objects.)

To anyone who views Image's operations strictly as an information-based parallel to the traditional chemical process, the company's value chain merely looks far more efficient than other companies' physical value chains. However, considering how value is added in the information world, Image has in fact reinvented the business model for the capture and display of images. To create and process a photo, Image gathers information (finds subjects and takes photographs); organizes information (creates the photo database); selects information (chooses images to produce from the database); synthesizes information (processes images for different media); and distributes information (outputs images to relevant platforms). Image does not make and process the digital equivalent of photographic film and ancillary products. It parlays its digital assets across many forms, from newsprint to catalogs to videos. That is, by thinking in terms of a virtual value chain *and* a physical value chain, the company's managers look at far more opportunities for creating and extracting value than they would have by considering the business exclusively from the point of view of a traditional physical value chain. Thinking about a business in terms of its value matrix can allow managers to go beyond changing the rules of the game: They can reinvent an industry.

Such thinking is springing up around the world as new ways of creating and extracting value in the marketspace become clear. For example, the China Internet Company, backed by the Xinhua News Agency, will roll out a network of Internet sites for 40 industrial cities in China before the end of 1995. On this network will be multimedia documents that describe a wide range of products, from toys to towels to auto parts. The China Internet Company will also provide a complete catalog of Chinese laws pertaining to trade and export, a translation service, and news. Because the Chinese do not have an adequate physical infrastructure for information about exports, they hope to create a virtual platform *first*. This new information infrastructure could easily become the basis for a whole new transaction and communications infrastructure into and out of China. After all, unlike a company entering the physical marketplace, the China Internet Company will have global reach the very instant it goes on-line.

Implications for Management

What all this means for managers is that they must consciously focus on the principles that guide value creation and extraction across the two value chains separately and in combination. These two value-adding processes are fundamentally different. The physical value chain is composed of a linear sequence of activities with defined points of input and output; in Geffen's case, it runs from locating new bands to manufacturing and distributing CDs of a band's music. By contrast, the virtual value chain is nonlinear—a matrix of potential inputs and outputs that can be accessed and distributed through a wide variety of channels. USAA can meet customers' needs wherever and however they are manifested. Image can deliver images and data on a wide variety of platforms and across a wide variety of distribution infrastructures. The China Internet Company may perform similar functions for an entire burgeoning national economy.

How can we make sense of this new realm of activity—the information space that allows for the creation of a virtual value chain and the exploitation of a value matrix? To succeed in this new economic environment, executives must understand the differences between value creation and extraction in the marketplace and in the marketspace; they must manage both effectively and in concert. More specifically, a company's executives must embrace an updated set of guiding principles because in the marketspace many of the business axioms that have guided managers no longer apply. We offer five new principles here.

THE LAW OF DIGITAL ASSETS

Digital assets, unlike physical ones, are not used up in their consumption. Companies that create value with digital assets may be able to reharvest them through a potentially infinite number of transactions, thus changing the competitive dynamics of their industries. For example, when Image Technology gathers and organizes a million images of hardware, it will have the dominant digital asset in that industry. Companies using traditional chemical-based processes will have a difficult time competing with Image because the variable cost of creating value using digital-information assets is zero or close to it. Therefore providers of products or services that must price according to the traditional variable-cost model—based on the consumption of the underlying materials—will have a tough time competing against companies that, by exploiting their virtual value chains, can price aggressively and still make margin.

NEW ECONOMIES OF SCALE

The virtual value chain redefines economies of scale, allowing small companies to achieve low unit costs for products and services in markets dominated by big companies. The U.S. Postal Service, which views the world according to an industrial paradigm, could never afford to build a post office in every one of the nation's homes. But FedEx has done exactly that in the marketspace by allowing individuals with access to the Internet to track packages through the company's site on the World Wide Web. (Customers can also request software from FedEx that allows them not only to track their parcels but also to view at any time the entire history of their transactions with FedEx.) The new economies of scale make it possible for FedEx to provide what are, in effect, mini-storefronts to each and every customer, whether millions of users request the service at any given moment or just one.

NEW ECONOMIES OF SCOPE

In the marketspace, businesses can redefine economies of scope by drawing on a single set of digital assets to provide value across many different and disparate markets. USAA dominates the insurance market for military officers with a 97% segment share, a scale of operations built on direct marketing. Now, through the new customer relationships made possible by its digital assets (the information USAA collected about its customers), the company is expanding its scope. Using its virtual value chain, USAA can coordinate across markets and provide a broader line of high-quality products and services.

TRANSACTION-COST COMPRESSION

Transaction costs along the VVC are lower than their counterparts on the PVC, and they continue to decline sharply as the processing capacity per unit of cost for microprocessors doubles every 18 months. In the 1960s, it cost about $1 to keep information about an individual customer. Today it costs less than 1¢ per customer. Lower transaction costs allow companies to control and track information that would have been too costly to capture and process just a few years ago. For instance, lower transaction costs made it possible for Frito to monitor its value chain from shipments of corn to in-store inventory.

REBALANCING SUPPLY AND DEMAND

Taken together, these four axioms combine to create a fifth: The world of business increasingly demands a shift from supply-side to demand-side thinking. As companies gather, organize, select, synthesize, and distribute information in the marketspace while managing raw and manufactured goods in the marketplace, they have the opportunity to "sense and respond" to customers' desires rather than simply to make and sell products and services. (See "Managing by Wire," by Stephan H. Haeckel and Richard L. Nolan, *Harvard Business Review* September–October 1993.) USAA senses a demand in its customer base and then connects that demand to a source of supply. In today's world of overcapacity, in which demand, not supply, is scarce, managers must increasingly look to demand-side strategies.

Senior managers must evaluate their business—its strengths and weaknesses, its opportunities and risks—along the value chains of both worlds, virtual and physical. Today events in either can make or break a business.

PART

II

Whither the Firm?

1
The Dawn of the E-Lance Economy

Thomas W. Malone and Robert J. Laubacher

In October of 1991, Linus Torvalds, a 21-year-old computer-science student at the University of Helsinki, made available on the Internet a kernel of a computer operating system he had written. Called Linux, it was a rudimentary version of the ubiquitous UNIX operating system, which for more than a decade had been a mainstay of corporate and academic computing. Torvalds encouraged other programmers to download his software—for free—and use it, test it, and modify it as they saw fit. A few took him up on the offer. They fixed bugs, tinkered with the original code, and added new features, and they too posted their work on the Internet.

As the Linux kernel grew, it attracted the attention of more and more programmers, who contributed their own ideas and improvements. The Linux community grew steadily, soon coming to encompass thousands of people around the world, all sharing their work freely with one another. Within three years, this loose, informal group, working without managers and connected mainly through the Internet, had turned Linux into one of the best versions of UNIX ever created.

Imagine, now, how such a software development project would have been organized at a company like IBM or Microsoft. Decisions and funds would have been filtered through layers of managers. Formal teams of programmers, quality assurance testers, and technical writers would have been established and assigned tasks. Customer surveys and focus groups would have been conducted, their findings documented in thick reports. There would have been budgets, milestones, deadlines, status meetings, performance reviews, approvals. There would have been turf wars, burnouts, overruns, delays. The project would have cost an enormous amount of money, taken longer to complete, and quite possibly produced a system less valuable to users than Linux.

For many executives, the development of Linux is most easily understood (and most easily dismissed) as an arcane story of hackers and cyberspace—a neat *Wired* magazine kind of story, but one that bears little relevance to the serious world of big business. This interpretation, while understandable, is shortsighted. What the Linux story really shows us is the power of a new technology—in this case, electronic networks—to fundamentally change the way work is done. The Linux community, a temporary, self-managed gathering of diverse individuals engaged in a common task, is a model for a new kind of business organization that could form the basis for a new kind of economy.

The fundamental unit of such an economy is not the corporation but the individual. Tasks aren't assigned and controlled through a stable chain of management but rather are carried out autonomously by independent contractors. These electronically connected freelancers— e-lancers—join together into fluid and temporary networks to produce and sell goods and services. When the job is done—after a day, a month, a year—the network dissolves, and its members become independent agents again, circulating through the economy, seeking the next assignment.

Far from being a wild hypothesis, the e-lance economy is, in many ways, already upon us. We see it not only in the development of Linux but also in the evolution of the Internet itself. We see it in the emergence of virtual companies, in the rise of outsourcing and telecommuting, and in the proliferation of freelance and temporary workers. Even within large organizations, we see it in the increasing importance of ad hoc project teams, in the rise of "intrapreneurs," and in the formation of independent business units.[1]

All these trends point to the devolution of large, permanent corporations into flexible, temporary networks of individuals. No one can yet say exactly how important or widespread this new form of business organization will become, but judging from current signs, it is not inconceivable that it could define work in the twenty-first century as the industrial organization defined it in the twentieth. If it does, business and society will be changed forever.

Businesses of One

Business organizations are, in essence, mechanisms for coordination. They exist to guide the flow of work, materials, ideas, and money, and the form they take is strongly affected by the coordination technologies available. Until a hundred or so years ago, coordination technologies were primitive. Goods and messages were transported primarily by foot, horse, or boat, and the process was slow, unreliable, and often dangerous. Because there was no efficient way to coordinate disparate activities, most people worked near their homes, often by themselves, producing products or services for their neighbors. The business organizations that did exist—farms, shops, foundries—were usually small, comprising a few owners and employees. When their products had to reach distant consumers, they did so through a long series of transactions with various independent wholesalers, jobbers, shippers, storekeepers, and itinerant peddlers.

It was not until the second half of the nineteenth century, after railroad tracks had been laid and telegraph lines strung, that large, complex organizations became possible. With faster, more dependable communication and transportation, businesses could reach national and even international markets, and their owners had the means to coordinate the activities of large and dispersed groups of people. The hierarchical, industrial corporation was born, subsuming a broad array of functions and, often, a broad array of businesses, and it quickly matured to become the dominant organizational model of the twentieth century.

Despite all the recent talk of decentralized management, empowered employees, and horizontal processes, the large, industrial organization continues to dominate the economy today. We remain in the age of multinational megacompanies, and those companies appear to be rushing to meld into ever larger forms. The headlines of the business press tell the story: Compaq buys Digital. WorldCom buys MCI. Citibank merges with Travelers. Daimler-Benz acquires Chrysler. British Airways allies with American Airlines (which in turn allies with US Airways). Some observers, projecting this wave of consolidation into the future, foresee a world in which giant global corporations replace nations as the organizing units of humanity. We will be citizens of Sony or Shell or Wal-Mart, marching out every day to do battle with the citizens of Philips or Exxon or Sears.

Such a scenario certainly seems plausible. Yet when we look beneath the surface of all the M&A activity, we see signs of a counter-phenomenon: the disintegration of the large corporation. People are leaving big companies and either joining much smaller companies or going into business for themselves as contract workers, freelancers, or temps. Twenty-five years ago, one in five U.S. workers was employed by a *Fortune* 500 company. Today the ratio has dropped to less than one in ten. The largest private employer in the United States is not General Motors or IBM or UPS. It's the temporary-employment agency Manpower Incorporated, which in 1997 employed 2 million people. While big companies control ever larger flows of cash, they are exerting less and less direct control over actual business activity. They are, you might say, growing hollow.

Even within large corporations, traditional command-and-control management is becoming less common. Decisions are increasingly being pushed lower down in organizations. Workers are being rewarded not for efficiently carrying out orders but for figuring out what needs to be done and then doing it. Some large industrial companies like Asea Brown Boveri and British Petroleum have broken themselves up into scores of independent units that transact business with one another almost as if they were separate companies. And in some industries, like investment banking and consulting, it is often easier to understand the existing organizations not as traditional hierarchies but as confederations of entrepreneurs, united only by a common brand name.

What underlies this trend? Why is the traditional industrial organization showing evidence of disintegration? Why are e-lancers proliferating? The answers lie in the basic economics of organizations. Economists, organizational theorists, and business historians have long wrestled with the question of why businesses grow large or stay small. Their research suggests that when it is cheaper to conduct transactions internally, within the bounds of a corporation, organizations grow larger, but when it is cheaper to conduct them externally, with independent entities in the open market, organizations stay small or shrink. If, for example, the owners of an iron smelter find it less expensive to establish a sales force than to contract with outside agencies to sell their products, they will hire salespeople, and their organization will grow. If they find that outside agencies cost less, they will not hire the salespeople, and their organization will not grow.

The coordination technologies of the industrial era—the train and the telegraph, the automobile and the telephone, the mainframe computer—made internal transactions not only possible but also advantageous. Companies were able to manage large organizations centrally, which provided them with economies of scale in manufacturing, marketing, distribution, and other activities. It made economic sense to directly control many different functions and businesses and to hire the legions of administrators and supervisors needed to manage them. Big was good.

But with the introduction of powerful personal computers and broad electronic networks—the coordination technologies of the twenty-first century—the economic equation changes. Because information can be shared instantly and inexpensively among many people in many locations, the value of centralized decision making and expensive bureaucracies decreases. Individuals can manage themselves, coordinating their efforts through electronic links with other independent parties. Small becomes good.

In one sense, the new coordination technologies enable us to return to the preindustrial organizational model of tiny, autonomous businesses—businesses of one or of a few—conducting transactions with one another in a market. But there's one crucial difference: electronic networks enable these microbusinesses to tap into the global reservoirs of information, expertise, and financing that used to be available only to large companies. The small companies enjoy many of the benefits of the big without sacrificing the leanness, flexibility, and creativity of the small.

In the future, as communications technologies advance and networks become more efficient, the shift to e-lancers promises to accelerate. Should that indeed take place, the dominant business organization of the future may not be a stable, permanent corporation but rather an elastic network that may sometimes exist for no more than a day or two. When a project needs to be undertaken, requests for proposals will be transmitted or electronic want ads posted, individuals or small teams will respond, a network will be formed, and new workers will be brought on as their particular skills are needed. Once the project is done, the network will disband. Following in the footsteps of young Linus Torvalds, we will enter the age of the temporary company.

The Temporary Company

From the 1920s through the 1940s, the movie business was controlled by big studios like MGM and Columbia. The studios employed actors, directors, screenwriters, photographers, publicists, even projectionists—all the people needed to produce a movie, get it into theaters, and fill the seats. Central managers determined which films to make and who would work on them. The film industry was a model of big-company, industrial organization.

By the 1950s, however, the studio system had disintegrated. The power had shifted from the studio to the individual. Actors, directors, and screenwriters became freelancers, and they made their own choices about which projects to work on. For a movie to be made, these freelancers would join together into a temporary company, which would employ different specialists as needed from day to day. As soon as the film was completed, the temporary company would go out of existence, but the various players would, in time, join together in new combinations to work on new projects.

The shift in the film business from permanent companies to temporary companies shows how entire industries can evolve, quite rapidly, from centralized structures to network structures. And such transformations are by no means limited to the idiosyncratic world of Hollywood. Consider the way many manufacturers are today pursuing radical outsourcing strategies, letting external agents perform more of their traditional activities. The U.S. computer-display division of the Finnish company Nokia, for example, chose to enter the U.S. display market with only five employees. Technical support, logistics, sales, and marketing were all subcontracted to specialists around the country. The fashion accessories company Topsy Tail, which has revenues of $80 million but only three employees, never even touches its products through the entire supply chain. It contracts with various injection-molding companies to manufacture its goods; uses design agencies to create its packaging; and distributes and sells its products through a network of independent fulfillment houses, distributors, and sales reps. Nokia's and Topsy Tail's highly decentralized operations bear more resemblance to the network model of organization than to the traditional industrial model.

For another, broader example, look at what's happened to the textile industry in the Prato region of Italy. In the early 1970s, Massimo Menichetti inherited his family's business, a failing textile mill. Menichetti quickly broke up the firm into eight separate companies. He sold a major portion of equity—between one-third and one-half—to key employees, and he required that at least 50% of the new companies' sales come from customers that had not been served by the old company. Within three years, the eight new businesses had achieved a complete turnaround, attaining significant increases in machine utilization and productivity.

Following the Menichetti model, many other big mills in Prato broke themselves up into much smaller pieces. By 1990, more than 15,000 small textile firms, averaging fewer than five employees, were active in the region. The tiny firms built state-of-the-art factories and warehouses, and they developed cooperative ventures in such areas as purchasing, logistics, and R&D, where scale economies could be exploited. Textile production in the area tripled during this time, despite the fact that the textile industry was in decline throughout the rest of Europe. And the quality of the products produced in the Prato region rose as innovation flourished. Textiles from Prato have now become the preferred material for fashion designers around the world.

Playing a key role in the Prato textile industry are brokers, known as *impannatori*, who act as conduits between the small manufacturing concerns and the textile buyers. The impannatori help coordinate the design and manufacturing process by bringing together appropriate groups of businesses to meet the particular needs of a customer. They have even created an electronic market, which serves as a clearinghouse for information about projected factory utilization and upcoming requirements, allowing textile production capacity to be traded like a commodity.

The Prato experience shows that an economy can be built on the network model, but Prato, it could be argued, is a small and homogeneous region. How would a complex, diverse industry operate under the network model? The answer is: far more easily than one might expect. As a thought experiment, let's take a journey forward in time, into the midst of the twenty-first century, and see how automobiles, the archetypal industrial product, are being designed.

General Motors, we find, has split apart into several dozen separate divisions, and these divisions have outsourced most of their traditional activities. They are now small companies concerned mainly with managing their brands and funding the development of new types and models of cars. A number of independent manufacturers perform fabrication and assembly on a contract basis for anyone who wants to pay for it. Vehicles are devised by freelance engineers and designers, who join together into small, ever shifting coalitions to work on particular projects. A coalition may, for example, focus on engineering an electrical system or on designing a chassis, or it may concentrate on managing the integration of all of the subsystems into complete automobiles.

These design coalitions take many forms. Some are organized as joint ventures; some share equity among their members; some are built around electronic markets that set prices and wages. All are autonomous and self-organizing, and all depend on a universal, high-speed computer network—the descendant of the Internet—to connect them to one another and exchange electronic cash. A highly developed venture-capital infrastructure monitors and assesses the various teams and provides financing to the most promising ones.

In addition to being highly efficient, with little managerial or administrative overhead, this market-based structure has spurred innovation throughout the automotive industry. While much of the venture capital goes to support traditional design concepts, some is allocated to more speculative, even wild-eyed, ideas, which if successful could create enormous financial rewards. A small coalition of engineers may, for example, receive funds to design a factory for making individualized lighting systems for car grilles. If their idea pans out, they could all become multimillionaires overnight. And the next day, they might dissolve their coalition and head off to seek new colleagues and new challenges.

Over the past few years, under the auspices of the Massachusetts Institute of Technology's initiative on Inventing the Organizations of the 21st Century, we have worked with a group of business professors and executives to consider the different ways business might be organized in the next century.[2] The automotive design scenario we've just laid out was discussed and refined by this group, and we subsequently shared it with managers and engineers from big car companies. They not only agreed that it was a plausible model for car design but also pointed out that the auto industry was in some ways already moving toward such a model. Many automakers have been outsourcing more and more of their basic design work, granting ever greater autonomy to external design agencies.

A shift to an e-lance economy would bring about fundamental changes in virtually every business function, not just in product design. Supply chains would become ad hoc structures, assembled to fit the needs of a particular project and disassembled when the project ended. Manufacturing capacity would be bought and sold in an open market, and independent, specialized manufacturing concerns would undertake small batch orders for a variety of brokers, design shops, and even consumers. Marketing would be performed in some cases by brokers, in other cases by small companies that would own brands and certify the quality of the merchandise sold under them. In still other cases, the ability of consumers to share product information on the Internet would render marketing obsolete; consumers would simply "swarm" around the best offerings. Financing would come less from retained earnings and big equity markets and more from venture capitalists and interested individuals. Small investors might trade shares in ad hoc, project-based enterprises over the Internet.

Business would be transformed fundamentally. But nowhere would the changes be as great as in the function of management itself.

The Transformation of Management

In the mid-1990s, when the Internet was just entering the consciousness of most business executives, the press was filled with disaster stories. The Internet, the pundits proclaimed, was about to fall into disarray. Traffic on the World Wide Web was growing too fast. There were too many Web sites, too many people on-line. Demand was outstripping capacity, and it was only a matter of months before the entire network crashed or froze.

It never happened. The Internet has continued to expand at an astonishing rate. Its capacity has doubled every year since 1988, and today more than 90 million people are connected to it. They use it to order books and flowers, to check on weather conditions in distant cities, to trade stocks and commodities, to send messages and spread propaganda, and to join discussion groups on everything from soap operas to particle physics.

So who's responsible for this great and unprecedented achievement? Who oversaw what is arguably the most important business development of the last 50 years? No one. No one controls the Internet. No one's in charge. No one's the leader. The Internet grew out of the combined efforts of all its users, with no central management. In fact, when we ask people whether they think the Internet could have grown this fast for this long if it had been managed by a single company—AT&T, for example—most say no. Managing such a massive and unpredictable explosion of capacity and creativity would have been beyond the skills of even the most astute and capable executives. The Internet *had* to be self-managed.

The Internet is the greatest model of a network organization that has yet emerged, and it reveals a startling truth: in an e-lance economy, the role of the traditional business manager changes dramatically and sometimes disappears completely. The work of the temporary company is coordinated by the individuals who compose it, with little or no centralized direction or control. Brokers, venture capitalists, and general contractors all play key roles—initiating projects, allocating resources, and coordinating work—but there need not be any single point of oversight. Instead, the overall results *emerge* from the individual actions and interactions of all the different players in the system.

Of course, this kind of coordination occurs all the time in a free market, where products ranging from cars to copying machines to soft drinks all get produced and consumed without any centralized authority deciding how many or what kinds of these products to make. More than two hundred years ago, Adam Smith called this kind of decentralized coordination the invisible hand of the market, and we usually take for granted that it is the most effective way for companies to interact with one another.

But what if this kind of decentralized coordination were used to organize all the different kinds of activities that today go on *inside* companies? One of the things that allow a free market to work is the establishment and acceptance of a set of standards—the "rules of the game"—that governs all the transactions. The rules of the game can take many forms, including contracts, systems of ownership, and procedures for dispute resolution. Similarly, for an e-lance economy to work, whole new classes of agreements, specifications, and common architectures will need to evolve.

We see this already in the Internet, which works because everyone involved with it conforms to certain technical specifications. You don't have to ask anyone for permission to become a network provider or a service provider or a user; you just have to obey the communication protocols that govern the Internet. Standards are the glue that holds the Internet together, and they will be the glue that binds temporary companies together and helps them operate efficiently.

To return to our auto industry scenario, car designers would be able to work independently because they would have on-line access to highly detailed engineering protocols. These standards would ensure that individual component designs are compatible with the overall design of the vehicle. Headlight designers, for example, would know the exact space allocated for the light assembly as well as the nature of any connections that need to be made with the electrical and control systems.

Standards don't have to take the form of technical specifications. They may take the form of routinized processes, such as we see today in the medical community. When doctors, nurses, and technicians gather to perform emergency surgery, they usually all know what process to follow, what role each will play, and how they'll interact with one another. Even if they've never worked together before, they can collaborate effectively without delay. In other cases, the standards may simply be patterns of behavior that come to be accepted as norms—what might today be referred to as the culture of a company or "the way things are done" in an industry.

One of the primary roles for the large companies that remain in the future may be to establish rules, standards, and cultures for network organizations operating partly within and partly outside their own boundaries. Some global consulting firms already operate in more or less this way. For example, McKinsey & Company has established a strong organizational culture with well-understood norms for how people are selected and promoted and how they are expected to work with others in the company. But the top managers do not tell individual partners what kind of work to do, which clients to work for, or which people to select for their consulting teams. Instead, the partners make largely autonomous decisions about what they will do and how they will do it. In other words, the value the firm provides to its members comes mainly from the standards—the rules of the game—it has established, not from the strategic or operational skills of its top managers.

As more large companies establish decentralized, market-based organizational structures, the boundaries between companies will become much less important. Transactions within organizations will become indistinguishable from transactions between organizations, and business processes, once proprietary, will freely cross organizational boundaries. The key role for many individuals—whether they call themselves managers or not—will be to play their parts in shaping a network that neither they nor anyone else controls.

Thinking About the Future

Most of what you've just read is, of course, speculative. Some of it may happen; some of it may not. Big companies may split apart, or they may stay together but adopt much more decentralized structures. The future of business may turn out to be far less revolutionary than we've sketched out, or it may turn out to be far more revolutionary. We're convinced, though, of one thing—an e-lance economy, though a radical concept, is by no means an impossible or even an implausible concept. Most of the necessary building blocks—high-bandwidth networks, data interchange standards, groupware, electronic currency, venture capital micromarkets—either are in place or are under development.

What is lagging behind technology is our imagination. Most people are not able to conceive of a completely new economy where much of what they know about doing business no longer applies. Mitch Resnick, a colleague of ours at MIT, says that most people are locked into a "centralized mind-set." When we look up into the sky and see a flock of birds flying in formation, we tend to assume that the bird in front is the leader and that the leader is somehow determining the organization of all the other birds. In fact, biologists tell us, each bird is following a simple set of rules—behavioral standards—that result in the emergence of the organization. The bird in the front is no more important than the bird in the back or the bird in the middle. They're all equally essential to the pattern that they're forming.

The reason it's so important for us to recognize and to challenge the biases of our existing mind-set is that the rise of an e-lance economy would have profound implications for business and society, and we should begin considering those implications sooner rather than later. An e-lance economy might well lead to a flowering of individual wealth, freedom, and creativity. Business might become much more flexible and efficient, and people might find themselves with much more time for leisure, for education, and for other pursuits. A Golden Age might dawn.

On the other hand, an e-lance economy might lead to disruption and dislocation. Loosed from its traditional moorings, the business world might become chaotic and cutthroat. The gap between society's haves and have-nots might widen, as those lacking special talents or access to electronic networks fall by the wayside. The safety net currently formed by corporate benefit programs, such as health and disability insurance, might unravel.[3] E-lance workers, separated from the communities that companies create today, may find themselves lonely and alienated. All of these potential problems could likely be avoided, but we won't be able to avoid them if we remain blind to them.

Twenty-four years from now, in the year 2022, the *Harvard Business Review* will be celebrating its 100th year of publication. As part of its centennial celebration, it may well publish a series of articles that look back on recent business history and contemplate the massive changes that have taken place. The authors may write about the industrial organization of the 20th century as merely a transitional structure that flourished for a relatively brief time. They may comment on the speed with which giant companies fragmented into the myriad micro-businesses that now dominate the economy. And they may wonder why, at the turn of the century, so few saw it coming.

Notes

1. For more about the influence of information technology on business organizations, see Thomas W. Malone, "Is 'Empowerment' Just a Fad? Control, Decision-Making, and Information Technology," *Sloan Management Review,* Winter 1997, p. 23; Thomas W. Malone, JoAnne Yates, and Robert I. Benjamin, "Electronic Markets and Electronic Hierarchies," *Communications of the ACM,* June 1987, p. 484; and Thomas W. Malone and John F. Rockart, "Computers, Networks, and the Corporation," *Scientific American,* September 1991, p. 128.

2. See Robert J. Laubacher, Thomas W. Malone, and the MIT Scenario Working Group, "Two Scenarios for 21st Century Organizations: Shifting Networks of Small Firms or All-Encompassing 'Virtual Countries'?" MIT Initiative on Inventing the Organizations of the 21st Century Working Paper No. 001 (Cambridge, Mass.: January 1997) available on the World Wide Web at http://ccs.mit.edu/21c/21CWP001.html.

3. Workers' guilds, common in the Middle Ages, may again rise to prominence, taking over many of the welfare functions currently provided by big companies. See Robert J. Laubacher and Thomas W. Malone, "Flexible Work Arrangements and 21st Century Worker's Guilds," MIT Initiative on Inventing the Organizations of the 21st Century Working Paper No. 004 (Cambridge, Mass.: October 1997) available on the World Wide Web at http://ccs.mit.edu/21c/21CWP004.html.

2
The Real Virtual Factory

David M. Upton and Andrew McAfee

By now, the monolithic factory was supposed to have given way to the virtual factory: a community of dozens, if not hundreds, of factories, each focused on what it does best, all linked by an electronic network that would enable them to operate as one—flexibly and inexpensively—regardless of their locations. This network would make it easy for companies with dissimilar computer systems to exchange information about inventory levels and delivery schedules. It would allow companies with different CAD systems to collaborate electronically on designs. It would permit potential suppliers to gain entry to the system in order to bid on jobs with minimal hassle and little or no investment. And finally, it would allow a small manufacturer to have the same access to information as a large partner.

For most companies, however, true electronic collaboration remains elusive. Networks for producing autos, textiles, and many other products do exist. But when one looks at how they share information, one is reminded of what Dr. Samuel Johnson said: "It is not done well; but you are surprised to find it done at all." Even highly sophisticated companies have found—and continue to find—the task of creating seamless electronic networks of lean, computer-integrated manufacturing operations to be frustrating and difficult. Managers at most of these companies are still struggling to make their information systems more flexible. They are perplexed about why so much paper is still being shuffled around. They are desperate to figure out how to extend the network to more of their partners without causing costs and overhead to balloon. And they do not understand why their heavy investments in IT have not radically changed the way their companies work.

Clearly, the three main technologies that companies have employed to create the virtual factory—electronic data interchange (EDI), proprietary groupware (such as Lotus Notes), and dedicated wide-area networks—are not complete solutions. Although that conclusion is hardly a revelation, many managers do not understand exactly why these technologies are not delivering. The reasons become clearer if one thinks about the different demands a network must meet for a large-scale virtual factory to succeed.

Working with companies in industries such as electronics, white goods, paper, and aerospace, we discerned three basic demands on such a network:

- It must be able to accommodate network members whose IT sophistication varies enormously—from the small machine shop with a single PC in the corner to the large site that boasts an array of engineering workstations and mainframes.

- While maintaining a high level of security, it must be able to cope with a constantly churning pool of suppliers and customers whose relationships vary enormously in intimacy and scope.

- It must give its members a great deal of functionality, including the capacity to transfer files between computers, the power to access common pools of information, and the capability to access and utilize all the programs on a computer located at a distant site.

EDI, groupware, and wide-area networks can each deal with some of these demands, but none can deal with all of them, nor can combinations of the three technologies. Does this sad fact mean that the virtual factory remains a mirage—a wonderful destination that can't ever be reached? The answer is no. *Real* virtual factories are now being built. For example, AeroTech, a small, relatively young information-services company, has built one for McDonnell Douglas Aerospace that represents a radical departure from the approaches that others have taken. (See "The Real Virtual Factory That AeroTech Built" on page 85.) AeroTech has created a networked manufacturing community that is open and friendly to even the most unsophisticated users, provides a very high degree of functionality, and works even though the community's membership is constantly changing.

Two critical elements make this type of networked manufacturing community possible: a function we call an information broker and open standards based on the protocols established for the Internet. As anyone who has used the Internet's World Wide Web knows, open standards make it relatively easy for members of a community to share information regardless of differences in their individual IT systems. In addition, they make it possible for members to use one another's computing power. Finally, the Internet's open standards permit each member of an *internetwork* to pick the communication channels—from a normal phone line to a high-speed connection—that are best suited for it to carry out its role in the virtual factory. In a real virtual factory, the network is the factory.

The information broker, which is an outside vendor in McDonnell Douglas's virtual factory, performs a variety of functions. It signs up new partners. It keeps track of the network's members and the number and level of relationships that each has with others in the network. It oversees security, constantly ensuring that each partner has the proper security clearance and access codes. Although AeroTech does not yet do so, an information broker could also serve as a converter, employing powerful conversion software to permit partners who have different formats or proprietary software to exchange information.

The Demands of a Virtual Factory

Before laying out the mechanics of an information-brokered manufacturing internetwork—a real virtual factory—it might help if we first explored why existing forms of EDI, groupware, and wide-area networks are inadequate. To that end, let's examine how each can or cannot satisfy the three main demands on a virtual factory:

1. that it be able to incorporate partners at any *stage* of a relationship,
2. that it be able to incorporate partners with all *levels* of IT sophistication, and
3. that it be able to provide all required *functionality*.

DIFFERENT STAGES

Like people in a romantic relationship, manufacturing partners typically move through progressively closer stages—from dating through engagement to marriage. During the exploratory stage, companies learn about each other and establish norms of interaction and bases for further involvement. For companies, exploratory activities include requesting, sending, and obtaining information about products and services; distributing requests for bids and receiving quotes; and establishing contracts and purchase orders. Collaboration entails more sharing and planning. Companies at this stage have agreed, for example, to work together as customer and supplier and therefore want to exchange and review more detailed data, such as CAD/CAM files and manufacturing-process documentation. Integrated manufacturing partners expect a continuing relationship—for example, in a joint venture. Their activities include sharing data about production, inventory, and schedules and accessing the information and applications resident on each other's machines.

At any one moment, it is common for a company to be at different stages with its various partners. It may have several joint-venture partners and at the same time may be constantly shuffling customers and making changes in its relationships with suppliers. To support many relationships at all stages, information systems must be easy to enter and leave: a network that is expensive or difficult to join will discourage exploration. In addition, networks must be secure: potential participants will not join a system that will expose their internal networks or their transmissions to spies and hackers.

DIFFERENT LEVELS OF IT SOPHISTICATION

Regardless of the stage of their relationship, participants in a virtual factory will vary greatly in their level of sophistication about information technology. That level is a combination of several factors, including the type and power of installed hardware and software; the average and highest level of computer expertise among site personnel; and the degree to which people on the site are already connected to one another by an internal network.

Within the typical large manufacturing company, different groups are themselves at different levels. A design group might have a cluster of linked workstations running advanced drawing and modeling software. The production control function might access mainframe manufacturing-resource-planning (MRP) software from dumb terminals. A sales manager might have a lone PC. And it would not be unusual if none of the three could interact with the others electronically, even if they were all on the same site.

There is also tremendous variation across smaller companies. For example, a subcontractor specializing in finite element analysis or other modeling techniques is likely to have an advanced computing environment, whereas a supplier of packaging materials may have only rudimentary systems. The wide range means that any technology underpinning a real virtual factory must be easy to implement, even on low-end hardware.

HIGH FUNCTIONALITY

Manufacturing groups have both heavy and complex information-sharing requirements. By *heavy*, we mean the great volume of information involved in any manufacturing process. For example, consider the body of documentation needed to specify how to build even a relatively simple part, the different information formats typically used, and the information required to move the item through the production process. As the part moves among partners' sites, this ever mounting pile of information must go with it. For complex parts, the amount of information required can be staggering. The paper required to fully describe the production of a Boeing 747 undoubtedly would not fit inside the airplane itself.

Information-sharing requirements within manufacturing are also complex. The IT process required to send a purchase order, for example, is very different from the process required to send an assembly. The former is a simple transmission of text, whereas the latter is an interactive manipulation of graphical data. Both, however, are common activities that a real virtual factory should support.

Sharing and manipulating all information on a network involve three distinct types of functionality. In ascending order of complexity, they are: simple data transmission, data access, and access to applications, or what we call *telepresence*.

Transmission is the most straightforward; it is simply sending a packet of information from one place to another. Partners in a virtual factory need to exchange all kinds of information, from E-mail to purchase orders to numerical control programs. Transmissions such as videoconferences need to occur in real time, but most do not.

Data access capabilities permit members of the community to share common pools of information in more sophisticated ways than simply by passing messages to one another. For example, by creating virtual bulletin boards and file cabinets that authorized users can open, companies can make sure that all participants in a product development project are abiding by the same schedule, that updated CAD files are always available to suppliers, or that regulators can monitor emissions levels. A real virtual factory must be able to permit some users to add or change information in databases in addition to viewing it.

The highest level of required functionality is telepresence, a capability that allows all authorized people to see and use the programs resident on a given computer, whether the users are company insiders or outsiders and whether they are on-site or far away. This attribute is one of the key advantages of the Internet, which lets cybernauts jump from machine to machine around the world, making use of the information and applications on each.

Telepresence is extraordinarily useful within a virtual factory. For example, it allows small companies to use the number-crunching power of a large partner for computationally intensive simulations, and it permits a customer to check the status of an order by logging on to a supplier's order-management system. That kind of activity can even be performed by means of a home page on the World Wide Web. (See "Virtual Factories, the World Wide Web, and Java" on page 88.)

A real virtual factory, then, provides all this functionality to its partners, regardless of the stage of their relationships or their level of IT sophistication. Exhibit 2-1, "Three Factors Determine the Ease of Information Sharing," provides a framework that can help managers analyze whether their current solutions are adequate for their needs. The exhibit shows, for example, that it is much easier for companies at the integrated stage to agree on and build an information sharing structure than it is for companies that are only at the cooperative stage. Similarly, it shows that it is much harder to connect naïve IT users than sophisticated ones or to provide access to applications—real telepresence.

Current Approaches

To compare different approaches to electronic collaboration, note how much of the cube each fills. A system that fills a lot of the space, especially one that reaches close to the back corner (where unsophisticated companies at the exploratory stage can transparently use others' machines), makes real virtual factories possible. Let's take a look at the three different categories of technology currently in use and see how they stack up.

ELECTRONIC DATA INTERCHANGE

EDI is the oldest form of electronic collaboration among manufacturers; it grew out of a need to simplify the paperwork for administer-

Exhibit 2-1   Three Factors Determine the Ease of
Information Sharing

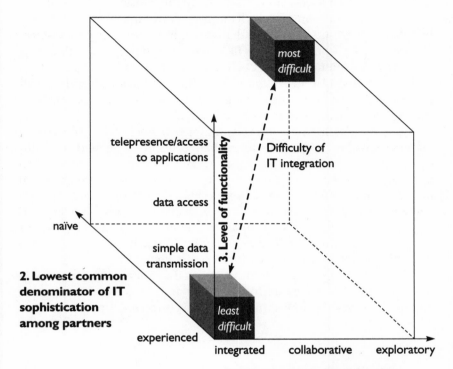

ing the Berlin airlift. Today's EDI uses a collection of common formats for communicating data between companies. It is used most frequently to exchange data such as purchase orders, to execute transfers of electronic funds, or to provide delivery information to customers. EDI standards specify how each of these information transfers should be structured so that any party using those formats can accept transmission from any other party using them.

However, conventional forms of EDI cannot satisfy all the demands of a virtual factory. Despite the existence of some common standards, many systems are still inflexible and proprietary. As a consequence, it is expensive and time consuming both to add new members to such a network and to expand the types of information exchanged on it. Depending on the particular network, it can cost tens of thousands of dollars to add an EDI link and to mold one's own computer protocols to those used by the dominant customer. Such attributes mean that conventional EDI is best suited for linking the members of a relatively small, stable community—particularly a community in which one member is powerful enough to demand adherence to its communications standards. Conversely, it is ill suited for communities with a large number of transient members or members with limited IT resources. With traditional EDI, every time a new member is added to the existing system, a dedicated line—and in many cases, a special terminal on the member's premises—must be installed.

Conventional EDI has other limitations. It does not easily permit members of the community to exchange information with one another, because the system has to be specially configured to create each link between each pair of members that want to communicate. EDI networks tend to be used only to send information in batches and are awkward for creating real-time links between sites. Also, current EDI systems are not designed to allow members to operate a partner's computer from a remote location in order to use its applications software and computing power or to access its files.

Current EDI fills very little of the virtual factory's requirements. It provides only a low level of functionality and, because of its expense and fixed costs, is appropriate only for integrated partners. (See Exhibit 2-2.)

GROUPWARE

The class of software known as groupware addresses some of EDI's drawbacks and has become popular for building collaborative environments. Groupware applications help coordinate work in three ways. First, they make available a common body of information so that, for example, a salesperson on the road can check the in-stock status of an item for a customer. Second, they track work flows so that group members can—from a remote location—collaborate on documents and projects; all members of a design team, for example, can use proprietary groupware to make sure they are working with the most recent version of a drawing. Finally, the software provides a platform for communication and interactive discussions, from E-mail and bulletin boards to on-screen video. A major advantage of groupware is that all links do not need to be preestablished; authorized users can access and leave the system at will.

*Exhibit 2-2   Electronic Data Interchange and the
Virtual Factory's Needs*

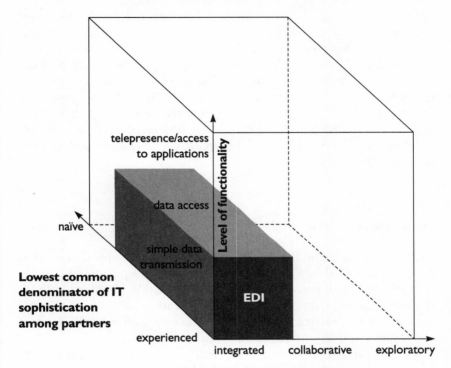

On the downside, groupware can be expensive. Each individual user must purchase a copy of the groupware application, and training and administration expenses for the new platform are high. Lotus Notes, for example, costs between $1,000 and $5,000 per user over a three-year period (*PC Week,* January 30, 1995).

A further drawback is that groupware cannot be used to gain access to remote computers that are not groupware servers. For example, it is not possible to use Lotus Notes to connect to another site's manufacturing information system to review inventory policies or to use its CAD software to work on the drawings of a part.

In summary, traditional groupware has many of the transmission and data access capabilities that an effective virtual factory needs. In addition, it requires a relatively low level of IT sophistication: people comfortable with PCs, for example, can use it without much difficulty. But groupware lacks adequate telepresence capabilities. Partners cannot use each other's applications. And because groupware entails a significant amount of administration and overhead, companies typically will not choose to use it to collaborate until it is clear that their relationship will continue. It will not be used by companies that are at the exploratory stage or anticipating a short relationship. If the community consists of a small number of partners that need to exchange only basic information such as orders, then EDI, because of its relative simplicity, is preferable to groupware. Although groupware is superior to traditional electronic data interchange in filling the requirements of a virtual factory, it nonetheless is far from perfect. (See Exhibit 2-3.)

WIDE-AREA NETWORKS

This class of technology provides dedicated high-speed links that connect individual local-area networks. Unlike groupware links, wide-area networks are permanent and usually provide members with all the transmission, data-access, and telepresence capabilities that a real virtual factory requires. They provide universal access to all data and applications resident on members' local-area networks.

Membership in a wide-area network, however, is exclusive and expensive to obtain. The high-bandwidth telecommunications lines that make up their backbones, for example, typically cost more than $1,000 per month. In addition, administration of a dispersed network is complicated, and a group needs a relatively high degree of IT sophistication to participate. Consequently, wide-area networks usually exist only within a company and are rarely extended to other partners.

Because of those constraints, even large manufacturers build wide-area networks between only a few of their large sites and exclude smaller sites and smaller partner companies. Wide-area networks fill a tall but narrow slice of the total requirements of a virtual factory and cannot be extended to support companies that are at the cooperative or exploratory stages. (See Exhibit 2-4.)

These limitations mean that proprietary wide-area networks are like an exclusive club. It is very difficult, for example, to use a wide-area network to share CAD data files with potential partners who might be interested in bidding for work. It also is difficult to add a new member

Exhibit 2-3   Groupware and the Virtual Factory's Needs

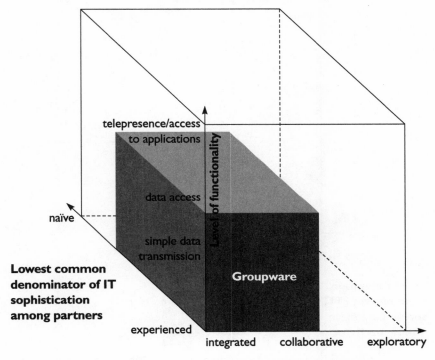

to the system quickly to exploit a new opportunity to codesign a product—a severe limitation in this age of rapid product development.

The Information-Brokered Internetwork

Could someone patch together EDI, groupware, and wide-area networks to create a mosaic that would fill the needs of a full-fledged virtual factory? No. Proprietary and disparate standards make such a network extraordinarily expensive, complex, inelegant, and, in the long run, dysfunctional. Moreover, none of the three conventional technologies accommodate exploratory relationships.

But a more flexible and less expensive alternative for carrying out collaborative manufacturing has just emerged—the information-

Exhibit 2-4   Wide-area Networks and the
Virtual Factory's Needs

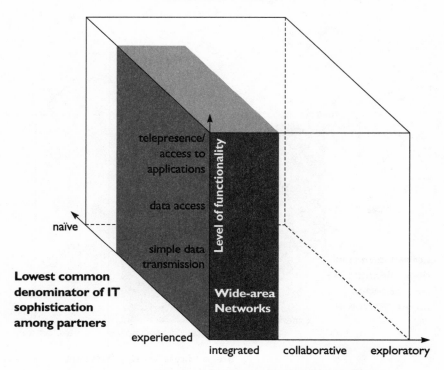

brokered internetwork. The confluence of several trends now makes this approach possible: the emergence of widely accepted, open standards; ever cheaper computing power; increasingly abundant bandwidth; the development of essentially unbreakable computer security; and accumulated expertise.

OPEN STANDARDS

Standards among computers are simply agreements about how data should be formatted or transmitted. The most important for the emerging virtual factories are the TCP/IP protocols developed for the Internet, which standardize how dissimilar computers and networks pass data among themselves. The TCP/IP protocols allow the three levels of functionality we have described: transmission, data access, and telepresence. As the unbelievable growth of the Internet attests, these increasingly dominant protocols have been helpful because they are comprehensive, open (published), and nonproprietary (free).

At the same time, standards for text files, spreadsheets, CAD drawings, and other electronic documents that make it easier for companies using different applications to exchange data also have emerged. Consequently, partners who share these standards on how to send information and what it should look like can communicate with confidence that nothing will be lost in the translation.

CHEAP, POWERFUL COMPUTING

Because of the phenomenal increase in computing power available per dollar, sufficient computing muscle for almost any information-sharing task in a virtual factory is now well within the financial reach of even the smallest companies.

ABUNDANT BANDWIDTH

The information-carrying capacity of a communications link, or its bandwidth, has been increasing at least as fast as computing power. For example, standard modems today provide as much bandwidth as the highest-speed links did ten years ago, and dedicated links between two partners now provide enough bandwidth for full-motion video conferences, a very high bandwidth application. And several emerging technologies promise to increase bandwidth dramatically in the near future.

SECURITY

Information security is understandably a major concern for companies seeking to build virtual factories. But despite the continuing tales of break-ins and hacker exploits, tools such as network fire walls—computers that act as bouncers and check all incoming data—provide the means to keep outsiders out and to limit or customize each insider's access. In addition, essentially unbreakable data-encoding schemes now guarantee that information sent over the Internet or any other network remains unreadable until it reaches its destination.

ACCUMULATED EXPERTISE

It takes time to master any emerging technology. But companies now are comfortably familiar with current open standards and the new technologies in computing, bandwidth, and security. Indeed, many businesses now have the skills required to innovate with these technologies and therefore the power to construct real virtual factories.

A network with the attributes listed above elegantly satisfies the demands of a virtual factory across all stages of relationships and all but the most naïve level of IT sophistication. (See Exhibit 2-5.) Transient or prospective partners as well as small companies and unsophisticated IT users will be willing and able to join the community because the costs and overhead of membership are very low. Once all these companies are connected, each one can access a wider pool of computing power and information. For example:

- A large company can quickly and inexpensively send bid-request packages to a much wider range of potential subcontractors than it could before.
- People can access other companies' on-line catalogs, get all required product specifications, and place orders from their desktops.
- A machine shop can use the three-dimensional modeling software resident on a distant mainframe to place the part it plans to make within a digital mock-up of a larger assembly and check that it fits—before the first one is produced.

These examples represent only a tiny fraction of the total uses that members will find for a virtual factory. Robert Metcalfe, inventor of the wide-spread Ethernet networking standard, contends that the utility of a computer network increases exponentially, not linearly, as the number of users expands. We are confident that real virtual factories will provide solid support for Metcalfe's Law.

The Information Broker

Of course, it is one thing for a networked factory to be possible or desirable, and it is quite another to create and maintain it and help

*Exhibit 2-5   The Brokered Internetwork and the Virtual
Factory's Needs*

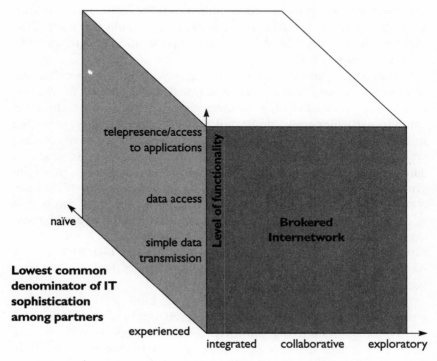

it evolve. Designing the system, administering it, updating its technology, maintaining security, and exploiting new opportunities as
they arise are collectively a huge job—and one that most companies
whose primary business is not IT will be loath to undertake. Indeed,
McDonnell Douglas has turned to what we call an information broker
to perform this function.

McDonnell Douglas's spin-off AeroTech developed the aerospace
company's virtual factory and, in its role as information broker, keeps
everything running smoothly. AeroTech maintains a database of all
users and of all the information to which each is allowed access. It also
has developed software packages and training manuals that allow
small companies to join the community easily and quickly. For larger,
more established partners, AeroTech builds gateways to their exist-

ing networks and establishes high-bandwidth links. Finally, AeroTech could eventually convert or translate the various data formats that exist across the virtual factory. For example, if one manufacturer's CAD data were written in Catia and another's is in Pro/Engineer, AeroTech could translate the data for them so that they could work together. More important, it could build a system that would perform this type of service automatically.

Potentially, an information broker can provide much more than the computer security, maintenance, and translation functions for the virtual factory. It can help the partners identify which information has value to particular constituents and how revenue might be generated from this information. For example, one company may have test data on the performance characteristics of its valve components, and that data might be tremendously useful to another company in its design process. Or the design department of a particular company might have ready-made CAD drawings of a wide range of electrical connectors and might choose to sell them to a partner that wanted to avoid drawing them from scratch. And a larger company might keep a list of suppliers that have been certified for meeting the ISO-9000 quality standards—a list that could be useful to others looking for such vendors.

Very few IT contractors presently have the kind of relationship that would allow them to explore and exploit opportunities like these jointly. Why? Identifying information-sharing opportunities on the network requires industry knowledge that is both broad and deep. Current systems integrators rarely have such knowledge.

The first generation of internetwork-building information brokers will probably be either spin-offs of larger companies, such as AeroTech, or completely new companies composed of computer networking experts and veterans of the particular industry who have a deep understanding of how the industry works. Real virtual factories are likely to proliferate first in environments where there is a large, dominant partner that can provide the impetus and the funding. McDonnell Douglas Aerospace, for example, had a clear idea of its requirements and was willing initially to assume all the costs of filling them, even though others also would reap benefits.

Eventually, however, many different models for building virtual factories are likely to arise. They may be star-like structures with dominant centers or manufacturing communities in which groups of small manufacturers band together for the same kinds of benefits available to large traditional factories with abundant resources for expanding information technology. The rigid formulation of traditional electronic data interchange will give way to a world of greater fluidity.

Once the benefits of the real virtual factory have been demonstrated, they will create a new manufacturing world. In this new world, companies that insist on remaining loners or that cling to today's closed, proprietary systems will find it increasingly difficult to survive.

The Real Virtual Factory That AeroTech Built

AeroTech Service Group, which is based in St. Louis, Missouri, has built a highly effective virtual factory with McDonnell Douglas Aerospace. The open and flexible network accommodates users whose IT sophistication and relationships with one another vary greatly. Moreover, it permits members to carry out a wide variety of collaborative tasks and is extremely secure.

Those attributes explain why the number of participants in this computer-linked manufacturing community has soared since mid-1993, when AeroTech, a McDonnell Douglas spin-off, began adding external suppliers to the network. Until then, the network had been limited to 50 or so McDonnell employees who used it to pass data between different computer systems within the organization. When external suppliers joined, they were so impressed with the way the network helped them work with McDonnell that they started to ask *their* suppliers and partners to join. By the fall of 1994, there were 400 internal and external users. There are now several thousand.

To accommodate a broad range of tasks and users, and to make the system as simple as possible to use, AeroTech employs protocols developed for the Internet, which itself is just an extra-large network that connects millions of dissimilar computers around the world. In addition, AeroTech permits members to choose from a wide assortment of telecommunication methods and speeds. Those members with minimal or sporadic needs access the system with modems, while more permanent participants, such as customers within other large aerospace companies or the U.S. government, use dedicated high-bandwidth links.

The network offers its members enormous advantages. Consider how McDonnell Douglas and UCAR Composites, a $12 million manufacturer of tooling for high-performance composite components based in Irvine, California, use the network to build prototypes of complex new parts rapidly. McDonnell wanted to send UCAR design updates electronically but could not allow UCAR to establish a direct link into its computers because of security concerns—namely, that an aggressive hacker might tap into such a link to access or modify data within McDonnell computers. (Although UCAR is a trusted supplier, McDonnell has a large number of suppliers of similar size and importance, and the cost of maintaining security if all had direct links would be prohibitive.)

AeroTech provided an alternative. At McDonnell, computer-aided design files are translated into the numerical-control machine code needed to operate UCAR's metal-cutting machines. Using standard Internet protocols over a dedicated high-speed link, McDonnell then transfers the CAD file and the metal-cutting program to AeroTech's secure network node. AeroTech's system then forwards them to UCAR on normal phone lines.

Once information on the job arrives in California, UCAR engineers can view it on their own CAD/CAM systems to make last-minute checks on the program. They then transfer the cutting program to their machines and begin manufacturing. The solution was particularly attractive for UCAR, which already had a paperless manufacturing operation. Now it could feed the data directly into its manufacturing and quality-assurance systems. As a result of the AeroTech system, the cost of these transfers has fallen from $400 per file (for tapes and express mail) to $4—and can be carried out in seconds rather than days.

This method of transferring cutting programs also is being used by hundreds of small machine shops, many of whose IT systems and expertise are much less sophisticated than UCAR's. These companies, which include many five- or six-person shops, can dial AeroTech using a regular modem, download a program or a drawing onto their PCs, and use the data to manufacture the parts.

This virtual factory also helps its members find the best suppliers much more quickly than before. In the past, McDonnell Douglas would invite representatives of qualified suppliers to come to St. Louis to view bid-request packages (containing engineering drawings and manufacturing-process specifications) so that they could decide whether and how much to bid for particular jobs. The groups would remain at the bidding table until all jobs were subcontracted—a process that often would take days.

Using the virtual factory's electronic bidding system, a McDonnell buyer now can E-mail qualified suppliers throughout the world that a job is available for bidding and let them access information about the job securely through the Internet. The suppliers then can use the system to return their bids to St. Louis. The system even ranks the bids for the buyer on the basis of cost. McDonnell estimates that the savings from electronic bidding alone pay for the operating costs of the entire system.

AeroTech also helps the electronic manufacturing community coordinate schedules better by allowing remote members to use scheduling software on one another's machines. A Department of Defense project manager in Washington, D.C., might use the system to access a McDonnell Douglas mainframe and run the graphics-based program that maintains a project's schedule. The manager then could get early warnings of time overruns by checking whether subcontractors were completing their subassemblies on time.

One of the most powerful functions that the AeroTech community provides is the ability to operate large, complex software programs securely from afar, without the need for sophisticated equipment on the local site. As a part of its contract with McDonnell Helicopter, for example, the U.S. Army periodically reviews engineering designs for the new Longbow helicopter. The army now can view these drawings by operating a McDonnell computer from a remote location, rather than by downloading the files, which would require the army to have the enormous CAD software systems on its own machines. The drawings and the graphics program to view them reside on a workstation in Phoenix, Arizona. AeroTech has configured the computer to serve this program to authorized clients, such as the army's reviewers. AeroTech maintains a database that constantly keeps track of which connections are allowed, by whom, into which computers, and with what level of functionality. All transmissions are routed in real time through AeroTech's watchdog computers to prevent Internet interlopers from breaking into the Phoenix computer or customers' computers on the network.

It's true that closed groups of technically sophisticated companies with long-standing partnerships carry out many of these same kinds of tasks. But, unlike them, AeroTech has made it possible for both longtime and casual partners to collaborate easily, securely, and cheaply, and without having to invest in new and proprietary information technology.

AeroTech and McDonnell are now exploring ways to generate even more value from this system. In particular, AeroTech is looking at how it might become an information broker for engineering data by providing a conduit through which McDonnell could sell and distribute drawings for the spare-parts business. Currently, spare parts are procured by the Defense Logistics Agency, which requests quotations for manufacturing them. Because many prospective manufacturers are unable to access the appropriate drawings quickly enough, a small number of companies, including McDonnell, end up with the business.

McDonnell, however, may choose to sell rapid access to the drawings and technical data so that a larger pool of qualified companies can bid on the jobs. By stimulating competition, this approach could improve the quality of its spares providers, allow McDonnell to manufacture only those spares that are most worth its while to make, and generate a higher return on the information systems that manage and store the technical data. AeroTech would help more producers of spares join the virtual factory, activate their access to the information required to make the spares, and bill the producer of the data, using whatever pricing model McDonnell Douglas chooses. Clearly, McDonnell Douglas, AeroTech, and the other members of this virtual factory have only begun to mine its vast potential.

Virtual Factories, the World Wide Web, and Java

Advances in internetworking technologies are making virtual factories easier to build. First, there is the much vaunted explosive growth of the World Wide Web. The Web's primary importance, from a manufacturing point of view, is that it provides a common visual interface to connect to a computer network.

Growing numbers of companies are embracing these standard browsers and protocols as the way for sites in different organizations to communicate with one another. This broad acceptance makes the World Wide Web an immensely powerful tool for intercompany transactions. The power and ubiquity of these protocols and interfaces will make the Web one of the mainstays of virtual factories to come. Web sites already can help buyers of electronic components find what they're looking for on the Web (see http://centralres.com) or match buyers and sellers from more than 26,000 companies in the apparel and textile industry (see http://www.apparelex.com). And Netscape is teaming up with General Electric Information Services to offer EDI services through the Web.

A second development ultimately may prove to be at least as important as the Web: the advent of languages such as Sun's Java, which will allow a user to connect to a remote site and grab tiny pieces of software (called *applets*) one at a time. Any computer that can run a Web browser can run this kind of software. Many people have speculated that this way of working will eventually challenge the existing methods of running programs on the desktop. Desktop users currently must buy increasingly large, complex program packages to perform tasks such as word processing or spreadsheet analysis. Those packages contain a vast array of functions that any individual user will never use. In contrast, Internet-based Java-like languages will allow customers to obtain modules for performing particular functions as they need them by downloading them across an increasingly fast and reliable Internet. Users will pay for the functions they need. For example, a customer purchasing a word-processing program will not have to buy a spelling checker as part of the package but, instead, can download an applet containing the checker from the Internet if and when needed. And Java was developed with security safeguards in place to foil viruses and other threats.

Consider what this capability will mean for the virtual factory. A company will be able to post work-sheet applets on its Web pages to allow customers to simulate the function of its products before buying them. For example, a valve manufacturer might supply an applet that allows engineers not only to see pictures and CAD drawings of the valves but also to use a working spreadsheet that would permit them to make key design calculations and show the results on-screen.

Such applets also will allow companies to deliver sophisticated bid requests over the Web. These requests could include a combination of moving diagrams of the product that they would like potential suppliers to bid on, along with bid forms and more traditional drawings.

A Java-based interface for a three-dimensional CAD system not only allows companies to put a catalog on the Web but also lets potential customers examine a three-dimensional representation of a product from any angle to see if it is right for their needs (see http://deneb.hbs.edu/public/javademo/viewer.html). If the user has to access a large legacy database at another company and doesn't happen to have the right kind of terminal, Java can even make a Web browser pretend to be that terminal by emulating it in software (see http://www.unige.ch/hotjava/Emulator3270.html). As network-based software becomes more and more sophisticated, it will present new opportunities to extract the power of the Web for manufacturing.

3
Developing Products on Internet Time

Marco Iansiti and Alan MacCormack

The rise of the World Wide Web has provided one of the most challenging environments for product development in recent history. The market needs that a product is meant to satisfy and the technologies required to satisfy them can change radically—even as the product is under development. In response to such factors, companies have had to modify the traditional product-development process in which design implementation begins only once a product's concept has been determined in its entirety. Instead, they have pioneered a *flexible* product-development process that allows designers to continue to define and shape products even after implementation has begun. This innovation enables Internet companies to incorporate rapidly changing customer requirements and evolving technologies into their designs until the last possible moment before a product is introduced to the market.

Flexible product development has been most fully realized in the Internet environment because of the turbulence found there, but the foundations for it exist in a wide range of industries where the need for responsiveness is paramount. Product developers in industries from computer workstations to banking increasingly face dynamic and unpredictable environments characterized by rapidly evolving technologies, changing customer tastes, and sweeping regulatory changes. In these industries, companies that have begun to adopt more flexible product-development approaches are setting new competitive standards.

What's involved in increasing the flexibility of the product development process? Many of the companies we studied have adopted a coherent set of mechanisms that allow product developers to gen-erate and respond to new information about what customers want and about how technology has evolved over the course of a project. These mechanisms not only enable a continuous flow of informa-tion about customer needs and new technologies but also reduce both the cost and the time it takes to integrate that information into the evolving product design. They allow designers continually *to sense* customer needs, *to test* alternative technical solutions, and *to integrate* the acquired knowledge into a coherent product design. This flex-ible process continues iteratively throughout the development process.

The traditional development processes that many companies use are highly structured. A future product is designed, developed, transferred to production, and rolled out to the market in clearly articulated, se-quential phases. Such processes usually begin with the identification of users' needs and an assessment of the various technological possi-bilities. Then a detailed set of product specifications is created and, once approved by senior management, is set in stone. At that point, attention shifts to implementation as a functionally integrated team translates the concept into reality. If the up-front work has been done correctly, inherently expensive changes to the product's specifications are kept to a minimum. Indeed, the number of engineering changes is often used as a measure of a project's effectiveness: many changes sig-nify an inferior effort.

In contrast, flexible product development delays until as late as pos-sible any commitment to a final design configuration. The concept de-velopment phase and the implementation phase thus overlap instead of following each other sequentially. By accepting the need for and re-ducing the cost of changes, companies are able to respond to new in-formation that arises during the course of a product's development. Systemic changes in a project's definition and basic direction are man-aged proactively; designers begin this process with no precise idea of how it will end. (See Exhibit 3-1.)

When technology, product features, and competitive conditions are predictable or evolve slowly, a traditional development process works well. But in turbulent business environments, a sequential approach to product development is more than inefficient; it risks creating an obsolete product—one that fails to address customer needs and to make use of the latest technologies. When new competitors and tech-nologies are likely to appear overnight, when standards and regula-tions are in flux, and when a company's entire customer base can

Exhibit 3-1   Two Approaches to Product Development

The Traditional Approach

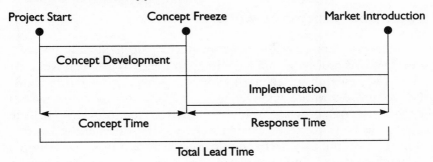

The Flexible Approach

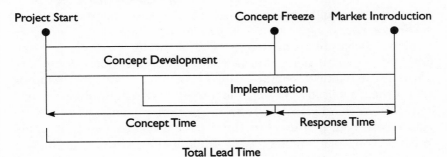

Speed is a subtle concept in this model. *Total lead time*—the time taken to fulfill the initial objectives of the project—is clearly important; but *concept time* and *response time* are critical measures themselves. Concept time is the window opportunity for including new information and for optimizing the match between the technology and its application context. Response time is the period during which the window is closed, the product's architecture is frozen, and the project is unable to react to new information. Although the total lead time is the same for both processes above, the flexible process has a shorter response time and is therefore preferable in rapidly changing environments.

easily switch to other suppliers, businesses don't need a development process that resists change—they need one that embraces it.

A Flexible Process at Work

Not every company interested in developing a flexible product-development process would have to go to the extremes that Netscape did. But by looking at Netscape's experiences, we can see how a highly flexible process works. Founded in 1994, the company pioneered the easy-to-use Web browser: a software interface that provides access to the World Wide Web. The Web browser has transformed the Internet from a communications channel for scientists and technicians into a network connecting millions of ordinary users across time and space—and thus into an industry in its own right.

But Netscape faced no easy task in developing its Web browser, Navigator. In the rapidly evolving Internet industry, many alternative technologies and applications compete for attention, and product development is a project manager's nightmare. The major challenge in the development of a Web browser is the level of technical complexity involved: a typical program rivals a traditional word processing or spreadsheet application in size, and it must work seamlessly with myriad different hardware and software platforms. The level of uncertainty is so high that even the most basic decisions about a product must be continually revised as new information arises. And the fact that industry giant Microsoft, which had already developed its own flexible product-development process, was readying a product to compete with Navigator only added to the complexity and urgency of Netscape's development effort.

Netscape introduced Navigator 2.0 to the market in January of 1996 and immediately thereafter began to develop the next version of the Web browser, Navigator 3.0, which was to be released in August of the same year. (See Exhibit 3-2.) The Netscape development group—which included staff from engineering, marketing, and customer support—produced the first prototype quickly. By February 14, just six weeks into the project, it had put a Beta 0 version of the program up on the company's internal project Web site for testing by the development staff. Although many of the intended functions were not yet available, the prototype captured enough of the essence of the new product to generate meaningful feedback from members of the development group. On February 22, less than two weeks later, the team

Exhibit 3-2   The Development of Navigator 3.0: A Timeline

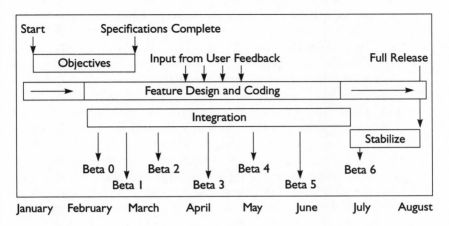

posed an updated version, Beta 1, again for internal development staff only. In early March, with major bugs in the product worked out, the first public release, Beta 2, appeared on Netscape's Internet Web site. Additional public releases followed thereafter every few weeks until the official release date in August, with gradual refinements appearing in each beta iteration.

The sequence of beta versions was extremely useful to Netscape because it enabled the development team to react both to feedback from users and to changes in the marketplace while the team was still working on the Web browser's design. Beta users by and large are more sophisticated than Netscape's broader customer base and therefore are a valuable source of information. Most useful among them are developers from other Internet software companies, who tend to be extremely vocal customers. Because many of these customers use the Navigator browser as part of the environment in which their own products operate, they are often the first to find the more complicated bugs—bugs that are revealed only when the product is stretched to the limits of its performance in complex applications.

Getting input from users was one way in which the Navigator team generated new information during the course of the project. During the seven-month development cycle, however, the team also paid careful attention to competing products. As the largest and most powerful software developer in the industry, Microsoft was considered a very serious threat to Netscape's then-dominant position in the

browser market. The software giant had just undertaken a dramatic—
and very public—switch in strategy, refocusing its formidable talents
squarely on the Internet. As a result, Netscape continually monitored
the latest beta versions of Microsoft's competing product, Explorer, to
compare features and formats. Based on the information that it gathered, the Netscape team would often add format or feature changes to
the current beta version of its own product.

In order to respond to the constant stream of new information being
brought into the development process, the team carried out extensive
experimentation and testing. Subgroups working on individual features went through numerous design-build-test cycles, gradually adding functionality to the product. As features were completed, the team
integrated them into the evolving product, then conducted tests to ensure that the new feature did not produce unwanted interactions with
other parts of the system. These so-called system builds occurred
with increasing frequency as the project progressed; they were performed at least daily in the run-up to the official release.

To facilitate the integration of the vast amounts of information generated during the project, Netscape set up a project Web site on its
intranet. The site contained the product's development schedule and
specifications, each of which was updated as target dates changed or
new features were added. In addition, it contained bulletin boards
through which team members could monitor the evolution of various
parts of the design, noting the completion of specific features and logging problems in the existing version. Once the Navigator moved to
public beta testing, these intranet features became especially valuable
because an increasing amount of information then had to be received,
classified, and processed.

Netscape built into its product-development process considerable
flexibility to respond to changes in market demands and technology.
And what is already true of companies in the Internet industry is becoming true of companies elsewhere. Our research on the computer-
workstation-and-server industry has shown that there, too, a more
flexible process is associated with greater performance. In this environment, companies with a faster response time, as measured from
the construction of the first physical prototype to commercial shipping, clearly outperform those with slower response times. The use of
sophisticated simulation tools allows teams to work with a virtual prototype for much of the project—in effect, creating a significant overlap
between the concept and the design implementation phases.

According to Allen Ward and his colleagues in "The Second Toyota Paradox: How Delaying Decisions Can Make Better Cars Faster" (*Sloan Management Review,* Spring 1995), there also is evidence that a more flexible model has emerged in the automotive industry. Toyota's development process allows it to delay many design decisions until later in the development cycle. The development team creates several sets of design options and, finally, through a process of elimination, selects only one for implementation. As a result, Toyota can respond to changing market conditions at a later stage than many of its competitors.

The Foundations of a Flexible Process

How should companies create a flexible development process? The experiences of leading companies suggest that senior managers first must understand what gives the process its flexibility. Product development flexibility is rooted in the ability to manage jointly the evolution of a product and its application context. The goal is to capture a rich understanding of customer needs and alternative technical solutions as a project progresses, then to integrate that knowledge into the evolving product design. The faster a project can integrate that information, the faster that project can respond to changes in the product's environment.

The value of flexible product development, however, is only as good as the quality of the process it uses to generate information about the interaction between technical choices and market requirements. Unlike traditional development projects, which rely on periodic bursts of input on users' needs, projects in turbulent business environments require continual feedback. To acquire and use this information, the development process must be able to sense customer needs, to test alternative technical solutions, and to integrate the knowledge gained of both markets and technologies into a coherent product. (See Exhibit 3-3.)

As we describe how leading companies have achieved a more flexible development process, many of the examples we cite come from our work with several software companies that have recently launched Internet products or services. But bear in mind that this is not the only industry in which these lessons apply. We also describe specific practices from other, more traditional industries to illustrate

Exhibit 3-3   The Structure of a Flexible Product-Development Process

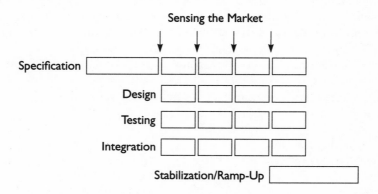

that the approaches used are not unique to the Internet. In fact, they represent cutting-edge practice across a range of environments where change is—or is becoming—the norm.

SENSING THE MARKET

The first element of a flexible process is sensing the needs of customers and the market. Flexible projects establish mechanisms for getting continual feedback from the market on how the evolving design meets customers' requirements. They do so by creating intensive links with the customer base—links that range from broad experimentation with many customers to selective experiences with a few lead users. Furthermore, these customers do not have to be external to the company: leading companies make extensive use of internal staff and resources to provide a test bed for evolving new products.

Gaining continual feedback from customers was particularly critical at Netscape because of its dramatic head-to-head race with Microsoft. Netscape's broad-based release of multiple beta versions to its entire customer base allowed users to play a significant role in the evolving product design. At the same time, it allowed Netscape to test an extremely complex technical product. Although not all Netscape's customers actually experimented with beta versions, the Web browser's most advanced users had to because they themselves were creating products that needed to work seamlessly with the Navigator release.

And their feedback clearly had an impact: a significant portion of the new code, features, and technology that were integrated into the new release was developed only after the first beta version went public.

Microsoft, Netscape's chief rival, was slow to recognize the opportunities offered by the World Wide Web. Not until the end of 1995 did the company begin to focus on developing Internet products. Yet when Bill Gates and the rest of the senior management team finally acknowledged the need for a strategic shift, Microsoft's development expertise was unleashed with astonishing speed. In the six months from the end of 1995 to the middle of 1996, the company went from having no presence in the critical browser market to offering a product that several industry experts claimed was comparable to or better than Netscape's Navigator.

Microsoft was able to react quickly because its existing product-development process had been founded on the rapid iteration of prototypes, early beta releases, and a flexible approach to product architecture and specification. (For a detailed account of Microsoft's development process, see Michael A. Cusumano and Richard W. Selby, *Microsoft Secrets* [Free Press, 1995].) The process that Microsoft followed in developing its Internet Explorer was similar to Netscape's but was more internally oriented. With more than 18,000 employees to Netscape's 1,000 at the time, Microsoft could test successive Explorer beta versions extensively just by putting them up on its own intranet. "Everyone around Microsoft is encouraged to play with it," explained a Microsoft program manager. "Internal testing means that we release it to thousands of people who really hammer away at it. We use the product much more heavily than the average Web user." Microsoft combined broad internal testing by employees with carefully staged external beta releases, using only two or three in contrast to Netscape's six or seven. The company thus limited the risk that imperfections in early releases might damage its reputation.

A similar flexible philosophy can be used in the development of services. Consider Yahoo!. Founded in 1995, the company offers search, directory, and programming services for navigating the World Wide Web. As a service provider, the company believes that before a new offering is released to the outside world, it needs to be more robust than the typical Internet software beta. The market risk of broad, public testing is too high: users who try a new service once and have an unsatisfactory experience with it either are unlikely to return or, worse, may defect to competitors. Furthermore, Yahoo! assumes that competing companies will copy the innovative features of a new service once it has been released. These factors suggest delaying external testing to late in the development cycle.

For these reasons, Yahoo! puts early versions of new services online for internal use only. Given its development team's technical skills and breadth of experience, these trials expose any major technical flaws in the service and provide additional suggestions for improving functionality. Only then does Yahoo! begin a "soft release" of the offering: the service is put up on Yahoo!'s Web site but without any links to highly frequented parts of the site. As a result, only the more technically aggressive users are likely to find and use the service at this stage. Yahoo! also asks some of the 30,000 users, who have volunteered to be beta testers, to try the new service—thus exposing the service to rigorous external testing without revealing it to unsophisticated users who might be frustrated by a slow, incomplete, or error-ridden version.

The Netscape, Yahoo!, and Microsoft examples illustrate several approaches to sensing customer and market needs: broad consumer testing, broad internal testing, and testing by lead users. Companies adopting a flexible development approach should consider the merits of each, as well as the potential for using a balanced combination of all. It is important to emphasize, however, that these techniques are not unique to the Internet. Advances in information technology now allow companies to sense customer needs in ways not possible a few years ago. Leading companies in many industries have begun to use these new capabilities.

Fiat, for example, used a broad, external testing approach, not unlike Netscape's, to evaluate several automobile concepts. A link on the company's Web site directed customers to a page aimed at evaluating users' needs for the next generation of the Fiat Punto, its highest-volume car, which sells about 600,000 units per year. Customers were asked to fill out a survey indicating their preferences in automobile design. They could prioritize the following five considerations: style, comfort, performance, price, and safety. Then they were asked to describe what they hated most in a car and to suggest ideas for new features. Next the software allowed customers to design a car themselves. They could select from a variety of body styles, wheel designs, and styles for the front and rear of the automobile. They also could examine different types of headlights, details, and features. In this way, users could experiment with different designs and see the results immediately on the screen. The software captured the final results; in addition, it traced the sequence that customers went through in evaluating and selecting options. This information told designers much about the logic customers used to evaluate features, styles, and characteristics in order to arrive at a given design solution.

Fiat received more than 3,000 surveys in a three-month period, each comprising about ten pages of detailed information. The ideas suggested ranged from clever (an umbrella holder inside the car) to significant (a single bench front seat). Fiat used the information to inform a variety of styling and concept decisions for the next-generation Punto. And the total cost of the exercise was only $35,000, about the cost of running a few focus groups. Moreover, Fiat executives claimed that the surveys provided them with precisely the data they needed. The profile of the survey's participants—trend-setting individuals with high incomes, who are 31 to 40 years old and frequent car buyers—was the target segment most useful to Fiat.

General Motors' Electro-Motive division has adopted a similar philosophy in its new virtual-product-development process. That process allows engineers to give customers digital tours of next-generation locomotives even as their development proceeds. Although the GM system is still evolving, the aim is to move to an all-digital environment in which the product moves electronically through concept design, analysis, prototyping, and manufacture, and along the way makes several stops on the customer's desktop for feedback.

TESTING TECHNICAL SOLUTIONS

Sensing customer and market needs as a project progresses is one element of a flexible development process. If companies are going to allow a product's design to evolve well into the design implementation phase, however, they also must adopt mechanisms that lower the cost of changes, speed their implementation, and test their impact on the overall system. Such mechanisms allow companies to evaluate and test alternative technical solutions at a rapid rate: the second element of a flexible development process.

Early prototypes and tests of alternative technologies are critical to establishing the direction of a project. Consider NetDynamics, a company that develops sophisticated tools for linking Web servers to large databases. The single most important technical decision confronting NetDynamics during the development of its second product release was the early choice of language in its product. Either the company could develop a proprietary language, or it could use Java. At that time, in early 1996, the Java programming language had received a lot of publicity, but it was still highly unstable, relatively immature, and little understood. "We knew Java was going to be big," recalled chief engineer Yarden Malka, "but it was still only available as a Beta 1 version. This meant that the development tools that went along with it were either terribly buggy or nonexistent. If we chose it, we knew we also had to develop many of our own tools."

NetDynamics' commitment to an open platform tended to favor Java. If there was a standard—either existing or emerging—it should be used, and Java appeared to be that standard. To make the decision, however, NetDynamics' engineers spent considerable time experimenting with various options, trying to become as comfortable as possible with the benefits and risks of each language. They began by developing simple prototypes and gradually migrated to more complex programs, attempting to gauge the advantages each would give the user. This "user-centric" approach to prototyping and experimentation was critical to the final choice and stands in stark contrast to the approach often adopted by high-tech companies in which technologies often are evaluated purely on the basis of the advantages they give the design team.

As a project progresses, the design team must have the capacity to evaluate and test alternative design solutions quickly and cheaply. Yahoo! can easily do just that because of the way it has elected to provide its Internet service. The company meets its processing needs with many inexpensive computers instead of a few large (and expensive) servers. The small investment required for each machine allows Yahoo! to scale up its capacity smoothly to meet new demand. It also means that Yahoo! can easily run experiments to test different design options. According to Farzad Nazem, the vice president of engineering, "Our Web site setup works just like a spigot valve. If we want to test out a new product or feature on several thousand users, we promote it on the home page of only a few machines. As users access the service and we reach the required volume, we can turn off the promotion on each machine. We can also conduct comparative experiments by running multiple versions of the same service on different computers in the network, then track the results to see which version attracts more customers."

To reduce the cost of testing alternative design choices, companies outside the software industry increasingly have invested in new technologies for virtual design. By designing and testing product designs through simulation, for example, companies achieve the flexibility to respond to new information and to resolve uncertainties by quickly exploring alternatives. Computer-aided design software also has dramatically reduced the cost of design changes, while at the same time speeding up experimentation. At Boeing, for example, the all-digital development of the 777 aircraft made use of a computer-generated "human" who would climb inside the three-dimensional design on-screen to show how difficult maintenance access would be for a live mechanic. Such computer modeling allowed engineers to spot design errors—say, a navigation light that would have been difficult to service —that otherwise would have remained undiscovered until a person negotiated a physical prototype. By avoiding the time and cost associated with building physical prototypes at several stages, Boeing's development process has acquired the flexibility to evaluate a wider range of design options than was previously possible.

INTEGRATING CUSTOMER NEEDS WITH TECHNICAL SOLUTIONS

It's no good knowing what customers want in a product under development if the development team can't integrate that information with the available technical solutions. As a result, all the organizations we discuss have established dynamic integration mechanisms. Some of them are based on well-understood concepts, such as using dedicated teams—an approach adopted by Netscape, NetDynamics, and Microsoft. Others are less traditional. All three companies, for example, use their intranets to integrate tasks, synchronize design changes, and capture customer information as projects evolve. Thus project teams are able to keep track of the evolving relationships among tasks, schedules, and design changes in a dynamic way. Such integrating mechanisms are essential for managing a flexible process, given the many rounds of experimentation and the wide range of information generated. Without a way of capturing and integrating knowledge, the development process can quickly dissolve into chaos, with ad hoc design changes creating masses of rework because of unanticipated interactions with other components in the system.

In the Internet world, integrating mechanisms are dictated by the nature of the product—software. Each of the projects we describe adopted sophisticated design-integration tools to hold the master version of the emerging product. As team members went to work on individual components, they checked out the code for that part of the system. Once finished, they had to run a series of tests to ensure that the component did not create problematic interactions with the rest of the system. Only then could they check in the new component. At the end of each day, when all the new components had been checked in, engineers ran the program. Any problems that occurred had to be corrected before new code could be permanently integrated.

Similar approaches are found in projects outside the Internet world where new information systems allow companies to share knowledge more effectively. At Silicon Graphics, a leading manufacturer of workstations and servers, a new product-introduction process makes extensive use of the company's intranet to coordinate development activities. Managers and engineers throughout the world, who respond daily to the problems of current customers, provide input during the concept-generation stage. In addition, lead users in target application segments (referred to as "lighthouse" customers) are linked directly to the development teams, allowing the teams to get fast and effective guidance on critical decisions as the project evolves. The intranet also is used to integrate design tasks on a daily basis. Project engineers work from a shared body of software that simulates the hardware design. As with the Internet projects, when team members want to make a change, they check out the relevant code, make the desired design improvements, test it for errors and unanticipated interactions, then check it back in.

Such approaches are not limited to high-technology products. Booz•Allen & Hamilton, a management consulting firm, approaches the problem of integrating a diverse and geographically dispersed knowledge base by using its intranet. The intranet allows consulting staff quickly to locate and contact industry experts with specific skills and to identify previous studies that are relevant to current projects. In this way, the collective experience of the organization is available to all employees on-line. The intranet also allows the company to develop its intellectual capital. In management consulting, new-product development consists of developing new frameworks, industry best practices, performance benchmarks, and other information that can be applied across projects. By having these products on-line during development and thereafter, Booz•Allen can integrate new information and experiences into its knowledge base.

Integrating within the company, however, is not always sufficient. In some cases, the ability to integrate knowledge across networks of organizations may also be important. For Internet software companies, given the novelty and complexity inherent in their products and the rapidity of their development cycles, no single organization can research, make, and market products alone. Instead, they take advantage of technical possibilities that are beyond the boundaries of any individual company; those technologies can then be integrated into their own core products. (Internet users will be familiar with Java applets and Web browser plug-ins.) Doing so, however, means that just as the technologies must be seamlessly integrated into a product, so must the organization accommodate a changing cast of players. The companies we describe have built alliances with third-party developers, engaged in joint development projects, and worked hard to foster open product architectures and modular designs. And such arrangements are not peculiar to software. Workstation manufacturers such as Sun, Hewlett-Packard, and Silicon Graphics frequently engage in joint development efforts with other hardware companies (such as Siemens, Intel, Fujitsu, Toshiba, and NEC) to leverage the performance of their systems.

Putting Flexibility to the Test

In combination, the foundations of a flexible product-development process allow a company to respond to changes in markets and technologies *during* the development cycle. We found a striking example of how that is done in a setting that is about as far from the typical high-tech world as one can get: the America's Cup. In 1995, a small team from New Zealand dominated the races from start to finish. Team New Zealand's effort shows how the mechanisms we have described can be combined to dramatic effect in a flexible process.

Team New Zealand recruited Doug Peterson, who had been on the winning America's Cup team in 1992, as its lead designer. It also recruited an experienced simulation team to make use of advanced design software. Although Peterson's extensive experience drove the initial concept design, once the team's yachts were constructed the emphasis shifted to evaluating design changes through thousands of computer-simulated design iterations. The simulations were run on a small network of workstations located a few feet from the dock. To ensure rapid feedback on the performance of design changes, the team built two boats. Each day, one of them was fitted with a design change for evaluation; then the two boats raced each other to gauge the impact of the change.

Team New Zealand's flexible process sensed "market needs" through the two-boat testing program, which generated feedback each day on how the evolving design fit the racing environment. It tested alternative designs through a simulation program that was directed by one of the world's most experienced yacht designers. And it integrated knowledge by making the resulting information available locally. The crew, design team, and management were therefore able to make suggestions for the design, to see the impact of potential changes, and to know what to expect when those changes were tested on the water.

The U.S. boat that Team New Zealand faced in the final race had been designed on the latest supercomputers with the support of large, well-heeled corporations. Although the U.S. team could test a massive number of experimental designs, the computers were located hundreds of miles from the dock. As a result, there were significant delays between detailing a design and getting feedback on results. Furthermore, the team had only one boat on which to test design changes; given the varying sea and wind conditions, it took far longer than its rival to verify the impact of a change.

Team New Zealand's approach had better mechanisms than its U.S. rival for sensing, testing, and integrating what it had learned. Its flexible process produced a yacht of superior design, which many observers believed to be a full generation ahead of its competitors' boats. As Paul Cayard, skipper of Team New Zealand's opponent in the final race, remarked, "I've been in some uphill battles in my life. But I've never been in a race where I felt I had so little control over the outcome. It's the largest discrepancy in boat speed I've ever seen."

We have seen a similar pattern throughout many environments we have studied. Organizations that have adopted a flexible product-development process have begun to transform the very industries that forced them to adopt it. They have implemented strategies that companies clinging to traditional approaches cannot follow. Competitors without flexible development processes will almost certainly find their industries growing more and more turbulent in appearance. And in such an environment, their products and services will always seem to be one step behind those of their more flexible rivals.

4

Trust and the Virtual Organization

Charles Handy

Not long ago, I found myself in the Laurentian Library, which Michelangelo built in Florence for the Medicis nearly 500 years ago. It is a special place, filled with the scent of learning; a place more restful and more uplifting, in many ways, than the Church of San Lorenzo, in whose cloister it stands. The Laurentian is no longer used as a library, however. It is visited only by tourists, and, as for its contents, they could all be fitted onto one CD-ROM disc.

Was this, I wondered, a symbol of what was coming to all our organizations? Their buildings turned into museums for tourists, their work on discs? And would we not lose something thereby, because, for all their probable efficiency, videoconferencing and cruising the Internet are not the same as working in Michelangelo's library?

Only the week before, in fact, I had been with a group of librarians, discussing the future of their modern-day libraries. Computer screens and keyboards, they agreed, were taking over from shelves of books and journals. A publisher revealed that he was no longer going to print and publish his journal but would instead enter it into the database of subscribing organizations. In that case, said one of those present, we need never visit a library again; we can get all that we want from the screen in our room. At the University of Virginia, added another, the change is already happening; all you need to access the library is a password and a modem. The library of the University of Dubrovnik was destroyed, someone else reported, but the gift of a computer terminal, linked to a host of foreign databases, more than compensated.

I watched the expressions of those in the room as they took in the implications of what was being said. They were coming face-to-face with the idea of the virtual library: a library as a concept, not a place; an activity, not a building. For the librarians, who were accustomed to seeing themselves as guardians of a special place, the idea was either frightening or exciting, depending on their ages and attitudes.

Libraries, whose lifeblood is information, were always likely to be among the first to confront the challenge and opportunity of virtuality, but as businesses become ever more dependent on information, they come up against the same dilemmas. An office is, at heart, an interpretative library geared to a particular purpose, and more and more of our economic activity is a churning of information, ideas, and intelligence in all their infinite variety—an invitation to virtuality.

It is easy to be seduced by the technological possibilities of the virtual organization, but the managerial and personal implications may cause us to rethink what we mean by an organization. At its simplest, the managerial dilemma comes down to the question, How do you manage people whom you do not see? The simple answer is, By trusting them, but the apparent simplicity disguises a turnaround in organizational thinking. The rules of trust are both obvious and well established, but they do not sit easily with a managerial tradition that believes efficiency and control are closely linked and that you can't have one without a lot of the other. Organizationally, we have to wonder whether a company is, in the future, going to be anything more than the box of contracts that some companies now seem to be. Is a box of contracts a sustainable basis for getting the work done in our society, or is it not, in fact, a recipe for disintegration? For society as a whole, the challenge will be to make sure that virtuality brings benefits to all and not just to a favored few. Organizations and, in particular, business organizations, are the linchpins of society. That gives them responsibilities beyond themselves, responsibilities that virtuality throws into high relief.

The Virtuality Dimension

If one ignores the technology, there is nothing new, conceptually, in the idea of an activity without a building as its home. Where information is the raw material of work, it has never been necessary to have all the people in the same place at the same time. A network of salespeople is the most common example—so ordinary and everyday an example that we would not think of giving it such a grandiose title as a virtual organization. Yet salespeople operate on their own, out of no common place—out of sight but not, one hopes, out of touch or, for that matter, out of line.

Journalism provides other examples. I myself fill an occasional slot on the BBC morning radio program *Today*. For many years, I did not meet my director, nor have I ever met any members of the production team. I communicate by telephone from wherever I happen to be, and my contributions are often broadcast from remote, unmanned studios. It is not in any way unusual.

The Open University in Great Britain, with counterparts all over the world, is perhaps the most ambitious example of a concept without a place. The Open University has a home base, to be sure, but none of the students and few of the faculty are to be found there. Its home base is merely the administrative hub of an unseen and sprawling empire. Its business school is already the largest in Europe, although few of the students have ever met any of the faculty or any of the other students. They used to meet at short residential summer schools, using the campuses of more traditional universities. This year, however, the university has created its first truly virtual summer school. The students will participate from their homes or places of work via E-mail, mobile phone, and videoconferencing. They will never be together in the same place at the same time. The technology has been provided by the university, which has thoughtfully included the mobile phone for students so that, as they sit with their computers beside them, still connected to their land telephone lines, they may converse with supervisors.

In my part of Great Britain, the central library in Norwich, serving the eastern region of the country, burned to the ground last summer. The librarian is considering replacing the grand building with a network of tiny libraries in every hamlet and town throughout the region, each linked to a central facility and, indeed, to every library in the world if need be. As in Dubrovnik, disaster can help us leap into the future before we ever intended. What will hold our librarian back, however, is not the technology or the money—both are potentially available—but the hearts and minds of his staff and his political masters. That's because what people cannot see they often cannot contemplate.

Business is creeping along behind such exemplars from the public sector. Large parts of organizations are now made up of ad hoc mini-organizations, projects collated for a particular time and purpose, drawing their participants from both inside and outside the parent organization. The projects often have no one place to call their own. They exist as activities not as buildings; their only visible sign is an E-mail address. Inside the buildings that *do* exist, so-called hot-desking is increasingly common. In international business, videoconferencing is the norm. The trains in Great Britain double as mobile offices, with the commuter's doze interrupted by the ringing of personal phones and the bleeping of portable computers.

One day soon, when everyone has a personal phone, the phone will no longer belong to a place. That will be more dramatically different than it sounds. We will be able to call anyone without knowing where they are or what they are doing. The office as the home of our telephone—with a secretary to answer it and a line plugged into the wall—will become an antiquated and very expensive notion. An office that is available 168 hours a week but occupied for perhaps 20 is a luxury that organizations can ill afford. If there is an office in the future, it will be more like a clubhouse: a place for meeting, eating, and greeting, with rooms reserved for activities, not for particular people.

Virtuality, however, isn't always as much fun as it is supposed to be. A room of one's own, or at least a desk of one's own, has been the executive security blanket for a century or more. A sense of place is as important to most of us as a sense of purpose. E-mail and voice mail have many attractions, including immediacy, but they are not the same as watching the eyes of others. The loneliness of the long-distance executive is well documented. Even office politics and gossip have their attractions, if only as an antidote to the monotony of much of what goes on in the name of work. Few are going to be eager advocates of virtuality when it really means that work is what you do, not where you go.

The Managerial Dilemmas

Like it or not, the mixture of economics and technology means that more and more of us will be spending time in virtual space—out of sight, if not out of touch. No longer will our colleagues be down the corridor, available for an unscheduled meeting or a quick progress check. Most meetings will have to be scheduled, even those on video, and will therefore become more infrequent. We will have to learn how to run organizations without meetings.

We will also have to get accustomed to working with and managing those whom we do not see, except on rare and prearranged occasions.

That is harder than it sounds. I once sat with a features writer of a daily paper. She was interviewing me in the newsroom, a place filled with smoke, noise, telephones, and the sweat of 100 journalists. I had to perch on the edge of her desk—there was nowhere else.

"Couldn't we have done this somewhere else?" I said over the hubbub. "Like at your home?"

"I wish we could," she said. "Indeed, I would do so much of my work a lot better if I could do it where it suited me. I could send it down the wire just as easily from home, or wherever, as from here."

"Why don't you, then?" I asked with surprise.

"Because *they* want me where they can see me." And she pointed down the long room to where two men sat behind large plateglass windows. They were the editors, she explained, and they liked to be able to see what everyone was doing, to check the work, or to interrupt it whenever they needed to give out a new assignment.

"The truth is," she said, "they don't trust us."

Trust is the heart of the matter. That seems obvious and trite, yet most of our organizations tend to be arranged on the assumption that people cannot be trusted or relied on, even in tiny matters. Oversight systems are set up to prevent anyone from doing the wrong thing, whether by accident or design.

The other day, a courier could not find my family's remote cottage. He called his base on his radio, and the base called us to ask directions. He was just around the corner, but his base managed to omit a vital part of the directions. So he called them again, and they called us again. Then the courier repeated the cycle a third time to ask whether we had a dangerous dog. When he eventually arrived, we asked whether it would not have been simpler and less aggravating to everyone if he had called us directly from the roadside telephone booth where he had been parked. "I can't do that," he said, "because they won't refund any money I spend." "But it's only pennies!" I exclaimed. "I know," he said, "but that only shows how little they trust us!"

Writ large, that sort of attitude creates a paraphernalia of systems, checkers, and checkers checking checkers—expensive and deadening. Some commentators have argued that *audit mania* (the urge to have some independent inspection) is a virus infecting our society. It exists, they suggest, because we no longer trust people to act for anything but their own short-term interests. That attitude becomes a self-fulfilling prophecy. "If they don't trust me," employees say to themselves, "Why should I bother to put their needs before mine?" If it is even partly true that a lack of trust makes employees untrustworthy, it does not bode well for the future of virtuality in organizations. If we are to enjoy the efficiencies and other benefits of the virtual organization, we will have to rediscover how to run organizations based more on trust than on control. Virtuality requires trust to make it work: Technology on its own is not enough.

The Rules of Trust

Common sense tells us that there are seven cardinal principles of trust we should keep in mind.

TRUST IS NOT BLIND

It is unwise to trust people whom you do not know well, whom you have not observed in action over time, and who are not committed to the same goals. In practice, it is hard to know more than 50 people that well. Those 50 can each, in turn, know another 50, and so on. Large organizations are not therefore incompatible with the principle of trust, but they have to be made up of relatively constant, smaller groupings. The idea that people should move around as much and as fast as possible in order to get more exposure and more experience— what the Japanese call the horizontal fast track—can mean that there is no time to learn to trust anyone and, in the end, no point, because the organization starts to replace trust with systems of control.

My title in one large organization was MKR/32. In that capacity, I wrote memos to FIN/41 or PRO/23. I rarely heard any names, and I never met the people behind those titles. I had no reason to trust them and, frankly, no desire to. I was a "temporary role occupant," in the jargon of the time, a role occupant in an organization of command and control, based on the premise that no one could really be trusted. I left after a year. Such places can be prisons for the human soul.

TRUST NEEDS BOUNDARIES

Unlimited trust is, in practice, unrealistic. By trust, organizations really mean confidence, a confidence in someone's competence and in his or her commitment to a goal. Define that goal, and the individual or the team can be left to get on with it. Control is then after the event, when the results are assessed. It is not a matter of granting permission before the event. Freedom within boundaries works best, however, when the work unit is self-contained, having the capability within it to solve its own problems. Trust-based organizations are, as a result, reengineering their work, pulling back from the old reductionist models of organization, in which everything was divided into its component parts or functions. At first sight, the new holistic designs for the units of the organization look more expensive because they duplicate functions and do not necessarily replicate each other. The energy and effectiveness released by the freedom within boundaries more than compensates, however. To succeed, reengineering must be built on trust. When it fails, it is because trust is absent.

TRUST DEMANDS LEARNING

An organizational architecture made up of relatively independent and constant groupings pushes the organization toward the sort of federal structure that is becoming more common everywhere. A necessary condition of constancy, however, is an ability to change: If one set of people cannot be exchanged for another set when circumstances alter, then the first set must adapt or die. The constant groups must always be flexible enough to change when times and customers demand it. They must also keep themselves abreast of change, forever exploring new options and new technologies. They must create a real learning culture. The choice of people for these groups is therefore crucial. Every individual has to be capable of self-renewal. Recruitment and placement become key, along with the choice of group leaders. Such topics will require the serious attention of senior management. They should not be delegated to a lower echelon of human resources.

TRUST IS TOUGH

The reality is, however, that even the best recruiters and the best judges of character will get it wrong sometimes. When trust proves to be misplaced—not because people are deceitful or malicious but because they do not live up to expectations or cannot be relied on to do what is needed—then those people have to go. Where you cannot trust, you have to become a checker once more, with all the systems of control that involves. Therefore, for the sake of the whole, the individual must leave. Trust has to be ruthless. It is incompatible with any promise of a job for life. After all, who can be so sure of their recruitment procedures that they are prepared to trust forever those whom they select? It is because trust is so important but so risky, that organizations tend to restrict their core commitments to a smaller group of what I call *trusties*. But that policy in turn pushes the organization toward a core/periphery model, one that can, if practitioners are not careful, degenerate into a set of purely formal contractual relationships with all the outsiders. Nothing is simple; there is paradox everywhere.

TRUST NEEDS BONDING

Self-contained units responsible for delivering specified results are the necessary building blocks of an organization based on trust, but long-lasting groups of trusties can create their own problems, those of organizations within the organization. For the whole to work, the goals of the smaller units have to gel with the goals of the whole. The blossoming of vision and mission statements is one attempt to deal with integration, as are campaigns for total quality or excellence. Such things matter. Or rather, if they did not exist, their absence would matter. They are not, however, enough in themselves. They need to be backed up by exhortation and personal example. Anita Roddick holds her spreading Body Shop together by what can best be called "personal infection," pouring her energies into the reinforcement of her values and beliefs through every medium she can find. It is always a dangerous strategy to personalize a mission, in case the person stumbles or falls, as The Body Shop nearly did last year after unfavorable publicity, but organizations based on trust need that sort of personal statement from their leaders. Trust is not and never can be an impersonal commodity.

TRUST NEEDS TOUCH

Visionary leaders, no matter how articulate, are not enough. A shared commitment still requires personal contact to make it real. To augment John Naisbitt's telling phrase, high tech has to be balanced by high touch to build high-trust organizations. Paradoxically, the more virtual an organization becomes, the more its people need to meet in person. The meetings, however, are different. They are more about process than task, more concerned that people get to know each other than that they deliver. Videoconferences are more task focused, but they are easier and more productive if the individuals know each other as people, not just as images on the screen. Work and play, therefore, alternate in many of the corporate get-togethers that now fill the conference resorts out of season. These are not perks for the privileged; they are the necessary lubricants of virtuality, occasions not only for getting to know each other and for meeting the leaders but also for reinforcing corporate goals and rethinking corporate strategies. As one who delivers the occasional "cabaret" at such occasions, I am always surprised to find how few of the participants have met each other in person, even if they have worked together before. I am then further surprised by how quickly a common mood develops. You can almost watch the culture grow, and you wonder how they could have worked effectively without it.

TRUST REQUIRES LEADERS

At their best, the units in good trust-based organizations hardly have to be managed, but they do need a multiplicity of leaders. I once teased an English audience by comparing a team of Englishmen to a rowing crew on the river—eight men going backward as fast as they can without talking to each other, steered by the one person who can't row! I thought it quite witty at the time, but I was corrected after the session by one of the participants, who had once been an Olympic oarsman. "How do you think we could go backward so fast without communicating, steered by this little fellow in the stern, if we didn't know each other very well, didn't have total confidence to do our jobs and a shared commitment—almost a passion—for the same goal? It is the perfect formula for a team."

I had to admit it—he was right. "But tell me," I said to him, "who is the manager of this team?" "There isn't one," he replied, after thinking about it. "Unless that is what you call our part-time administrator back in the office." Manager, he was reminding me, is a low-status title in organizations of colleagues.

"Well, then, who is the leader?"

"That depends," he said. "When we are racing, it is the little chap who is steering, because he is the only one who can see where we are going. But there is also the stroke, who sets the standard for all of us. He is a leader, too, in a way. But off the river, it's the captain of the crew, who selects us, bonds us together, builds our commitment to our goal and our dedication. Lastly, in training, there is our coach, who is undoubtedly the main influence on our work. So you see," he concluded, "there isn't a simple answer to your question."

A rowing crew, I realized, has to be based on trust if it is to have any chance of success. And if any member of that crew does not pull his weight, then he does not deserve the confidence of the others and must be asked to leave. Nor can all the leadership requirements be discharged by one person, no matter how great or how good.

The Organization's Dilemma

Racing crews row for the sake of glory, but it is not as clear what motivates the people in the virtual organizations of business. Why should the now smaller core of trusted individuals give so much of their lives and time and talent to an organization that they work for but do not live in, an organization that, significantly, someone else owns, someone whom they almost certainly do not know and have never met, because, for the most part, that someone is not an individual at all but an institution owned, in turn, by other anonymous people?

That question had a clear answer in times past. The organization was the instrument of its owners, and the individual was the instrument of the organization. The implied and the legal contracts were both instrumental. The individual was a hired hand, a human resource, employed to work the assets of the organization. Good pay, good prospects, and a challenging job were enough for most. The human resource, however, is now the human asset, not the human cost. That is not just refined semantics, it is the literal financial truth. The market value of the top 200 businesses on the London Stock Exchange is on average three times the worth of the visible fixed assets. In the case of the high-tech high fliers, it can be up to 20 times. If that means anything, it means that the market is valuing the intangible assets many times higher than the tangible ones. Whether those intangible assets are the research in a company's pipeline, the brands, the know-how, or the networks of experience, they amount in the end to one thing: the people.

Those people can and often do walk out the door. Whole teams of analysts nowadays shift themselves from one financial institution to another at the glint of a golden handshake or the lure of new pastures. If laborers are worthy of their hire, there is no reason to suppose that they won't go where the hire looks better. The assets of the new information-based corporations are, as a result, increasingly fragile. It is hard to measure assets in the present, harder still to gauge their future. Investing in information-based businesses will be even more of a gamble than it has been in the past.

The consequences of increased gambling are predictable: Investors will be in more of a hurry to get their money back; managers will be under pressure to milk their assets while they still have them; horizons will shrink; and the result will be that, even if the assets don't walk, they will wilt. Under those pressures, even inspired, articulate leaders will be hard-pressed to hold the virtual corporation together.

When laborers become assets, the underlying contract with the organization has to change. Trust inevitably requires some sense of mutuality, of reciprocal loyalty. Virtual organizations, which feed on information, ideas, and intelligence (which in turn are vested in the heads and hearts of people), cannot escape the dilemma. One answer is to turn the laborers into members; that is, to turn the instrumental contract into a membership contract for the smaller core. Members have rights. They also have responsibilities. Their rights include a share in the governance of the community to which they belong. No one can buy a club against the wishes of its members. Major capital investments and strategic initiatives require the agreement of the members. The terms and conditions of membership require members' agreement. Their responsibilities center on the need to make the business grow, because without growth there will be no striving and, ultimately, no point. Growth, however, can mean growth in quality, size, profitability, or desirability, and maybe in all four. People who think of themselves as members have more of an interest in the future of the business and its growth than those who are only its hired help.

Giving membership rights to key people is not the same as giving them ownership, but those membership rights inevitably diminish the powers of the owners. Shareholders become investors rather than owners. They are entitled to a reasonable return on their money—a return that takes the risk into account—but they are not entitled, for instance, to sell the company over the heads of its members or to dictate to management, unless the financial returns start to evaporate.

Major investors, however, who tend to be long-term investors, might also be included in the extended family of the business. Such a shift in the governance of the corporation would bring Anglo-American businesses more into line with the businesses of continental Europe or Japan. Companies there, paradoxically perhaps, are seeking to give more power to the investors as a discipline for the members and their management and as a way of increasing the financial base. The principle of requisite balance would suggest that all groups should meet halfway, and they probably will, as the world of business becomes increasingly linked and interdependent.

The concept of membership, when made real, would replace the sense of belonging to a *place* with a sense of belonging to a *community*, even if that community were a largely virtual one. A sense of belonging is something humans need if they are to commit themselves to more than simple selfishness. Families and family businesses know something about the sense of belonging and the motivating force of collective pride in the family tradition, as well as the responsibilities that go with belonging. Families, at their best, are communities built on mutual trust. If the family could be extended to include key contributors, the sense of belonging would be properly inclusive. Without some real sense of belonging, virtuality looks like a very precarious state and a perilous base for the next phase of capitalism, whatever the economic and technological advantages.

Society's Dilemma

An economy that adds value through information, ideas, and intelligence—the Three I Economy—offers a way out of the apparent clash between material growth and environmental erosion. Information, ideas, and intelligence consume few of the earth's resources. Virtuality will redesign our cities with fewer skyscrapers and fewer commuters, making a quieter and perhaps a gentler world. Our aspirations for growth in a Three I Economy would increasingly be more a matter for the mind than for the body. The growth sectors would be education in all its varied forms, health care, the arts and entertainment, leisure, travel, and sports. As the economic statistics show, the new growth is already happening, and the organizations that deliver it tend to be small groups of colleagues united by mutual trust. Small, growing companies often serve today's young people, who aspire to better music systems and computers rather than to faster cars or flashier clothes. The younger generation also relishes employment in the new and freer organizations.

Not all people do, however. If the Three I Economy is to take off in the First World and thus give hope of a sustainable future to others, everyone needs to be able to participate. Currently, there is in every country of the First World a growing underclass that knows little about the concepts behind the Three I Economy. For members of that underclass, such concepts are a joke. They want hamburgers and heating, not computers. In the short term, maybe, they should be helped with their hamburgers and heating, but they also need a hand up into the Three I Economy. Virtuality will be a recipe for a divided society unless we help everyone, and a society divided will not long survive. We have to take from the present to ensure our future, instead of borrowing from the future to ensure our present, as most countries do today.

Everyone has something to contribute to a Three I Economy. There is no unteachable group. Talent in some form or another exists in all human beings; it only needs to be detected and developed. Naturally, early education is crucial, but our future should not be determined by the time we are 16. Work can be a great laboratory of learning, and organizations, therefore, hold one of the keys to the future of society. But if they concentrate their efforts only on their core members, they will be throwing away that key. Who else will help those who are outside the organization—the independents, the part-timers, and the small contractors and suppliers?

Already, in the European Union, one half of the available workforce is outside the organization, not in full-time jobs. If organizations do not embrace the concept of an extended family and include their associated workers in their plans for their human assets, the workforce will become increasingly useless to them and to themselves. If a trust-based organization means trust for some and the old instrumental contract for the less able, then trust will become a dirty word, a synonym for selfishness. Some see the peripheral workforce as the responsibility of government—to train, to employ, or, if all else fails, to support. Governments, however, have their limits. They can pass laws, they can regulate, and they can sometimes find money to empower others; but they cannot and should not try to do it all themselves. They need help from the rest of society.

The hope for the future that is contained within the virtual organization will end in disillusionment unless we can mobilize society to think beyond itself to save itself. Governments in a democracy can move only as fast as the opinion leaders in society. Business has always been a major leader of opinion, but if business minds its own business exclusively or if it takes virtuality to extremes and becomes a mere broker or box of contracts, then it will have failed society. In the end, its search for wealth will have destroyed wealth.

5

Predators and Prey: A New Ecology of Competition

James F. Moore

Successful businesses are those that evolve rapidly and effectively. Yet innovative businesses can't evolve in a vacuum. They must attract resources of all sorts, drawing in capital, partners, suppliers, and customers to create cooperative networks.

Much has been written about such networks, under the rubric of strategic alliances, virtual organizations, and the like. But these frameworks provide little systematic assistance for managers who seek to understand the underlying strategic logic of change. Even fewer of these theories help executives anticipate the managerial challenges of nurturing the complex business communities that bring innovations to market.

How is it that a company can create an entirely new business community—like IBM in personal computers—and then lose control and profitability in that same business? Is there a stable structure of community leadership that matches fast-changing conditions? And how can companies develop leadership that successfully adapts to continual waves of innovation and change? These questions remain unanswered because most managers still frame the problem in the old way: companies go head-to-head in an industry, battling for market share. But events of the last decade, particularly in high-technology businesses, amply illustrate the limits of that understanding.

In essence, executives must develop new ideas and tools for strategizing, tools for making tough choices when it comes to innovations, business alliances, and leadership of customers and suppliers. Anthropologist Gregory Bateson's definition of *co-evolution* in both natural and social systems provides a useful starting place. In his book *Mind and Nature*, Bateson describes co-evolution as a process in which interdependent species evolve in an endless reciprocal cycle—in which "changes in species A set the stage for the natural selection of changes in species B"—and vice versa. Consider predators and their prey, for instance, or flowering plants and their pollinators.

Another insight comes from biologist Stephen Jay Gould, who has observed that natural ecosystems sometimes collapse when environmental conditions change too radically. Dominant combinations of species may lose their leadership. New ecosystems then establish themselves, often with previously marginal plants and animals at the center. For current businesses dealing with the challenges of innovation, there are clear parallels and profound implications.

To extend a systematic approach to strategy, I suggest that a company be viewed not as a member of a single industry but as part of a *business ecosystem* that crosses a variety of industries. In a business ecosystem, companies co-evolve capabilities around a new innovation: they work cooperatively and competitively to support new products, satisfy customer needs, and eventually incorporate the next round of innovations.

For example, Apple Computer is the leader of an ecosystem that crosses at least four major industries: personal computers, consumer electronics, information, and communications. The Apple ecosystem encompasses an extended web of suppliers that includes Motorola and Sony and a large number of customers in various market segments.

Apple, IBM, Ford, Wal-Mart, and Merck have all been or still are the leaders of business ecosystems. While the center may shift over time, the role of the leader is valued by the rest of the community. Such leadership enables all ecosystem members to invest toward a shared future in which they anticipate profiting together.

Yet in any larger business environment, several ecosystems may vie for survival and dominance: the IBM and Apple ecosystems in personal computers, for example, or Wal-Mart and Kmart in discount retailing. In fact, it's competition among business ecosystems, not individual companies, that's largely fueling today's industrial transformation. Managers can't afford to ignore the birth of new ecosystems or the competition among those that already exist.

Whether that means investing in the right new technology, signing on suppliers to expand a growing business, developing crucial elements of value to maintain leadership, or incorporating new innovations to fend off obsolescence, executives must understand the stages that all business ecosystems pass through—and, more important, how to direct the changes.

A business ecosystem, like its biological counterpart, gradually moves from a random collection of elements to a more structured community. Think of a prairie grassland that is succeeded by stands of conifers, which in turn evolve into a more complex forest dominated by hardwoods. Business ecosystems condense out of the original swirl of capital, customer interest, and talent generated by a new innovation, just as successful species spring from the natural resources of sunlight, water, and soil nutrients.

Every business ecosystem develops in four distinct stages: birth, expansion, leadership, and self-renewal—or, if not self-renewal, death. In reality, of course, the evolutionary stages blur, and the managerial challenges of one stage often crop up in another. Yet I've observed the four stages in many companies over time, across businesses as diverse as retailing, entertainment, and pharmaceuticals. What remains the same from business to business is the process of co-evolution: the complex interplay between competitive and cooperative business strategies (see Exhibit 5-1.).

During Stage 1 of a business ecosystem, entrepreneurs focus on defining what customers want, that is, the value of a proposed new product or service and the best form for delivering it. Victory at the birth stage, in the short term, often goes to those who best define and implement this customer value proposition. Moreover, during Stage 1 of a business ecosystem, it often pays to cooperate. From the leader's standpoint, in particular, business partners help fill out the full package of value for customers. And by attracting important "follower" companies, leaders may stop them from helping other emerging ecosystems.

The rise of the personal computer is a revealing example of ecological business development. In the early 1970s, a new technology—the microprocessor—emerged with the potential to spawn vast new applications and dramatically reduce the cost of computing. Yet this innovation sat dormant for several years. By 1975, hobbyist machines like the Altair and IMSAI had penetrated a narrow market. But these computers were not products that could be used by the average person.

Starting in the late 1970s, Tandy Corporation, Apple, and others introduced early versions of what would eventually become the personal computer. The seed innovation they all chose was the micropro-

Exhibit 5-1 **The Evolutionary Stages of a Business Ecosystem**

	Cooperative challenges	Competitive challenges
Birth	Work with customers and suppliers to define the new value proposition around a seed innovation.	Protect your ideas from others who might be working toward defining similar offers. Tie up critical lead customers, key suppliers, and important channels.
Expansion	Bring the new offer to a large market by working with suppliers and partners to scale up supply and to achieve maximum market coverage.	Defeat alternative implementations of similar ideas. Ensure that your approach is the market standard in its class through dominating key market segments.
Leadership	Provide a compelling vision for the future that encourages suppliers and customers to work together to continue improving the complete offer.	Maintain strong bargaining power in relation to other players in the ecosystem, including key customers and valued suppliers.
Self-renewal	Work with innovators to bring new ideas to the existing ecosystem.	Maintain high barriers to entry to prevent innovators from building alternative ecosystems. Maintain high customer switching costs in order to buy time to incorporate new ideas into your own products and services.

cessor, but these first designers also recognized that other products and services had to be created to bring the whole package together. These ranged from hardware components to software to services like distribution and customer support.

Apple and Tandy each had a different strategy for creating a full, rich ecosystem. Apple worked with business partners and talked about "evangelizing" to encourage co-evolution. While the company tightly controlled its basic computer design and operating system software, it encouraged independent software developers to write programs for its machine. Apple also cooperated with independent magazines, computer stores, and training institutions—and even seeded a number of school districts with Apple IIs.

Tandy, on the other hand, took a more vertically integrated approach. It attempted to buy and then own its software, ranging from the operating system to programming languages and applications like word processors. The company controlled sales, service, support and training, and market development by selling exclusively through its Radio Shack stores. At the same time, it discouraged independent magazines devoted to its TRS-80 machines. Therefore, Tandy's simpler and more tightly controlled ecosystem did not build the excitement, opportunities, and inner rivalries of Apple's, nor did it harness as much capital and talent through the participation of other companies.

Tandy's approach got the company out front fast; in 1979, it had sales of $95 million compared with Apple's $47.9 million. However, Tandy's tight control of its ecosystem ultimately led to slower growth at a time when establishing market share and a large user base was essential to success. By 1982, Apple's $583.1 million in sales had decisively passed Tandy's $466.4 million.

Meanwhile, a third business ecosystem emerged in the early days of personal computing. It never rivaled Apple's or Tandy's in size, but it did help IBM enter the fray. This third ecosystem centered around two software companies: Digital Research and Micropro. In 1977, Digital Research made its software operating system CP/M available independent of hardware. That separation allowed almost any small manufacturer to assemble components and put out a usable personal computer. Overnight, a variety of small companies entered the business, building on the same Zilog microprocessor used in the early Tandy machines.

In 1979, Micropro brought out a word processor that ran on CP/M-based machines. Wordstar was the first truly powerful word processor, and it took an important group of potential PC customers—writers and editors—by storm. Demand for CP/M machines soared, fueling the growth if not the fortunes of small companies like Morrow and Kaypro.

But during the first stage of any business ecosystem, co-evolving companies must do more than satisfy customers; a leader must also emerge to initiate a process of rapid, ongoing improvement that draws the entire community toward a grander future. In the Apple and Tandy ecosystems, the hardware companies provided such leadership by studying the market, defining new generations of functionality, and orchestrating suppliers and partners to bring improvements to market. In the CP/M ecosystem, however, the hardware companies were bedeviled by rivalry among themselves. Infighting kept down prices and profit margins, and none of the CP/M companies could afford heavy advertising programs.

In Stage 1, established companies like IBM are often better off waiting and watching carefully as a new market sorts itself out. The iterative process of trying out innovative ideas and discovering which solutions are attractive to customers is hard to accomplish in a traditional corporate culture. And the diverse experimentation that thrives in an entrepreneurial scene provides more "genetic diversity" from which the market can ultimately select the fittest offering.

Established companies can subsequently replicate successful ideas and broadcast them across a wider market. In other words, they can enter the market at Stage 2 by appropriating the developmental work of others. Meanwhile, original ecosystems that succeed, like Apple's, do so by consciously nurturing a full community of partners and suppliers right from the start.

In Stage 2, business ecosystems expand to conquer broad new territories. Just as grasses and weeds rapidly cover the bare, scorched ground left after a forest fire, some business expansions meet little resistance. But in other cases, rival ecosystems may be closely matched and choose to attack the same territory. Direct battles for market share break out. Fighting can get ugly as each ecosystem tries to exert pressure on suppliers and customers to join up.

In the end, one business ecosystem may triumph, or rival ecosystems may reach semistable accommodations. Think of a hardwood forest that borders a grassland. The zone of conflict at the boundary may shift from year to year, but it never completely wipes out either ecosystem.

In general, two conditions are necessary for Stage 2 expansion: (1) a business concept that a large number of customers will value; and (2) the potential to scale up the concept to reach this broad market. During the expansion stage, established companies can exercise enormous power in marketing and sales, as well as in the management of large-scale production and distribution, literally crushing smaller ecosystems in the process.

IBM, for example, entered the personal computer business in 1981. In contrast to its own history and culture of vertical integration, IBM followed and extended the Apple model of building a community of supporters. IBM took on partners and opened its computer architecture to outside suppliers. Moreover, it adopted a microprocessor from Intel that incorporated all of the instructions available in the Zilog microprocessor in Tandy and CP/M machines. And IBM licensed MS-DOS, a software operating system from then tiny Microsoft, which was almost a near clone of CP/M. As a result, Wordstar and other popular application programs could easily be ported over to the IBM PC.

One of the most important managerial challenges in Stage 2 is to stimulate market demand without greatly exceeding your ability to meet it. IBM certainly stimulated demand for its new machine through a combination of heavy brand advertising, distribution through Sears and other channels, and building its own network of specialty stores. By anyone's measure, IBM's approach to expanding its PC ecosystem was a major success. Its personal computing business grew from $500 million in 1982 to $5.65 billion by 1986, and IBM's ecosystem rapidly dominated the market.

However, IBM also generated much more demand than it could meet. The company maintained high prices, which encouraged others to enter the market by setting a high price umbrella under which they could thrive. Compaq, for example, became the fastest company to join the *Fortune* 500 based on supplying machines to meet demand in the IBM ecosystem.

IBM did its best to keep up with demand. In the early 1980s, it invested directly in several key suppliers to help it grow fast enough to meet the market. Intel, for example, received $250 million from IBM in 1983. Concerned about its image as an insensitive behemoth, as well as possible antitrust objections, IBM managers carefully assured these suppliers that the help came without any strings attached.

IBM's relationships with suppliers were basically nonexclusive. Obviously, suppliers like Intel, Microsoft, and Lotus were happy to help the success of Compaq and others because it allowed them to diversify the risk of overdependence on IBM. For its part, IBM was flush with more demand and success than it knew what to do with. Top managers didn't focus on slowing the development of clone makers and non-exclusive suppliers—or keeping crucial elements of value like the microprocessor in-house. At first, IBM didn't attack new competitors within its ecosystem through the courts, through special promotions, or by lowering its own prices.

However clear the threat from the rest of the pack appears to us now, at the time, IBM and its business partners were pleased. By 1986, the combined revenues of companies in the IBM ecosystem were approximately $12 billion, dwarfing the Apple ecosystem's revenues of approximately $2 billion. IBM's leadership also forced Tandy and essentially every other non-Apple maker of personal computers to dump their proprietary designs and offer IBM PC compatibles.

In contrast with IBM, the story of Wal-Mart's retailing ecosystem shows how top management can take the right precautions when a business is expanding (see "The Evolution of Wal-Mart: Savvy Expansion and Leadership" on page 137). In general, Stage 2 rewards fast expansion that squeezes competing ecosystems to the margin. But managers must also prepare for future leadership and leverage in the next stage. To do so, companies need to maintain careful control of customer relationships and core centers of value and innovation. Moreover, they must develop relationships with their suppliers that constrain these followers from becoming leaders in Stage 3.

While the lion and antelope are both part of a healthy savanna ecosystem, they also struggle with each other to determine to what extent each species expands within it. Similarly, in business ecosystems, two conditions contribute to the onset of the leadership struggles that are the hallmark of Stage 3. First, the ecosystem must have strong enough growth and profitability to be considered worth fighting over. Second, the structure of the value-adding components and processes that are central to the business ecosystem must become reasonably stable.

This stability allows suppliers to target particular elements of value and to compete in contributing them. It encourages members of the ecosystem to consider expanding by taking over activities from those closest to them in the value chain. Most of all, it diminishes the dependence of the whole ecosystem on the original leader. It's in Stage 3 that companies become preoccupied with standards, interfaces, "the modular organization," and customer-supplier relations.

For example, by the mid-1980s, the IBM PC technical architecture defined the de facto business structure for the personal computer business as a whole. Virtually any company could figure out how to make components and services that would dovetail effectively with other elements of the PC ecosystem. Of course, this was a mixed blessing for IBM. The openness of its computer architecture encouraged third parties to support it, dramatically accelerating the ecosystem's growth. Yet this same openness decreased the dependence of suppliers on IBM's leadership, laying the foundations for Stage 3 "clone wars."

Lotus, Intel, Microsoft, and other suppliers started working together to determine common standards for hardware and software, with and without IBM's involvement. Other ecosystem members welcomed this new leadership since it seemed fairer to suppliers and more innovative than IBM's.

Belatedly, IBM sought to enforce its patents against clone makers, seeking licenses from major players—one of the many strategies that failed. A grim milestone of sorts was achieved in 1989 when clone shipments and product shipments from other smaller companies bypassed those of major personal computer manufacturers. Thus IBM was relegated to competing head-on with myriad "box makers." IBM still retained a large share of the market but only through offering extensive discounts to large volume purchasers.

Which brings us to the new structure of today's "Microsoft-Intel" ecosystem: Microsoft, with gross margins estimated at 80%; Intel, with gross margins of 40% and 50% on its new chips; and IBM's PC business with margins of about 30%, a far cry from the 70% to 90% margins in its mainframe business.

In Stage 3, bargaining power comes from having something the ecosystem needs and being the only practical source. Sometimes this sole-source status can be established contractually or through patent protection. But fundamentally, it depends on constant innovation—on creating value that is critical to the whole ecosystem's continued price/performance improvement. During expansion, IBM didn't find a way to keep innovating or even to achieve economies of scale. Power shifted to chips and software, areas in which IBM did not excel.

Now both Intel and Microsoft have bargaining power through control of a critical component. Each is a strong leader and plays the role of *central ecological contributor.* Central contributors maintain the much-coveted chokehold within a business ecosystem. In short, other members can't live without them. This central position enables them to bargain for a higher share of the total value produced by the ecosystem. For example, Intel and Microsoft have gross margins that are almost double the average for their whole ecosystem.

Central contributor status is maintained in part by the investments others have made in being followers. Hardware and software vendors have made heavy investments in Microsoft operating systems and in applications that work with Intel chips. Switching to other vendors would be risky and expensive; if possible, other co-evolving companies don't want the burden of learning how to work with a new leader.

In addition, central companies reinforce their roles by making important innovative contributions to the performance of the ecosystem as a whole. Intel, for instance, has enormous scale advantages in the fabrication of microprocessors. Its chip volumes allow it to work out fabrication-process advances sooner than other chip vendors. Ironically, IBM held a license to manufacture Intel-designed microprocessors. With its large volumes during the expansion stage, IBM could have been the one taking the fabrication and price/performance lead in chips—and it could have denied Intel the scale to keep up.

Finally, followers value a central contributor because of its grip on customers. End users are drawn to Microsoft operating systems and Intel chips because so many software applications are available for them. In turn, developers keep turning out such applications because they know Microsoft and Intel are customer gateways.

To some extent, these two companies achieved their current central position by being in the right place at the right time—that is, by serving IBM. Intel and Microsoft clearly appreciate what they have now and are working effectively to maintain their central contributions. Still, some companies like Wal-Mart have systematically gone about building a strong ecosystem, one that guarantees a leading role for themselves.

In any case, for dominant companies, the expansion and leadership stages of an ecosystem can make or break them. In Stage 3, lead producers must extend control by continuing to shape future directions and the investments of key customers and suppliers. And for healthy profits, any company in the ecosystem—leader or follower—must maintain bargaining power over other members.

Stage 4 of a business ecosystem occurs when mature business communities are threatened by rising new ecosystems and innovations. Alternatively, a community might undergo the equivalent of an earthquake: sudden new environmental conditions that include changes in government regulations, customer buying patterns, or macroeconomic conditions. Moreover, these two factors reinforce each other. An altered environment is often more hospitable to new or formerly marginal business ecosystems.

In fact, how a dominant company deals with the threat of obsolescence is the ultimate challenge. Just because Microsoft and Intel are leaders now doesn't mean their current ecosystem is immortal. Nor does it mean that Microsoft NT ("New Technology" operating software) will form the basis for its successor. After all, Novell and UNIX Systems Laboratories have merged and will put forth a new generation of software, looking to strengthen a new ecosystem. Both Hewlett-Packard and Sun Microsystems remain strongly entrenched. And Motorola is now manufacturing a new generation microprocessor to be sold by both IBM and Apple, along with a jointly developed new software operating system.

Leading successive generations of innovation is clearly crucial to an ecosystem's long-term success and its ability to renew itself. Today's pharmaceutical companies provide some interesting insights into three general approaches to self-renewal, which can be used alone or in combination: (1) dominant companies can seek to slow the growth of a new ecosystem; (2) they can try to incorporate new innovations into their own ecosystems; or (3) they can fundamentally restructure themselves to try coping with a new reality.

During the past few decades, pharmaceutical companies have operated under a relatively consistent, if largely implicit, social compact with government regulators. In exchange for investing heavily in product and process innovation, drug companies have been allowed comparatively high margins and protection from competition through patent laws and lengthy approval processes. Traditional pharmaceutical ecosystems, therefore, have evolved around three major functions: R&D, testing and approval management, and marketing and sales. Each of these functions is expensive, hard to perfect, and thus presents a barrier to new competitors. In the past, these functions were carried out within large, vertically integrated companies that did not, until recently, consider themselves networked organizations.

In the 1980s, generic drug manufacturers that specialized in producing off-patent drugs posed a threat to the established pharmaceutical houses. The dominant companies responded by blocking these rival ecosystems in order to minimize their expansion. This included lobbying to slow generic-drug enabling legislation and to reinforce the natural conservatism of the U.S. Food and Drug Administration. Well-funded marketing and sales efforts convinced thousands of individual physicians to continue prescribing mostly branded drugs. While the generic drug manufacturers were able to establish alternative ecosystems, their penetration of the market has been held to about 30%, with little price cutting by the dominant companies.

Meanwhile, a variety of small biotechnology start-ups posed an even greater threat to the traditional pharmaceutical powerhouses. In general, biotech researchers concentrate on isolating complex substances that already exist in the human body and finding ways to manufacture them—for example, human insulin and human growth hormone. As many as one biotech try in ten may prove successful, which keeps the R&D cost down to between $100 million and $150 million per marketable product. Compare this with the traditional pharmaceutical average of 10,000 chemical tries to identify one marketable drug—and R&D costs of $250 million to $350 million per product.

Many of the founders of and investors in biotechnology start-ups believed that low R&D costs would provide the basis for creating whole new business ecosystems that could compete with the established drug companies. For example, Genentech, one of the pioneering biotech companies, clearly intended to establish itself as a full competitor. By the mid-1980s, Genentech had five products in the market and was marketing three itself. It licensed its first two products: alpha-interferon to Hoffmann-LaRoche and insulin to Eli Lilly. Using the cash from these licenses, Genentech sought to manufacture and market human growth hormone and tissue plasminogen activator on its own. Yet in 1990, 60% of Genentech was sold to Hoffmann-LaRoche for $2.1 billion. A similar fate has befallen almost all of the original biotech companies.

In essence, these companies misjudged the difficulties of mastering the testing and approval process. The first biotech managers bet on the assumption that testing and approval would, like R&D, be less expensive and problematic than it was for their traditional competitors. Since biotech products were existing molecules already resident in the human body, these products would presumably require much less testing than synthetic chemical compounds. However, the FDA approval process in the United States, which grants access to the most important market worldwide, has not borne this out. From 1981 to 1991, only 12 biotech products were approved for general marketing.

Strapped for cash and unable to raise much more from their original investors, most biotech companies ended the 1980s in no position to lead their own business ecosystems. Biotech managers and investors were attracted to alliances with traditional companies and thus merged new business ecosystems with powerful existing ones. In turn, dominant companies like Merck, Eli Lilly, and Bristol-Myers began to think like business ecosystem builders. In order to snap up licenses, patents, and talent to strengthen their own R&D, these companies affiliated themselves with the biotech companies rather than simply blocking their new rivals.

Of course, the leaders of a mature business ecosystem sometimes have no choice but to undertake profound structural and cultural changes. Pharmaceutical ecosystems now face new threats and a profoundly altered environment. The social compact to protect drug company profits in exchange for product and process innovation is breaking down. The public, government, and corporations all want health care costs reduced. Drug company leaders see lean times ahead as they confront the possibility of price and profit caps, as well as consolidated purchasing of drugs by HMOs and government agencies.

Responding to this environmental shift will force changes across all major functions. Companies will probably have to limit R&D spending and focus it carefully. Managers are likely to design a testing and approval process that highlights not only efficacy but also cost/benefit performance of new treatments. Finally, companies will probably market and sell less directly to individual physicians, focusing instead on negotiations with experts who represent third-party payers and government.

But despite the difficulties of such a complex business environment, managers can design longevity into an ecosystem. During the expansion and leadership stages, for instance, companies can work hard to micro-segment their markets, creating close, supportive ties with customers. These customers will then remain committed to a particular ecosystem long enough for its members to incorporate the benefits of new approaches.

And visionary executives like Merck's Roy Vagelos can sometimes lead an ecosystem so that it rapidly and effectively embraces anticipated developments—be they new technologies, regulatory openings, or consumer trends. Ultimately, there is no substitute for eternal vigilance. As Intel's Andy Grove noted recently, "Only the paranoid survive."

Clearly, pharmaceutical companies—and any other venture threatened by continual innovations—can no longer allow their particular ecosystems to evolve without direction. Using an ecological approach, executives can start making strategic changes by systematically questioning their company's current situation: Is the company linked with the very best suppliers and partners? Is the company betting its future on the most promising new ideas? Are suppliers leading the way in commercializing innovation? Over the long run, how will the company maintain sufficient bargaining power and autonomy to guarantee good financial returns?

Examining a company's key competitors from a business ecological point of view is also important: What hidden web of customer and supplier relationships have competitors worked to develop? Who do they depend on for ideas and supplier support? What are the nature and benefits of those relationships? How do these compare with what the company has?

And to prepare the ground for organizational breakthroughs, managers need to consider how the work of their company might be radically different: What seed innovations might make current businesses obsolete? What would it take to catalyze a cluster of ideas into a new and vital business ecosystem? What type of community would be required to bring these new ideas to the widest possible market?

Asking these questions, let alone acting on the answers, has become a difficult necessity for all companies. Superficially, competition among business ecosystems is a fight for market share. But below the surface, these new competitive struggles are fights over who will direct the future.

Yet it's precisely in the role of conscious direction that a strictly biological metaphor is no longer useful. Business communities, unlike biological communities of co-evolving organisms, are social systems. And social systems are made up of real people who make decisions; the larger patterns are maintained by a complex network of choices, which depend, at least in part, on what participants are aware of. As Gregory Bateson noted, if you change the ideas in a social system, you change the system itself.

I anticipate that as an ecological approach to management becomes more common—as an increasing number of executives become conscious of co-evolution and its consequences—the pace of business change itself will accelerate. Executives whose horizons are bounded by traditional industry perspectives will find themselves missing the real challenges and opportunities that face their companies. Shareholders and directors, sensing the new reality, will eventually remove them. Or, in light of the latest management shifts, they may have already done so.

Unfortunately for employees and investors, this often occurs only after the companies involved have been deeply damaged. Companies that once dominated their industries, as traditionally defined, have been blindsided by new competition. Whether such companies can find the appropriate leadership to renew the ecosystems on which their future depends remains an open question. If they cannot, they'll be supplanted by other companies, in other business ecosystems, that will expand and lead over the next few years.

For the individuals caught up in these ecosystem struggles, the stakes are high. As a society, we must find ways of helping members of dying ecosystems get into more vital ones while avoiding the temptation of propping up the failed ecosystems themselves. From an ecological perspective, it matters not which particular ecosystems stay alive; rather, it's only essential that competition among them is fierce and fair—and that the fittest survive.

Automobiles: An Old-Fashioned Timeline

An ecological approach can be used to analyze the evolution of any major business. However, a look at how the old-line automobile companies evolved reveals a different time scale than that of almost any new business today. Historically, the evolutionary stages of an established ecosystem like Ford's or GM's often took decades to play out; but now businesses can be born and die in a matter of years. Managers used to focus on directing the action within a particular stage rather than on how to move from one stage to another. Yet transition between stages has currently become a managerial fact of life.

The major U.S. automobile ecosystems took about three-quarters of a century to evolve, a phenomenal length of time compared with the rise and fall of high-tech businesses like personal computers. However, early automobile executives were well aware of the need to forge a community of suppliers and customers.

Birth of the Horseless Carriage. The late 1800s were a time of experimentation, as the first automobile pioneers struggled to grasp the potential of individualized, motorized transportation. Ransom E. Olds and a handful of others established viable automobile business ecosystems by the turn of the century. Their machines worked reasonably well, were accepted by a small but dedicated number of customers, and could be profitably produced.

Expansion Battles. The next 20 years carried the automobile business deep into the second stage of ecological competition. In 1904, William C. Durant began building what would become General Motors. Henry Ford founded the Ford Motor Company, and, in 1908, he introduced his mass-produced, mass-marketed Model T. Near-legendary battles between Ford and GM ensued—struggles as much for soul and future definition of the business as for simple market share.

Ford's approach was based on vertical integration, carefully engineered production, and product simplicity. Ford's ecosystem had what we now would call "scalability"; by 1914, his company produced over 267,000 cars and held 48% of the market.

Durant's strategy for GM, however, was based on acquisitions of early companies, marketing might, sales coverage, and product variety. Durant's ecosystem captured market share by pooling and integrating the markets and the production facilities of a variety of smaller companies. However, by 1920, General Motors had nearly collapsed because of the inability of Durant's management systems to control such a complex collection of business entities.

From about 1910 to 1930, industry leaders directed the large expansion of the automobile market, reconfiguring the major ecosystems in the process. Alfred P. Sloan's design for General Motors, initiated in 1920, is most notable and involved the simultaneous ouster of Durant. Sloan's design specifically allowed for the management of a complex business ecosystem by breaking up the diverse company into product lines, which, in turn, could be focused like Ford's mass-produced lines. Sloan also centralized financial oversight of decentralized product lines, and GM became the prototype of the modern multidivisional company.

Community Leadership. By the 1930s, battles for community leadership and bargaining power revolved around the principal supplier to the auto industry: labor. In the late 1920s, around 500,000 people worked in the Detroit area car factories. Working conditions were dangerous; one auto body plant was known as "the slaughterhouse." But by the mid-1930s, the United Auto Workers Union had formed. In 1937, the UAW achieved a landmark victory when GM recognized the union as an official representative of its employees.

Over time, organized labor brought workers crucial bargaining power, which the union used to force the companies to share the spoils of victory. The tug-of-war between workers and companies continued for decades, mediated with varying effectiveness by the U.S. government. While it protected workers, this form of ecosystem struggle also carried with it high costs: work-rule rigidity and the polarization of workers and management. These costs would come back to haunt the U.S. automobile business in the next stage of ecosystem development.

The Threat of Obsolescence. Labor-management struggles continued into the 1970s, until both sides were driven together by a much deeper crisis: the obsolescence of the management approaches, business practices, and systems of production that had been only incrementally improved since the 1920s. The near collapse of the U.S. automobile business came, of course, at the hands of the Japanese. The Toyota ecosystem, for one, was capable of unheard-of levels of product variety, quality, and efficiency at the time. This powerful new business ecosystem was based on a combination of customer-focused design, concurrent engineering, flexible manufacturing, dedicated workers, and networks of suppliers, all tied together through statistically refined management practices.

Therefore, the automobile industry, as traditionally defined, found itself in a full-fledged ecological war, defending against a new wave of business ecosystems. Self-renewal proved difficult, and companies like Ford and Chrysler had nearly collapsed by the late 1970s. The superiority of Japanese approaches ultimately forced the transformation of the world automobile business into what we know today.

The Evolution of Wal-Mart: Savvy Expansion and Leadership

An ecological analysis of Wal-Mart reveals how a relatively small company, starting in a rural area of the United States, could turn its original isolation to advantage by creating a complete business ecosystem. Wal-Mart developed and continues to refine an offer that customers find nearly irresistible: low prices on a variety of brands as diverse as Gitano jeans and Yardman lawn mowers. Moreover, CEO Sam Walton managed the company's expansion superbly and increased bargaining power during the leadership stage.

The Birth of Discounting. In the early 1960s, Kmart, Wal-Mart, and other discounters recognized that the Main Street five-and-dime was giving way to the variety store. And variety stores, in turn, were threatened by the large discount store. In order to buy a wide range of goods at low prices in one location, customers were increasingly willing to get into cars and drive to malls or other non-Main Street locations.

Kmart and Wal-Mart appeared on the discount scene at about the same time. The Kmart stores were actually owned by old-style S.S. Kresge, which reinvented itself as a suburb-oriented discount retailer, with big stores located near existing malls and towns of more than 50,000 people. Kmart stores carried items aimed at the lower end of suburban tastes.

By the late 1960s, Wal-Mart had worked out the basic structure of its own business ecosystem: Wal-Mart stores, which supplied a variety of well-known brands, were located in relatively sparsely populated areas. The company went into towns of 5,000 people, particularly where several of these towns might be served by one store. Wal-Mart products were up to 15% cheaper than those available in "mom-and-pop" stores.

While the original Wal-Mart locations could support one store, the customer population wasn't large enough to maintain two rival discounters. Thus once Wal-Mart established a store in a particular area and had beaten back weak local retailers, it was seldom threatened with future local competition from other discounters, including Kmart.

Expansion: Planning for a Chokehold. Once its business strategy was up and running in a number of discount stores in the American South and Mid-West, Wal-Mart's top executives concentrated on developing organizational capabilities that would let it scale up successfully. They were obsessed with three things:

- Building a set of incentives that would ensure employee commitment to local stores, which led to a complex system of training, oversight, bonuses, and stock-purchase plans for workers.
- Managing communication and control of a network of remotely located stores, which required close monitoring of a carefully drawn set of measures that were transmitted daily to Wal-Mart headquarters in Bentonville, Arkansas.
- Setting up an efficient distribution system that allowed for joint purchasing, shared facilities, systematic ordering, and store-level distribution of a large number of different goods. This third obsession ultimately became Wal-Mart's trademark hub-and-spoke distribution system: warehouses served constellations of stores located no more than a day's drive from the center.

In 1970, Wal-Mart went public to raise funds for its expansion. That same year, the company built its first hub-and-spoke distribution center—embarking on a strategy of targeting a large geographic area, setting up a distribution center, and then populating the area with as many stores as the territory would support. Wal-Mart not only filled the needs of customers in small towns but also saturated entire regions, making it uneconomical for competitors to enter as either distributors or local store owners.

The number of Wal-Mart stores grew rapidly, from 32 in 1970 to 195 in 1978—when the first fully automated distribution center opened—to

551 in 1983—when Wal-Mart launched its own satellite, creating a communication network to keep in daily touch with its now far-flung empire.

Leadership: Building Bargaining Power. By 1984, Wal-Mart's managerial agenda changed. What was in the birth and expansion stages a race to develop systems and conquer territory now became a concerted effort to build bargaining power. As the leaders of a highly successful and visible business ecosystem, Wal-Mart managers worked on continuing to assert the company's vision over other community members, including suppliers like Procter & Gamble, Rubbermaid, and Helene Curtis Industries.

First, Wal-Mart resisted the temptation to charge higher prices in the markets and regions it dominated. Instead, top managers still viewed each market as "contestable"—as a potential opening for rivals if Wal-Mart ceased to give the maximum possible value to customers. Continued customer leadership, in turn, enhanced the Wal-Mart brand and further cemented the company's place in the minds and buying habits of consumers. Wal-Mart's system of "everyday low prices," in which there's no need for weekly sales or special promotions, has now become a standard in discount retailing.

Second, Wal-Mart—now a very large and powerful channel to customers—started putting heavy pressure on suppliers to keep their prices down. Moreover, Wal-Mart compelled its suppliers to set up cross-company distribution systems to attain maximum manufacturing efficiency. For example, in 1987, Wal-Mart and Procter & Gamble reached an unprecedented accord to work together through extensive electronic ordering and information sharing between the companies. In return, Wal-Mart gives better payment terms than the rest of the retailing industry: on average, Wal-Mart pays its suppliers within 29 days compared with 45 days at Kmart.

Third, Wal-Mart continued to invest in and enhance its own fundamental economies of scale and scope in distribution. By the leadership stage, distribution had become the crucial ecological component of the Wal-Mart ecosystem. In fact, Wal-Mart's distribution chokehold has allowed the ecosystem as a whole to triumph over others like Kmart's. While suppliers, big and small, may chafe under Wal-Mart's heavy hand, it's also clear that most of them need this particular leader to survive. The graph "Wal-Mart Takes Off" is a testament to the company's dominance and bargaining power in the leadership stage.

Finally, Wal-Mart has extended its reach into adjacent territories and ecosystems. In 1983, Wal-Mart entered the membership discount market with its Sam's Club, which by 1992 included 208 clubs that contributed over $9.4 billion in revenues. In 1990, Wal-Mart incorporated another

Exhibit 5-2 Wal-Mart Takes Off

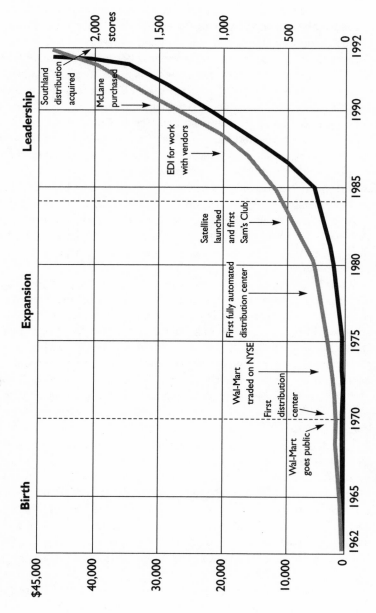

Birth   Expansion   Leadership

■ Growth in sales (millions of dollars)   ■ Growth in number of stores

ecosystem by acquiring McLane Company, the nation's largest distributor to the convenience store industry. McLane, under Wal-Mart's control, now serves about 30,000 retail stores, including 18,000 convenience stores. And in 1992, Wal-Mart also acquired the distribution and food processing divisions of Southland Corporation. Southland operates a large chain of 7-Eleven convenience stores, and this acquisition added as many as 5,000 more 7-Eleven stores to the McLane/Wal-Mart customer base.

PART

III

The Customer in a
Network Economy

1
Real-Time Marketing

Regis McKenna

It's no secret that managing a brand in today's chaotic marketplace is a daunting task. Long-established brands such as IBM and Apple battle for customers against makers of computer clones with uncertain pedigrees. Even hallowed name brands like Tide and Budweiser are not immune from upstart competitors. In fact, in the 1990s, "other" has become the fastest-growing category in the market-share figures of many product groups.

At the same time, consumers have more information about products and more products to choose from than ever before. They have more ways to shop: at giant malls, specialty shops, and superstores; through mail-order catalogs, home shopping networks, and virtual stores on the Internet. And they are bombarded with messages pitched through a growing number of channels: broadcast and narrowcast television, radio, on-line computer networks, the Internet, telephony services such as fax and telemarketing, and niche magazines and other print media. Given the proliferation of choices, it's no wonder consumers view brand names with growing indifference. For the producer, establishing a new brand is a herculean task. The noise level of the media is deafening, and it takes longer to break through and develop the market. Maintaining an existing brand isn't much easier.

But there is an upside to the brand dilemma. Information technology, which brought about much of the complexity in today's marketplace, can also become a tool for rebuilding the power of brands. Using current and emerging technologies, such as high-speed communications, computer networks, and advanced software programs, companies can start real-time dialogues with their customers and provide interactive services. Technology-facilitated conversation and service will allow companies to cut through the market chaos and establish binding relationships with their customers.

To understand how brand building will change, consider the way Philips NV, the Netherlands-based electronics giant, developed an on-line product for children, soon to be available in Europe. Philips sent industrial designers, cognitive psychologists, anthropologists, and sociologists in mobile vans to communities in Italy, France, and the Netherlands. The researchers invited adults and children to help brainstorm for ideas for new electronics products to meet customers' changing needs. The Philips employees did not conduct a survey of these volunteer product designers. Rather, they hosted a dialogue in which specialists and customers interactively imagined new possibilities. Philips looked at all the ideas, narrowed them down, and settled on one new on-line interactive product for children. The researchers then went back out into the communities and tested the new product idea on the same children.

Philips's direct contact with consumers is not unique. As many companies have discovered, interactions between designers and customers during the development of new products can provide managers with information that can help make the products more acceptable in the marketplace. But, for marketing professionals, there is more to the story. The children who advised Philips in developing its on-line product not only helped make the product acceptable but also became potential customers for it. Providing these customers with the experience of participating in the design of a product wins their loyalty. Right now, most companies can provide such experiences directly to only a handful of customers. The challenge for marketers is to use information technology to create similarly binding experiences for hundreds of thousands of customers. By doing so, companies can speed up the time it takes for the marketplace to accept a new product—what I call *time to acceptance*—thereby improving the chances for the product's success.

Today marketing sits at the end of the production chain. Companies strive to reduce time to market—the time it takes to design and manufacture new products and push them out the door. They expect marketing professionals to make the product succeed once it's in the marketplace. But time to acceptance is what determines success in a crowded marketplace, not time to market. A product that cannot win customers quickly will not compete well against a product that has a ready base of customers. Improving time to acceptance means integrating marketing with design and manufacturing. That's done by involving potential customers as early as possible in the development process.

Information technology can help companies with time to acceptance and more. To build customer loyalty—to build brand—companies need to keep their customers engaged in a continuous dialogue. The conversation between customers and the organization should not be limited to the development cycle. How the product works, the customer's experiences with the product, and how the company supports the product after the sale also contribute to customer loyalty. Companies must keep the dialogue flowing and also maintain conversations with suppliers, distributors, and others in the marketplace. To do this effectively, the technology linking these groups to the company must be integrated with internal systems managing production and design schedules, field sales information, and even competitive intelligence. Combined, these systems allow companies to interact with their customers and the marketplace in real time and to incorporate into their products the service experiences that will keep customers loyal. Dialogue will become the way companies build brand.

Marketing must take responsibility for managing these systems. Although real-time marketing has a growing number of supporters (see B. Joseph Pine II, Don Peppers, and Martha Rogers, "Do You Want to Keep Your Customers Forever?" *Harvard Business Review* March–April 1995), few people recognize how dramatically marketing organizations must change in order to engage the customer in an effective conversation. Real-time marketing requires

- replacing the broadcast mentality that has long dominated marketing with a willingness to give consumers access to the company and to view their actions and feedback as integral to developing or improving products
- focusing on real-time customer satisfaction, providing the support, help, guidance, and information necessary to win customers' loyalty
- being willing to learn how information technology is changing both customer behavior and marketing, and to think in new ways about the role of marketing within the organization

Although no company has yet begun to rebuild its brand through real-time marketing, the seeds of such an approach are germinating in a number of organizations, including Apple Computer, Levi Strauss, and Federal Express.

From Broadcast to Dialogue

If companies treat new communications media such as the Internet and even established media such as 800 numbers simply as channels for broadcasting messages, distributing products, and processing transactions, they will fail to gain the real benefits of the technology. The power of the new media lies in their ability to draw the individual customer into a conversation with the company.

Marketing executives are not used to thinking about how to build and manage dialogue with their customers. Marketing has long been a broadcast discipline, rooted in practices developed for selling mass-produced goods to broad, homogeneous markets. For nearly half a century, companies have targeted products at customers. The most important role of marketing in the process has been to create and broadcast messages about those products through the mass media. Product awareness has been synonymous with brand building. Marketing departments would develop a positioning theme for a product and advertise it. For each of the dozen toothpaste brands available in the 1960s and 1970s, for example, customers knew a jingle or a slogan and little more. The brand name connoted reliability, quality, value, or a host of other associations.

The environment has changed, but the marketing model hasn't. Marketing staffs know full well that the explosion of products and media outlets has made the job of message making and brand building extraordinarily difficult. Yet as they search for solutions, they rarely look beyond broadcasting. Instead, they try to improve the quality or increase the number of the messages. When that fails, they blame their advertising agencies. The ultimate brand and demand generators, advertising agencies receive almost $140 billion per year from companies for their services. Such expenditures put the agencies squarely in the sights of performance-minded managers. Agencies that fail to produce results are fired overnight. But the issues behind a product's failure or a brand's decline are deeper than the failure of one season's ad campaign.

Even recent approaches to the discipline, such as micromarketing, perpetuate the traditional model. Drawing on the power of information technology to zero in on specific households and individuals, micromarketers can send personalized advertisements to a carefully selected audience. But these are still one-way messages, and they must compete against all the other messages bombarding the marketplace. In each of the past three years, marketers sent more than 60 billion direct mail packages to homes in the United States. As every marketer gets access to the same tools, the market of one will collapse, smothered in messages, catalogs, and phone calls. Customers will be overloaded, and dissatisfaction will rise.

Marketing's traditional connections to customers are no longer sufficient in a real-time world. Focus groups, market research, consumer surveys, and other tools for probing the consumer's wants and needs are—and always have been—limited. The drawbacks to focus groups are well-known: A handful of carefully selected individuals, paid for their time and plied with questions in an artificial setting, hardly represent the marketplace. Similarly, customer surveys must be viewed with skepticism: Digital Equipment Corporation's minicomputer business faltered in the late 1980s, but customers rated DEC their top vendor in survey after survey.

By contrast, more continuous connections with customers can provide information that focus groups and surveys cannot. Many companies already have systems in place that could begin providing more reliable information right now. Apple Computer, for instance, collects information from customer hot-line calls for its Macintosh Performa home and education computers. Customer service staff use the phone interaction to tell customers about new products that make computing easier. From this dialogue, the staff members also identify the top ten customer issues for the week. Apple treats the information seriously. Customer service staff meet regularly in planning sessions with Apple's design staff to discuss what they are hearing from customers. Design engineers use the weekly top ten list to improve new releases and also to identify customers' wishes for new products. In this way, Apple now responds more rapidly and more accurately to customer input than it could when relying on periodic market research studies.

For instance, customers unacquainted with computers contacted Apple early on with surprisingly basic questions about how to set up their systems. Several thought the mouse was a foot pedal. Although Apple's instruction manuals clearly explained how to use a mouse and perform other basic functions, the hot-line questions prompted the company to build a simple solution into the computer itself. Engineers designed a software welcome mat, which appears on the screen when a Macintosh Performa customer first turns on the system. It introduces computer users to system basics. Apple continually makes such simple design changes in direct response to customer feedback.

But that is just half the picture. Companies like Apple can do more than use information systems to sense the needs of their customers.

They can also use technology to respond to customers by creating service experiences for them. By closing the interactive loop, marketers can establish and maintain a dynamic brand in a noisy marketplace.

Levi Strauss offers one example. The California-based apparel company has begun marketing a made-to-order service for customizing women's jeans in selected U.S. locations. Salesclerks measure customers and feed the data into a computer-aided-design information system. They let a customer try on sample jeans in the store—to perfect the fit—and they feed the additional data into the system. The system forwards the information to a computerized fabric-cutting machine at the factory, and the jeans are made to order. The custom jeans cost only $10 more than Levi Strauss's mass-produced products.

In this real-time system, the transaction (selling the jeans) is also a service experience for the customer. Technology allows companies to bundle services into every product and turn every sale into a conversation. The interaction allows the customer and the producer to learn from each other and to respond to each other.

Where does this leave the brand? Without a doubt, it is still the patch on the back of the jeans. Yet the electronic conversation that surrounds it has grown in importance. The shopper will still expect high quality jeans at a reasonable price, but she will also help Levi Strauss design her product, and she'll define specific elements of the product—measurements, color, and texture—that satisfy her. The brand, in this case, is no longer the static image it was during the age of mass marketing. Instead it becomes an ongoing dialogue, the interactive experience of buying and using the product.

In the future, Levi Strauss could use this system to broaden its dialogue with the customer. Customers could order new jeans over the phone; Levi Strauss could make them using the customer's measurements, stored in a database, and ship them out quickly. The company could also send information on new products to repeat customers. And, as the company's database grows, it will have useful information about the sizes and styles of jeans that its customers are ordering.

The knowledge of individual customer needs that companies can capture through technology harkens back to the days when the butcher, baker, and candlestick maker knew their clientele personally. In that setting, customer service relationships were built in face-to-face transactions. A cabinetmaker designed and manufactured a product by interacting constantly with the customer. The customer got immediate responses and assurances. The service provider learned firsthand what customers wanted, how they liked the offered products and services, and even how they felt about issues seemingly unrelated to the specific transaction, such as lifestyle questions. Today's technology can recreate the conversation between the shopkeeper and the customer. The only difference is that the conversation today can and does happen electronically, in real time.

The information revolution has made possible a new kind of relationship among strangers, based not on physical proximity but on the speed of electronic information. Today companies and customers, doctors and patients, students and teachers, and architects and clients can know more about one another and work more closely together than they ever could before. Virtual intimacy, electronic collegiality, instant familiarity, call it what you will: There's a new and evolving relationship that defines brand in the information age.

Access and Acceptance

For marketing managers to shift the focus of their efforts from broadcast to dialogue, they need to consider in particular how to initiate dialogue and sustain it. Companies initiate dialogue by opening themselves to consumer access; they sustain it by involving consumers as partners in development and production.

Dialogue begins with access. To converse with customers, companies must build interactive links to the marketplace. One of the easiest links a company can establish is an 800 number. Consumer goods companies could stamp the digits of an 800 number on every product next to the serial number and purchase codes, eliminating the need for warranty and registration cards, providing help and information, and perhaps even drawing customers into an interactive service. For instance, Kellogg has begun to place an 800 number on the inside top of its cereal boxes. Prompted by recent Food and Drug Administration labeling rules requiring food product companies to include more information about nutrition on their packages, Kellogg invites customers to call for help reading and understanding the new labels. The company considers this a temporary program, but conceivably it could build on it to offer additional information about the nutritional content of Kellogg's products and to solicit product ideas from customers.

There are other ways to give customers access to the company. Federal Express provides its customers with specially developed software and computer terminals so that they can track the delivery of their own packages. The technology links customers to a network that

Federal Express maintains and that provides real-time information about where their packages are. One Federal Express customer, National Semiconductor, uses the technology as the basis of its own delivery network to ensure that each of its customers worldwide receives ordered parts within 24 hours. A computer company in Taiwan, for example, can look at an on-line catalog of inventory at National Semiconductor's warehouse in Alaska, order a part directly from Federal Express, and track the part as it moves from inventory to the Taiwanese company's doorstep. The billing for the delivery is also automated. Soon, even individual customers will be able to use Federal Express's tracking software through an on-line service such as America Online or the Internet. In fact, Federal Express hopes that by the end of the decade it will be communicating with most of its customers by using real-time systems.

Once such a network of systems is in place, Federal Express can sell additional services to customers. Customers might purchase travel information through the Federal Express network. Or use it for sending secure E-mail messages. Companies might even use the technology to track the delivery of complex shipments such as displays for trade shows and conventions.

Access can happen anywhere in our changing world. Consider banking. Customers can bank by phone or by computer, from home or the office, on board a jet over the Rockies or at a street corner ATM, or even, occasionally, in person at a branch bank. Information and communications technologies have turned homes into workplaces and both homes and offices into shopping centers or entertainment, education, financial, and medical centers. The space where companies and consumers interact is no longer fixed and distinct. But although marketing managers must begin to understand how to use points of access as opportunities for dialogue, they must also recognize the difficulties: Once companies open themselves up to customers, they must have the systems, processes, and people in place to support the interactions fully. If customer requests fall into a black hole, if customized jeans are shipped late, if dental information is inaccurate, or if Federal Express cannot quickly repair system outages, the frustrated customer will not be patient. Access raises the stakes in the company's relationship with its customers: Shattered expectations will do more harm to the relationship than not providing access at all.

But, ultimately, marketing should involve the customer as a partner in development and production. It won't be easy to do, because most companies today have focused their processes on improving time to market and, by inclination and culture, see the customer as an end target rather than a partner. Companies develop new products based on information gathered from focus groups, surveys, and research; they push them to market quickly and then expect marketing departments to create awareness for the new product. But the concept of time to acceptance includes the customer as an integral, contributing partner. A product launch is not an isolated event but a milestone in a relationship with the customer—a relationship that begins with design and continues long after the product passes into the customer's possession. As we saw with Philips in the development of its new on-line offering for children, companies can foster interest in the product before it reaches the market. Customer acceptance of a new product is part of the process of developing it.

Consider how time to acceptance might work. Suppose I purchased a Sony tape recorder at a local appliance store and Sony took the information about my purchase and added it to a database. If I needed additional tapes or software, I could call an 800 number stamped on the product. Or, if the tape recorder was defective, I could call the 800 number and ask for a new one. Sony representatives also might decide to call me a month, say, after my purchase to see how I like the recorder and to sound me out on other features. Have I had any problems with the product? In what ways do I use it? Is there anything Sony could do to help me get greater satisfaction from it? Would I like to try out new Sony products under development and give the company feedback? And, of course, Sony can keep track of all this follow-up information, too. Eventually, Sony will build an upgraded model or attachments for the model I own, and I will be ready to buy them before Sony is ready to ship them.

There are precedents for the time-to-acceptance model. In business-to-business relations, the very nature of the marketing transaction encourages a dialogue between customer and company that fosters mutual loyalty during the development stage and beyond. Intel, for example, discusses plans for new microprocessors with engineers who design computers for Intel's customer companies. "If you could do thus and so in the next generation," an engineer might say, "it would make our life easier." The dialogue serves several purposes. It fosters good relationships with important clients, it prepares Intel's market for its new product, and it helps Intel refine its future development goals. From this dialogue, the company can sense market opportunities and shape designs with realistic parameters.

Still, as evidence of how difficult it can be to make the transition from a broadcast model to a dialogue model, Intel has stumbled in its dealings with its customers' customers. When computer users first discovered a programming error in the Intel Pentium chip, Intel did not rush to address their concerns. The users took their complaints to the Internet, and soon the error was a cause célèbre. Although the media tended to discuss the Pentium issue in terms of good and bad public relations, it was, in fact, an illustration of the power of dialogue with customers. Vocal customers pushed Intel to change its programs and policies. What Intel had long practiced with original equipment manufacturers, it had not extended to the end user. Had Intel incorporated the end users' comments as part of its usual development process, the problem might have been addressed earlier.

Time to acceptance begins by integrating customers as key partners in development and production, but it doesn't end there. Let us return to my Sony example. The company could make further efforts to draw me into the development of new tape recorder upgrades or attachments. Then, when the new products become available and I have purchased them, Sony should continue to provide me with the service experiences that will keep me loyal. The conversation must continue. The dialogue is the brand.

Technology Literacy

For brand rebuilding or for spotting new opportunities, marketing professionals must gain a far better understanding of how technology is changing their customers and their business. Marketing professionals must stand with one foot in the market, observing the opportunities, and one foot in the technology, applying the tools for better time to acceptance. In my experience, marketing managers remain aloof from information technology. Perhaps they are afraid of technology, daunted by its complexity, and reluctant to trust what they don't understand. They seem to expect technologists to do their thinking for them, to dream up and sell to the organization systems to connect them to the customer. But that isn't the technologist's job. Chief information officers and outsourcing partners build and maintain business systems, but business leaders must invent them. If companies aren't building real-time marketing systems, the fault lies with technologically diffident marketing managers, not with the CIO. This has to change.

Marketers do not need to know technical details about information systems—the bits, bytes, and baud rates. But they must develop a *business* understanding of technology and how to use it strategically. For instance, consider how ATMs have changed banking or how point-of-sale scanning technologies have changed retail businesses. Marketers must be able to see how today's technology, including the Internet, CD-ROM catalogs, and interactive television, will shape tomorrow's businesses. In my opinion, managers think very superficially about these things, gathering ideas from newspaper or trade-journal articles or simply adapting broadcast media models for the new generation of technology.

Just as important, marketing professionals must recognize how technology is changing customers' behavior in order to assess how to meet their needs tomorrow. Today's semiconductor and software technology allows consumers to adapt products to their individual needs—by programming the functions built into the product—or to manage their lives better. The average home now contains more than 100 microchips, in everything from home computers and video games to automatic defrost mechanisms in refrigerators. Microchips give consumers options. Taking advantage of the microprocessors embedded in some heating and air-conditioning systems, home owners can control temperature room by room. They can program the chimes in microprocessor-based doorbells to ring out Christmas carols or the notes to "Happy Birthday." They can program their VCRs, compact disc players, televisions, microwave ovens, bread makers, and clocks. As the performance of microprocessors continues to improve and their cost falls, appliances will perform more functions, contain more intelligence, display more options. New advances in software technology, such as object-oriented programming (a method of making software modular and portable), also will help consumers select from a wider range of programming options in order to customize products.

Consumers are using smart products to take more control over their lives. Home-diagnostic products, for instance, provide consumers with more control over their health. Diabetics can now use small test instruments the size of ballpoint pens to check their glucose levels, anywhere and anytime. They use the information to adjust the insulin shots they give themselves using another instrument that looks like a beeper. Such advances mean that diabetics no longer need to visit a lab once a week or rely on professionals to test their blood and give them information about their health. (Glucose levels can change hour by hour, so weekly readings were never especially accurate anyway.) Now diabetics can manage their health themselves—in real time.

Technologies that give consumers greater options and control are changing buyers' behavior in subtle ways. On the Internet, consumers can trade product information with other consumers, experiment with new software programs before they buy them, or join forums. Reebok recently hosted one such forum, in which consumers asked questions about products, checked out sporting events, and exchanged E-mail with Reebok endorsers such as Shaquille O'Neal and Nancy Kerrigan.

Broadcast approaches are inferior to such one-on-one communications. Not long ago, a couple in Nevada ran an ad on the Internet advertising their legal services to millions of Internet users. The response to the broadcast ad was overwhelmingly negative. Consumers sent back a stream of irate messages, overloading the Nevada couple's system. The old media don't work for the new consumer. The new media are about dialogue, communication, and consumer control—not about passivity or broadcasting.

Managers can develop a sense of technology's potential only by using it. When executives sign on to the Internet, they discover firsthand how chaotic it is. They experience, as a customer might, what it's like to visit the numerous corporate sites on the network (home pages) and may begin to think of better ways to use the technology. How might real-time marketers create access in such a chaotic world? They could provide something more than simple linkages and try leading a potential customer from somewhere else on the Internet straight to the company's home page. Compaq has seen to it that its customers can connect from several software companies' home pages to Compaq's. But this doesn't really tie the customer closer to Compaq. The customer still does all the work, hunting and pecking for information. But a real-time marketer would bring the information to the customer. Marketers can create an on-line community of interest for customers, which would link distributors, retailers, software companies, customer advocates, user groups, research organizations, and media databases in an electronic service, support, and development infrastructure. Such ideas will flow when managers engage with the technology. Reading about it is not enough.

One way managers can gain business experience with technology is to partner with technology organizations, including telecommunications companies such as AT&T and regional Bell operating companies, computer systems suppliers such as Sun Microsystems and Silicon Graphics, or systems integrators such as Andersen Consulting and EDS. There is an abundance of good potential partners in the information systems industry. Design, manufacturing, finance, and other functional groups in many companies have often forged successful partnerships with technology vendors to develop customized systems. Marketing-technology alliances might focus on developing systems that will help the company learn how to shift from broadcast to access. These systems might include kiosks at point of sale, 24-hour help lines, or new after-sales and follow-up systems. In the process, marketers could learn a great deal about the capabilities, directions, and opportunities of new and evolving technologies.

Marketing professionals also must begin to rethink their role within the real-time marketing organization. For instance, they must take responsibility for drawing together from departments throughout the company all the information necessary for brand building. They need to use customer information gathered from help services and other points of access: design and production schedules, inventory data, field sales reports, sales transaction data from point-of-sale scanners, and competitive intelligence. The marketing professional is now a marketing systems integrator.

Wal-Mart offers one example of what real-time marketing might entail. The giant retail chain provides its regional managers with daily information about sales, recorded product by product at the checkout counter. But that isn't enough information. Regional managers travel throughout their territories during the week, visiting Wal-Mart stores and stores of competitors, gathering personal knowledge of the market. They compare the personal knowledge they have gained with the data collected at point-of-sale scanners. At the end of one week, they plan the following week with their store managers, sometimes using Wal-Mart's television network to conduct virtual meetings. That is a real-time business environment—composed of information about customers, competitors, products, sales, inventory, and anything else that might help regional managers make sound decisions. In a real-time environment, managers do not need to conduct focus groups. The information they can obtain daily from a greater number of sensors in the marketplace is far richer.

How will marketing in general accomplish all this? Unquestionably, companies need to begin considering new designs for their marketing organization. Perhaps senior executives might shift large portions of their marketing units into the product design organization. Or marketing executives could head up the company's information technology function, guiding efforts to reshape systems so that they help build brands. Or perhaps the marketing organization will disappear as marketing becomes the work of every employee in the company, not just of those in a single department. One thing is certain: Marketing will change, and managers must be prepared to change with it.

2
The Coming Battle for Customer Information

John Hagel III and Jeffrey F. Rayport

Companies have good reason to collect information about customers. It enables them to target their most valuable prospects more effectively, tailor their offerings to individual needs, improve customer satisfaction and retention, and identify opportunities for new products or services. But even as more and more managers begin to build strategies based on capturing information about their customers, a major change is under way that may undermine their efforts. We believe that consumers are going to take ownership of information about themselves and demand value in exchange for it. As a result, negotiating with consumers for information will become costly and complex. That process has already begun to unfold, but it could take several years to play out across broad segments of customers and products.

It is no secret that consumers are becoming increasingly edgy about the amount and depth of information businesses collect about them. The popular press regularly chronicles the public's growing concern about privacy in an information-rich era. More specifically, people are starting to realize that the information they have divulged so freely through their daily commercial transactions, financial arrangements, and survey responses has value and that they get very little in exchange for that value. Why? Because the balance of power currently rests with companies, not consumers.

The balance could tip in favor of consumers, however, thanks to new technologies such as smart cards, World Wide Web browsers, and personal-financial-management software. These technologies make it possible for users to obtain much more comprehensive and accurate profiles of their own commercial activities than any individual vendor—or plausible combination of vendors—could hope to collect. Through these technologies, users will be able to choose whether to release or withhold information about themselves. Their decision will hinge, in large part, on what vendors offer them in return for the data.

Consumers probably will not bargain with vendors on their own, however. We anticipate that companies we call *infomediaries* will seize the opportunity to act as custodians, agents, and brokers of customer information, marketing it to businesses on consumers' behalf while protecting their privacy at the same time. Only a handful of companies with unique brand franchises, strong relationships with their customers, or radically new strategies will be positioned to become infomediaries; but they will be the catalyst for people to begin demanding value in exchange for data about themselves.

What will this shift in power mean for most other companies? In general, businesses in industries that cater to consumers, whether they are product manufacturers or service providers, will need to rethink how they obtain information about their customers and what they do with it. That is, they will need to understand what information they must collect and how they will acquire it and use it to find new customers more efficiently, improve products and services or tailor them to individual needs, and build loyalty. Those companies that do the best job of using information to provide value to customers will be positioned to gain access to more of it.

Privacy Isn't the Issue

We are witnessing the growth of a "privacy" backlash among consumers, which we believe has less to do with the desire to keep information about themselves confidential and more to do with the pragmatic assessment that the returns for the information they divulge are, simply put, unsatisfactory. Consumers increasingly recognize that they are selling their "privacy" cheaply to companies that are using it to forward corporate interests. More broadly, consumers regularly decry the invasion of their privacy by the government and the press. In those instances, too, they are outraged that those collecting the information are using it to create value only for themselves—or, in some cases, to damage the interests of the people surrendering the information.

These concerns are being voiced with increasing frequency. For example, consumer activists and the press attacked Lotus Development

Corporation in 1991 when they learned that the software company was planning to release a CD-ROM product for direct marketers. Called Marketplace, the product would allow ordinary PC users to search across the country for the names, addresses, and phone numbers of individuals who matched specified demographic or psychographic characteristics. Although all the information contained in Marketplace could be obtained either from sources in the public domain such as the U.S. Census Report or, for a price, from market research firms, critics argued that the product's low cost and user-friendliness would invite marketers and others to deluge private citizens with junk mail or telemarketing calls. In the face of considerable negative publicity, Lotus dropped the product and spun off Marketplace as a separate company.

Microsoft sparked a tempest in 1995 when it was revealed that its Registration Wizard, which allowed users of Windows 95 to register on-line, was automatically collecting information about customers' software without their knowledge or permission. When users registered with Microsoft, going on-line for the first time, Microsoft took the opportunity to "read" the configuration of their PCs. The company gained instant knowledge, subscriber by subscriber, of the major software products running on its customers' systems. When members of the on-line world got wind of what Microsoft was doing, they protested publicly. Microsoft quickly abandoned the practice.

Netscape faced a similar storm early last year over its "cookie" technology, which is embedded in its popular Internet software for accessing the World Wide Web. The cookie software enabled the Netscape browser to obtain automatically a record of Web sites visited and of the specific pages clicked to at each site; the software would store this information on the user's own PC. Netscape intended the cookie technology to allow Web sites to do more than tabulate hits, however; it enabled them to develop profiles of the sites' visitors. When a user arrived at a site, the cookie software on the user's PC downloaded a record of any previous visits made to that site, making the data available to the site's owner. (Even though the cookie software obtained an integrated profile of the user's visits to all Web sites, Netscape designed the technology to download information only about the user's previous visits to that specific site.)

When Netscape users realized that the software itself was divulging information about their behavior on the Web, they reacted much as Microsoft's users had—and Netscape quickly announced that in subsequent releases of its browser software, users would have the option of turning off the cookie function and denying Web sites access to the information it contained. In other words, consumers once again rebelled when they realized that information about them was flowing to businesses—providing them with commercial resources—while the consumers themselves were getting nothing in return.

But to view such rebellions as concerns about privacy is to misunderstand them. Of course, some individuals consider privacy an absolute right, and many people are concerned about their privacy in an abstract sense. However, most consumers have shown that they are willing to release personal information if they can profit by doing so. We are all familiar with the success of frequent-flier programs, which have passengers clamoring to hand over detailed information about their flight histories to airlines in return for something of tangible value, such as discounts on future flights or, increasingly, the ability to purchase a broad range of other products and services at a discount.

Consumers appreciate—and often pay premium prices for—the customized products and services companies can deliver when making thoughtful use of personal information. For example, car rental companies frequently collect highly detailed information for programs like Hertz Corporation's #1 Club Gold and National Car Rental's Emerald Club. Application forms request several credit-card account numbers and expiration dates, frequent-flier numbers for a dozen airlines, business and home addresses with phone and fax numbers, and E-mail addresses, not to mention driver's license and Social Security numbers, insurance providers and policy numbers, and estimated frequency of travel. Consumers surrender this information willingly, knowing that they will receive substantial benefits in return, such as a wider choice of vehicles, more favorable rates, and fast, hassle-free pickups and returns. For most people, the benefits gained by providing such potentially invasive information far outweigh any of their concerns.

Benefits such as these, however, highlight the overall problem. Whereas Hertz and a handful of other businesses may compensate customers for information by providing elevated levels of service, most companies these days do not. For example, although consumer electronics companies capture valuable product information from customers who fill out registration forms, they fail to reward those customers with even a note of appreciation, let alone anything of tangible value. Automobile companies, through their dealers, know a great deal about their average customer, but when was the last time an auto company offered its customers anything of value, such as tailored services or promotional discounts? (Lexus, of course, is one notable exception.)

Indeed, some companies do not even intelligently organize and use the information they collect, much less deliver value to people in return for it. We are all familiar with hotels that make the weary traveler reenter basic information such as home and business addresses, telephone numbers, place of employment, and method of payment, even though the guest has supplied it repeatedly during previous stays. And many banks acquire broad profiles of their customers across multiple financial-service areas but have difficulty merging that information to present a single face to those customers.

Consumers have become aware that the ability of companies to collect information far outstrips their ability—or inclination—to deliver meaningful value in return. And the gap is widening as vendors amass huge databases of detailed information about their customers and wrestle with the challenge of mining the data for value. It is precisely consumers' recognition of this growing imbalance that has begun to fuel their resentment over giving away still more information.

Consider how this resentment has already changed the way information is collected. Not long ago, many consumers regularly would respond to surveys, motivated by little more than a note of thanks for their efforts. Today they often will complete surveys only if they receive rewards in cash or in kind. For instance, hotels and restaurants once used comment cards in rooms and on tables to obtain feedback. Now response rates for such surveys are in the single digits, and hospitality companies such as Ritz-Carlton and British Airways frequently compensate customers who have experienced poor service not only to satisfy them on the spot but also to gain the trust and information necessary to customize services.

Similarly, customers once provided companies with referrals for new business; today they rarely give out such information freely. MCI Communications Corporation is, in effect, purchasing such referrals: its Friends & Family program rewards customers with discounts on long-distance calls for revealing whom they call frequently, thus helping MCI to acquire new customers. And consider this: ten years ago, many consumers responded politely to telemarketers who called them at home during the dinner hour to conduct surveys. Today people resent the imposition on their time. Can it be long before consumers demand that telemarketers compensate them, just as people now routinely receive compensation for participating in focus groups? Signs of consumers' changing attitudes are everywhere, and they provide a warning to managers about the seismic changes ahead.

Power Shifts to the Consumer

Even as consumers grow more restive about giving away personal information for free, several new technologies enable them to challenge companies for ownership of this valuable asset. To understand the potential of these technologies, consider again the cookie software that Netscape has agreed to modify. What appeared to be a fairly modest compromise by Netscape—certainly in comparison with the nearly total capitulation of Lotus and Microsoft—in fact represents a major step toward a new approach to obtaining information about consumers.

Netscape had anticipated from the outset that as commercial transactions over the Internet became more common, the cookie technology would capture information about those transactions, including the amounts users spent and the items they purchased. Users would have on their PCs detailed profiles of all the activities they conducted on the network, including (in addition to a record of the sites they visited) a log of the amount of time they spent at each site, the resources they accessed there, and any transactions they made. Because these profiles would cover all sites, not just one, they would provide rich portraits of individual users' interests and needs in a way that no single Web site could hope to duplicate.

Contrast the information collected by Netscape's cookie software with the more fragmentary data that companies acquire today. For instance, the typical point-of-sale (POS) scanner in a retail store obtains detailed information about the items purchased and prices paid by a customer on one shopping trip, but what if the customer returns to the store the next day and makes another purchase or buys something at another retail store owned by the same chain? Most POS scanners would not be able to connect the two transactions. Whereas vendors might make the connection if the customer used the same credit card on both occasions, what if the customer used the card for one article and paid for the second with cash? The most sophisticated retail technology available can develop an integrated profile of a customer's purchases from multiple stores in a chain, but what can the retailer hope to discover about goods the customer buys in a competing store? Of course, the customer's credit-card issuer could track his or her purchases from different retail outlets (assuming the same card is used for each transaction), but even it cannot learn certain details about the specific items and prices.

The broad, cross-category profiles of consumer behavior collected by Netscape users themselves promise to offer much more valuable information. Internet browsers are just one of the new technologies that allow consumers to obtain comprehensive information about their own activities using their own devices. Personal finance software, such as Intuit's popular product Quicken, is another.

Used by roughly 11 million households around the world, Quicken helps people write and print checks from their PCs; it also lets them collect and organize information about their purchases, expenditures, and investments so that they can more adequately prepare their budgets, plan their finances, and do their taxes. Quicken users also can do their banking and pay bills electronically. Last year, Intuit even introduced a Quicken affinity card so that its customers would be able to download the details of their credit card transactions directly into the record-keeping software.

Intuit's success is compelling evidence that at least some consumers —concentrated in high-income households and most likely to be the first to engage in electronic commerce—want to acquire information about themselves because it lets them monitor their own activities and become more thoughtful about how they spend and invest their money.

Smart cards are another technology that is changing the balance of power. Used frequently in place of pocket money by consumers in Denmark and some parts of Germany, smart cards are essentially electronic cash that can be used as readily as credit or debit cards. Consumers buy cards configured for a fixed value; each time the user makes a purchase, the amount can be electronically deducted from the card until the card is used up. Smart cards easily could be enhanced to capture and store the names of vendors and transaction amounts. (The ability to obtain details about the specific items a consumer buys will require a common set of standards and protocols.) The smart-card user then could routinely download this information into a PC to produce an integrated profile of his or her purchases.

More ambitious cardholders could potentially merge this information with data collected on viewing meters attached to television sets in their homes (similar to the meters used by A.C. Nielsen's TV-viewing survey families) to obtain a profile that combined viewing habits with purchasing patterns. What would the value of this information be? Advertisers might be willing to pay handsomely for it. Such easily collected profiles would provide explicit measures of how advertising drives purchasing activities.

Other technologies for acquiring and storing information conveniently no doubt will appear when more people begin to buy goods and services over interactive networks such as the Internet and the commercial on-line services. In the world these new technologies are creating, consumers will carry their histories on their persons as well as in their hard drives, just as they carry a recollection of their activities in their memories. Collecting such information would be difficult for companies, but for consumers it is simple. The technology is already in many homes—especially the homes of those affluent consumers whom marketers most want to reach.

These technologies, alone or in combination, enable consumers for the first time to seize control of information about themselves and to choose whether to transmit it to a vendor or a third party. Consumers can turn off the cookie or refuse to share smart-card or personal finance information. Thus, in one elegant stroke, these technologies also offer a solution for people worried about privacy. If they do not wish to reveal information, the technology makes denial possible. But if they choose to make information available in return for something of tangible value—as the evidence suggests most consumers will—they can hardly be concerned about their privacy, except for the possibility that information released to one vendor might be resold to other, less desirable vendors. Even that concern could be addressed: contractual provisions accompanying the release of information could prohibit its resale. Some customers might even be willing to permit resale for a fee. However, such secondary information may have little value in a world where companies can bargain for real-time data.

The Information Bargain Is Struck

With these new technologies, consumers will be able to collect information more easily than vendors will, to update the information instantly, and to collect both broad and deep information specific to an individual—literally, a segment of one. However, consumers won't have the time, the patience, or the ability to work out the best deals with information buyers on their own. In order to help them strike the best bargain with vendors, new intermediaries will emerge. They will aggregate consumers and negotiate on their behalf within the economic definition of privacy determined by their clients.

These infomediaries would, in fact, play a very traditional role. When ownership of information shifts to the consumer, a new form of supply is created. By connecting information supply with information demand and by helping both parties involved determine the value of that information, infomediaries would be building a new kind of information supply chain.

Intuit could evolve into such an infomediary. In the future, the company could easily offer to help users obtain information about on-line or smart-card transactions and automatically incorporate it into their Quicken records. Intuit even might act as an integrated payment and billing service for purchases on the Internet. By broadening the scope of transactions that it helps its customers capture and by deepening its understanding of their needs and preferences, the company could position itself to become a trusted intermediary and bargaining agent for cross-category information about its customers.

For example, Intuit might offer to screen commercial Internet messages, weeding out "junk" E-mail while reordering the remaining messages according to customers' evolving preferences. The company also might introduce services that use software agents to search for information about products and services that meet users' prespecified (and eventually learned) preferences, such as credit cards with the best combination of membership fees and interest charges, checking and money market accounts with the best features and interest rates, automobile loans, and leases or mortgages.

As customers begin to understand how software agents can provide enhanced services, Intuit might offer to train and activate personal agents that could draw on a broader understanding of an individual's profile. For instance, if an Intuit user started to download information on home remodeling from the network, an agent might determine where to get remodeling supplies in the local area; and if the user's financial profile suggested that financing might be necessary for the remodeling, the agent could start to poll banks offering home improvement loans to determine the range of fees and rates that might be involved. Agent-based services also could give customers access to a broader range of vendors that could meet their needs, and could supply the information necessary for choosing the best offerings at the lowest prices.

There are other ways in which Intuit, acting as an information conduit, could help its customers obtain value from vendors. The company could package elements of a customer's preference-and-transaction profile and, based on his or her instructions, selectively make that information available to favored vendors that agree to use it to tailor or enhance their products or services for that customer. For example, if a hotel in London knew that a guest had a passion for Thai food and collected stamps as a hobby, it might provide the guest with a list of good Thai restaurants within walking distance of the hotel and with a directory of stamp dealers and stamp collectors' clubs active in the city. Intuit also might draw on the experiences of its customers with such vendors to provide advisory services. On the one hand, it could advise customers on vendors' behavior; on the other, it could help vendors develop the skills to serve its clients better.

Of course, Intuit also might help customers receive payments from vendors in return for information. For instance, it could offer an airline the opportunity to deliver a targeted advertisement to those customers in Intuit's database who are the most frequent fliers across all airlines. The advertising airline would not get a list of the customers but, instead, would give its message to Intuit, which in turn would deliver it to the appropriate customers. The airline might pay one fee if the message is delivered to an Intuit customer, a higher fee if the customer actually clicks to read the advertisement, and an even higher fee if the customer clicks on an icon requesting more information or purchases a ticket. Those fees ultimately would be paid to the customer, and Intuit would take a management fee.

Intuit could become an infomediary not only because its software captures a broad range of financial data about its user base but also because the company has developed a unique brand franchise with a specific audience and long-standing relationships with customers who trust and are loyal to Intuit. Other potential infomediaries share similar relationships with customers.

Nordstrom, the high-end retailer whose commitment to the well-being and satisfaction of customers is legendary, could begin to manage its customers' information. Nordstrom already understands the buying preferences of its most active customers across a broad range of retail product categories. It might offer to equip its customers with credit cards or smart cards, television-viewing meters, or other tools for acquiring data, which would allow customers to build much broader profiles of their own activities, preferences, and transactions. Like Intuit, Nordstrom could manage, enhance, and broker this information on behalf of its customers. Of course, it also could use the data to offer tailored services that meet customers' current and future needs.

But very few companies will be able to become infomediaries. The best candidates to play this role are companies that have ongoing relationships with customers in a variety of commercial activities and have earned those customers' trust. Through such relationships, these businesses have the opportunity to collect detailed information. A bank will know a lot about a longtime customer's financial transactions; a clothing store will know a lot about a customer's taste in clothes and frequency of purchase; and a health maintenance organization will know a lot about a patient's medical history and risk profile. But having the trust of customers is equally important for would-be infomediaries. If customers question a company's professionalism, integrity, or commitment to high-quality service, they will be unwilling to entrust it with information—especially sensitive information such as financial data or medical records.

For that reason, banks are better positioned to become infomediaries than, say, airlines or high-end clothing stores. Banks collect information that provides a broader view of a customer's purchases and needs. Also, it may be easier for a bank to persuade customers to entrust it with information on their travel preferences than for an airline to persuade them to entrust it with information about their financial transactions. Clearly, the role of infomediary is not for everyone.

Still, predicting exactly how infomediaries will emerge and evolve is difficult at this stage. We suspect that infomediaries initially will specialize in managing information for general, albeit vertical, product categories. For example, we could see some infomediaries helping customers manage only their financial data and others focusing on addressing their travel information. But we also might expect to see such vertical infomediaries evolve over time into broad-based partners with their customers, managing more integrated and comprehensive profiles. That is likely to occur both because customers will find it inconvenient to deal with multiple infomediaries and because infomediaries will be able to offer even more value to their customers by exploiting cross-category information in their profiles.

The point is that a handful of elite service companies could work on behalf of their customers to force a shift toward the ownership of information by consumers. They would, in effect, become catalysts for change and thus accelerate the shift.

What Managers Can Do

We believe that the shift in ownership of information to the consumer creates an urgent need for businesses in a variety of industries to refocus their approach to such information. Companies today have every incentive to overinvest in collecting information about their customers and to underinvest in using it. Information has long been something that companies have obtained for free as a by-product of their transactions with customers. But when companies have to "pay" for information, the incentives will change. As a result, companies will have to become more selective about the information they collect, focusing on what they must know in order to understand and fulfill customers' needs. They also will have to develop the skills to use the information to create value for the customer. Finally, they will have to manage partnerships with their customers to ensure continuing access to information.

How companies accomplish this will vary by product and customer segment. For instance, businesses that deal directly with consumers, such as retailers, hotels, and airlines, will be able to continue collecting information about their customers in the near term just as they do today. However, as more consumers purchase goods and seek information over networks, or as they begin to use smart cards or other forms of electronic cash (which preserve their anonymity), it may become harder for those businesses to obtain information without the assistance of infomediaries.

Consider how that might work: if a book retailer wanted to know the names of customers using various forms of electronic currency to buy a certain book, the infomediary would provide that information for a fee—or for a higher fee might arrange for the bookseller to reach those customers with targeted advertisements. What if the bookseller wanted to learn more about each customer's reading preferences and buying habits—information formerly obtained through a simple survey? The infomediary would want to know what specific additional services or discounts the bookseller would offer in return. Would the bookseller want access to information that is not available to other booksellers? Well, perhaps the infomediary could arrange to provide it if the bookseller were prepared to pay a sufficiently high fee to ensure exclusivity.

To forestall or limit their dependence on infomediaries, such businesses could begin to think now about how they will obtain information about their best customers and forge strong relationships with them to earn their trust and loyalty. They also should start to consider how they will develop the capabilities to provide customized services that address their customers' future needs and desires.

Product manufacturers, on the other hand, should begin to think about what it may mean to make the relationship with the customer —rather than with the product—the central focus of their business. Generally speaking, product manufacturers do not currently have direct contact with the end customer, but in a world of infomediaries, that could change.

Infomediaries could help manufacturers identify their most loyal customers and target them with customized services. For instance, automakers could offer their customers more than extended-warranty plans. Using information about them, they could offer targeted customers such products or services as auto insurance, travel services, customized maps, driving schools, auto-maintenance or safety tutorials, and even outdoor gear or travel apparel. In the long run, offering such extras could enhance the vendor's clout in the market while diminishing the strength of dealers, agents, brokers, and retailers. Manufacturers can plan for these changes now by looking at the combinations of products and services their customers will want and deciding whether to make them or source them.

Finally, companies that have close relationships with their customers, such as banks and high-end retailers, may face the greatest challenges of all. They currently collect detailed data about their customers, so access to information isn't their primary concern. But we suspect that they will come under pressure to offer their customers increasingly more. The more these companies profit from a customer over time, the more they can afford to "bid" for information about prospective new customers. One can imagine that expectations of service will continue to rise in these industries. How companies in them will create value with information will be critical to their success—and will also conceivably position them, more than others, to become infomediaries.

A sea change is upon us. We cannot discern its exact nature and shape, but the broad outlines are already visible. Businesses have generally assumed that information about customers is a resource waiting to be claimed, like land in the western United States during the great land rush of the mid-nineteenth century. But as consumers take control of the information about themselves, access to it could become more difficult and costly. Those alert to the potential for change will be able to ensure that they continue to obtain the information they need in order to compete in the next century.

3

The Real Value of On-Line Communities

Arthur Armstrong and John Hagel III

The notion of community has been at the heart of the Internet since its inception. For many years, scientists have used the Internet to share data, collaborate on research, and exchange messages. In essence, scientists formed interactive research communities that existed not on a physical campus but on the Internet. Within the last few years, millions of computer users worldwide have begun to explore the Internet and commercial on-line services such as Prodigy and America Online. Many have joined one or more of the communities that have sprung up to serve consumer needs for communication, information, and entertainment. One of the oldest virtual communities is the Well, launched in 1985 by a group of high-tech enthusiasts located primarily near San Francisco. (See "Visit an Electronic Community.") Over the past decade, thousands of computer users have communicated with one another through the Well and, over time, developed strong personal relationships off-line.

Commercial enterprises—relative newcomers to the on-line world—have been slow to understand and make use of the unique community-building capabilities of the medium. Usually, businesses on the Internet today do little more than advertise their wares on the World Wide Web in the hope that somebody will buy something. For instance, flower distributors, booksellers, liquor companies, durable-goods manufacturers, and other businesses have sites on the World Wide Web where visitors can obtain information about the company and its products and send electronic messages to the company. Some of the more sophisticated sites allow visitors to play games and order products electronically. But rarely do these sites encourage communication among visitors to the site. (Meanwhile, most existing communities, such as the Well, are not business oriented; in fact, most strongly oppose the very idea of commercial activity on the Internet.)

Visit an Electronic Community

The Well
http://www.well.com

Virtual Vineyards
http://www.virtualvin.com

GardenWeb
http://www.gardenweb.com

Motley Fool
available on America Online

Red Dragon Inn
available on America Online

ESPNet
http://espnet.sportzone.com

Cancer Forum
available on CompuServe

Parents Place
http://www.parentsplace.com

By adapting to the culture of the Internet, however, and providing consumers with the ability to interact with one another in addition to the company, businesses can build new and deeper relationships with customers. We believe that commercial success in the on-line arena will belong to those businesses that organize electronic communities to meet multiple social and commercial needs. By creating strong on-line communities, businesses will be able to build customer loyalty to a degree that today's marketers can only dream of and, in turn, generate strong economic returns.

Consumers' Needs For Community

Electronic communities meet four types of consumer needs:
Communities of transaction primarily facilitate the buying and sell-

ing of products and services and deliver information related to those transactions. They are not communities in the traditional social sense. Participants are encouraged to interact with one another in order to engage in a specific transaction that can be informed by the input of other members of the community. Visitors to communities of transaction may want to buy a used car or a vintage wine, and they may want to consult with other community members before doing so.

Virtual Vineyards, a Web-based service that sells wines, is a community of transaction. The Virtual Vineyards site offers visitors information on wines and lists special deals on attractively priced offerings. Most of the wines that are listed are from small vineyards and are usually difficult to obtain. Visitors can purchase the wines directly from Virtual Vineyards, using an on-line form, or they can call the on-line service. Although visitors can post E-mail to the organizer of the site (and wine neophytes can post questions to the Cork Dork), they cannot yet trade information with one another. Adding that capability might add value for the site's visitors, making it a true community.

The organizer of a community of transaction does not need to be a vendor. Community organizers may simply bring together a critical mass of buyers and sellers to facilitate certain types of transactions. For example, a community organizer might offer electronic classified ads or provide a "marketspace" where everything from used construction machinery to financial investment products and services could be bought and sold.

Communities of interest bring together participants who interact extensively with one another on specific topics. These communities involve a higher degree of interpersonal communication than do communities of transaction. One community of interest is GardenWeb, where visitors can share ideas with other gardeners through GardenWeb forums; post requests for seeds and other items on the Garden Exchange; and post queries on electronic bulletin boards. GardenWeb also provides direct electronic links to other Internet gardening resources, including directories of sites relating to gardening. Participants communicate and carry out transactions with one another, but their interactions are limited to gardening. They do not discuss topics such as car care or parenting—topics which bring together people in other communities of interest. Nor do they share intensely personal information.

One of the most successful communities of interest is the Motley Fool, an electronic forum that two charismatic brothers, David and Tom Gardner, host on America Online. The Gardners began the Motley Fool for people interested in personal financial investment. They developed a portfolio of stock investments and invited people to comment on the choices made. The Motley Fool has become an engaging blend of information and entertainment. For example, in an area known as Today's Pitch, the organizers recently offered a short tutorial on why insider trading by managers of a company may be an important indicator of potential changes in stock value. They then provided a selection of companies in which insider trading had been particularly active and invited community participants to bet on which company would have the largest change in stock value over the next several weeks. The winner received several hours of free on-line time on America Online.

The Motley Fool has also aggressively leveraged user-generated content. Because the number of users and the extent of their participation have grown, the Motley Fool now offers extensive message boards organized by company, industry, and investment strategy. The forum also provides opportunities for participants to chat. The Motley Fool is one of the most rapidly growing communities within America Online, and it has spun off new communities that focus on entertainment (Follywood), sports (Fooldome), and popular culture and politics (Rogue).

Many people on-line today participate in *communities of fantasy*, where they create new environments, personalities, or stories. On America Online, a participant can pretend to be a medieval baron at the Red Dragon Inn. In this fantasy area, visitors exercise their imagination and participate (through typed, electronic chat) in the creation of an ongoing story of life at the inn. On ESPNet, an Internet-based sports community, participants can indulge their need for fantasy by creating their own sports teams (using the names of real players), which then compete against teams created by other participants. Winners are determined based on the performance of the real players during the season. Participants' real identities are not important in many of these communities, but interaction with others is at the heart of the appeal.

Finally, groups of people may feel a need to come together in *communities of relationship* around certain life experiences that often are very intense and can lead to the formation of deep personal connections. In communities of relationship, people often are aware of one another's actual identities—exceptions being communities formed around addictions (there is even a community of Internet addicts!), whose participants may prefer anonymity. The Cancer Forum on

CompuServe, for instance, provides support for cancer patients and their families. Participants talk about how they deal with the disease and exchange information on medical research, pain medication, test results, and protocols. The forum's library features literature on cancer, which participants can download. However, the primary value of this sort of community is that it gives people the chance to come together and share personal experiences. Other communities of relationship on the Internet include groups focused on divorce, widowhood, and infertility.

Clearly, the four sorts of community are not mutually exclusive. When consumers shop for goods and services, they often seek advice from others before they buy, essentially blending the needs met by communities of transaction with those met by communities of interest. But currently, most communities target only one of the four needs. In so doing, they are missing an opportunity to exploit the on-line medium fully (see "The Impact of Electronic Commerce on Marketing," on page 184). Imagine an on-line toy store that allows visitors only to enter, buy a toy, and then exit, without giving them the opportunity to connect with one another—an experience that might encourage them to return. Now consider Parents Place, an Internet-based community for parents. Parents can turn to the community for advice on such matters as whether an infant should be put on a schedule for meals and sleep. Parents Place also has a shopping mall equipped with catalogs, stores, and services such as on-line diaper ordering. Price and selection being equal, it is more likely that parents will shop at Parents Place than at a competing site that allows only for transactions.

Organizers offer participants the greatest range of services when they address all four needs within the same community. In practice, this may not be possible, but community organizers should strive to meet as many of the four needs as they can. By doing so, they will be able to develop new and stronger relations with participants. A travel community, for instance, could allow visitors to search for information about museums and special events in, say, London, and even to purchase airline tickets and make hotel reservations (community of transaction). The site could offer bulletin boards filled with tips from people who have traveled to London recently; it also could offer the opportunity to chat with travel experts, residents of London, and others (community of interest). Travelers might be invited to join a game hosted by an airline running a special deal (community of fantasy). The site even could make it possible for single travelers, such as elderly widows and widowers, to chat and perhaps find compatible travel companions for a trip to London (community of relationship).

By fostering relationships and networks of interest, organizers can make their communities highly competitive. First movers can build a critical mass of participants that has the potential to make it difficult for new entrants to lure customers away. When Apple Computer introduced its on-line service, eWorld, to compete with America On-line, CompuServe, and Prodigy, media and industry reviews generally agreed that it was an appealing environment and easy to use. But eWorld was not popular with consumers, who were frustrated to discover that when they entered chat areas, they could find no one to chat with, and when they accessed bulletin boards, they found few postings. A community full of half-empty rooms offers visitors a very unsatisfactory experience. The value of participating in a community lies in users' ability to access a broad range of people and resources quickly and easily.

Creating Value in Communities

What will be the likely sources of economic value in electronic communities? Most companies investing in an Internet presence today are doing so cautiously because they are uncertain about the payoff. Pundits point out that the only businesses currently making money on the Internet are those selling products and services to enable companies to develop their own sites. Certainly, even under the best of circumstances, electronic communities may take a decade to grow to sufficient scale to be significant contributors to the overall profitability of a large company.

In the short run, however, businesses that create communities that satisfy both relational and transactional needs will reap the benefits of greater customer loyalty and may gain important insights into the nature and needs of their customer base. In the long run, electronic communities are likely to create value in four different ways.

First, communities can charge *usage fees*. This is how on-line services such as America Online and Internet access providers such as Netcom make most of their revenues. (Typically, customers pay a fixed price to access the service for a certain number of hours per month; when customers use the service for additional hours, they are charged additional fees.) Time-based fees may make sense in the short run, given the relative absence of other sources of revenue. They make less sense in the long run. Communities will need to maximize the number of members and encourage them to spend increasingly more time on-line—posting messages on bulletin boards and chatting, for example—in order to make the community attractive to others. Usage fees do not encourage members to venture on-line and discourage them from lingering there. For this reason, we believe that most electronic communities will eventually turn away from usage fees.

Second, communities can charge users *content fees* for downloading an article or a picture from the service's library or for obtaining access to material. *Encyclopædia Britannica* offers on-line access to its content and varies its fees depending on how much information the user wants. Bill Gates has been assembling the electronic rights to a vast library of photographic and artistic images over the last several years, and one way for him to derive value from those assets is through content fees.

Third, communities can draw revenues from *transactions and advertising*. Advertising is already a significant source of revenue for many popular Internet sites. In 1995, on-line revenue from placement of advertising amounted to roughly $50 million to $60 million, according to best estimates. (The actual amount spent is not yet systematically tracked.) Still, this amount pales in comparison with the $140 billion spent annually in the United States on advertising overall to reach consumers in the home. It is even more difficult to assess—or define—the volume of transactions conducted in on-line environments. For instance, should estimates include business-to-business transactions conducted over private electronic-data-interchange networks? Jupiter Communications, a research company, has suggested that the value of all shopping transactions that took place over the Internet or through on-line services in 1994 amounted to roughly $500 million.

For most communities, revenue from transactions probably will be slimmer than those from advertising. Community organizers could take a substantial share of advertising revenues (although if they choose to offer their communities through an on-line service such as America Online, with its existing audience of 5 million subscribers, they may have to share the revenues with the service), but they will have to share a much greater portion of transaction revenues with the manufacturers and distributors of goods and services to the community. Currently, on-line services such as CompuServe usually receive commissions of 3% to 5% on transactions—not much more than commissions taken by credit card companies. These limited commissions reflect the fact that once the retailer's margins are factored in, additional margins are slim. Community organizers may be able to increase their cut of transaction revenues if they bypass retailers entirely and strike deals directly with product and service vendors. By doing so, a community organizer can become, in effect, the merchandiser and distribution channel for products and services and can command a retailer's share of the revenues (as much as 50%).

Finally, some electronic communities may be in a position to take advantage of *synergies* with other parts of their business. For a software company such as Microsoft Corporation, that could mean saving the cost of physically distributing new software or software upgrades. For some companies, it may mean reducing customer service costs. Federal Express Corporation allows customers to track a package on-line. This is convenient for the customer and saves money for Federal Express because it reduces the number of expensive calls to customer service representatives. Companies can benefit by following this model and moving activities from the physical world to the electronic world. (See "Exploiting the Virtual Value Chain," Part I, Chapter 3.)

How communities adopt these four models of value creation will vary, depending on the blend of needs the community addresses. Consider again the travel community that meets multiple needs. This community will probably derive most of its value from transactions and advertising, but it also may charge an access fee. A community for substance abusers, on the other hand, will probably have to derive its value primarily or even entirely from fees, given that its members are interested in a mutual support network rather than in buying goods or services.

Yet even though communities will rely primarily on just one of the four models of value creation, innovative community organizers will blend models. A canny organizer of the community of substance abusers, for instance, might find other sources of value to subsidize the cost of managing the community. Perhaps synergies for providers of health care services could be identified, for example.

Management Challenges

Before they can capture new sources of value, aspiring community organizers face a daunting array of issues, whether they are assessing strategies for competition or designing and managing the communities. Everyone needs to learn the new rules for managing in on-line communities.

ASSESSING STRATEGIES FOR COMPETITION

There are two strategic questions that a would-be community organizer must face up front: How large is the economic potential of the community and how intense is the competition likely to be?

The elements that make a community economically attractive include the potential for a large number of participants, the likelihood of frequent use and intense interaction among participants, the attractiveness the participants hold for advertisers, and the expectation that participants will want to engage in frequent or valuable transactions. When assessing those elements, managers might look to specialty-magazine advertising or product-category retail sales for indications of the overall economic potential of a target community. Additionally, they might explore whether the community they are considering could draw provocative gurus or personalities who would attract a broader range of participants and spur discussion on bulletin boards or chat lines.

When assessing potential competition, organizers must recognize that some communities may have "natural owners." For example, magazine publishers are likely to have a head start in some areas because of their strong understanding of particular groups of people (young women, for instance) or of a specific subject (such as boating). A boat manufacturer intent on launching a community could end up competing with a magazine in which its advertisements regularly appear. The magazine, for its part, could view the development of a community not simply as an opportunity but also as a mechanism for defending an existing business—because through an electronic community it would be able to collect, package, and offer to advertisers more detailed information about participants than it could before. If, however, the magazine fails to allow communication among members of its audience, or if it blocks participation by competing publishers, it will create opportunities for competitors. More fundamentally, natural owners of a community are those businesses that have a substantial economic incentive to exploit synergies between an on-line community and a preexisting business. For example, can the Walt Disney

Company afford not to organize one of the leading on-line communities that target children?

DESIGNING THE COMMUNITY

In order to decide how to structure their community, organizers must look at how they might segment the community over time. The finer the segmentation, the easier it will be to appeal to people's narrow (and probably more passionate) interests, but the smaller the community's size. For example, organizers of a travel community could divide the community by continent (Europe) or by type of travel (cruises). They could divide each continent into subcommunities for each country of interest (Italy) and sub-subcommunities for cities (Venice).

Another design dilemma the organizer faces is whether to locate the community directly on the Internet or within a proprietary service. On the one hand, a proprietary service provides, among other benefits not yet available on the Internet, a ready audience, a technology infrastructure, security for transactions, and billing processes. On the other hand, it also is a powerful business entity standing between the community organizer and subscribers. A proprietary service that builds a critical mass of subscribers and erects barriers to prevent those subscribers from switching may be able to renegotiate what share of revenues it takes from participating communities. At an extreme, the proprietary service could "backward integrate" by establishing communities of its own to compete with the communities it serves. Or it might try to disintermediate certain communities. For example, it might bypass a successful personal financial-investment community and offer subscribers direct access to checking accounts, credit cards, or mutual funds at an attractive discount.

OPERATING THE COMMUNITY

Electronic communities will involve a number of new roles. The "producer" (general manager) of any community or sub-community will play or oversee at least six roles, of which the first three are the most important.

The *executive moderator* will manage a large number of system operators ("sysops"), who in turn will moderate discussions on bulletin boards and chat lines. Sysops—such as the Gardner brothers—resemble radio or television talk-show hosts in that they are, at their best, conversation managers. They help to keep the discussion focused on the topic at hand, inject new topics or provocative points of view when discussion lags, and seed the discussion with appropriate facts or content. Sysops must be able to transform the random, low-quality interactions that one often finds on cyberspace chat lines and bulletin boards into engaging and informative forums that will keep people coming back for more.

Community merchandisers will identify goods and services that are likely to be attractive to community members, negotiate with the providers of those goods and services, and then market them creatively and unobtrusively to community members. The *executive editor* will develop a programming strategy for the community (including content, special events, and the overall look and feel of the community) and manage the external providers of content, information, and services.

That leaves the *archivist,* who will maintain and organize the content generated by participants over time; the *usage analyst,* who will study data on participants' behavior within the community and develop programming or editorial recommendations for the producer; and the *new-product developer,* who will keep the community fresh and distinct from its rivals.

PARTNERING TO COMPETE

Organizers must decide whether to build communities by themselves or to form alliances. Given the broad range of distinctive skills needed to manage a community successfully, it may make sense for many businesses to work with partners. For example, a magazine publishing company intent on forming a community will know its subscribers' interests and possess a large body of content, but will it know how to foster interaction among members of the potential community? The magazine may look to a large society, such as the American Association of Retired Persons, or to a smaller society focused on a specific hobby (depending on the nature of the community) for help. It also may look to those manufacturers or service providers that understand the key transactional needs of the members.

The value of successful electronic communities will be in the intense loyalty they generate in their participants, which is what favors first movers into this area. The organization of successful electronic communities will depend on skills and the right iconoclastic mind-set, not capital. As a consequence, this arena may favor bold entrepreneurs with constrained resources over established corporate titans.

Those titans who are tempted to wait and buy later should be warned that this market will not wait for slow learners. The skills required to participate successfully will be hard to learn quickly; and the premiums required to buy successful businesses will be very high. We therefore believe that any business marketing to consumers should make the small investment required to "buy an option" on electronic communities so that it can better understand both the potential value of communities and the radical changes they may cause.

The Impact of Electronic Commerce on Marketing

Most marketers today focus narrowly on consumers' needs within the parameters of their product category; at best, a marketer may analyze a few related categories. But few marketers (outside of advertising-supported media organizations) try to analyze the business of companies in unrelated industries that are targeting the same customers.

Marketers must expand their horizons as electronic communities emerge. They must learn how to cross-sell the products and services of the many providers within their community. Consider the role of marketing at a toy manufacturer that plans to participate in the organization of a parenting community. Marketers first must understand the full range of products and services that the community needs to provide if it is to attract on-line parents. These could include parenting magazines; access to book publishers, health care providers, and life insurance companies; links to brokers offering college savings plans; and even the products of competing toy manufacturers. Second, marketers must learn new ways to interact with the providers of those additional products and services in order to reach customers.

Also, marketers must learn how to take advantage of the technology that allows customers to move seamlessly from information gathering—finding out about a product through an advertisement or another user's on-line recommendation—to completing the transaction. This technology will transform today's marketing into tomorrow's direct selling. Marketers who are not currently in the business of direct selling, such as those in many consumer-goods companies, will need to learn the skills of fulfillment.

They also must come to understand the strategic impact of electronic communities, which in many cases will threaten the existing distribution channels of dealers, brokers, and retailers. Questions about channel strategy that marketers must answer include: What electronic communities might our customers belong to now or soon? Who will be organizing those communities? How can we use them to strengthen our relationships with our target customers—not just through advertising but as a means to stimulate greater trial and usage, or even to sell directly to the consumer? Communities affect the very nature of some products; they even can affect how marketers define their business. For a magazine publisher, is the product the on-line magazine or the on-line community? If the on-line community features content from competing publishers, what business is the community owner really in? New business definitions may emerge around the notion of owning a customer segment across the full range of its interests and needs, rather than focusing on owning products and services.

Finally, electronic communities will offer marketers a wealth of new and quite detailed information about their customers—even about individual customers. Marketers will need to learn how to use this information to anticipate a customer's needs and respond to them instantly. For example, if a greeting card company or a toy manufacturer knows the birthdays and ages of children in a given household, it could market to the parents two to three weeks before the birthdays. This means that marketers will need to wrestle with time-sensitive microsegmentation—marketing to the individual customer at specific points in time. Marketers therefore face several questions related to information: What kind of information can we capture in electronic communities? Are our information systems equipped to access and analyze this information? Are we organized to market both more broadly to specific customers and more narrowly to individual customers at particular points in time? Marketers who rise to meet these challenges will hold the business advantage.

4
Making Business Sense of the Internet

Shikhar Ghosh

The Internet is fast becoming an important new channel for commerce in a range of businesses—much faster than anyone would have predicted two years ago. But determining how to take advantage of the opportunities this new channel is creating will not be easy for most executives, especially those in large, well-established companies.

Three years after emerging into the spotlight, the Internet poses a difficult challenge for established businesses. The opportunities presented by the channel seem to be readily apparent: by allowing for direct, ubiquitous links to anyone anywhere, the Internet lets companies build interactive relationships with customers and suppliers, and deliver new products and services at very low cost. But the companies that seem to have taken advantage of these opportunities are start-ups like Yahoo! and Amazon.com. Established businesses that over decades have carefully built brands and physical distribution relationships risk damaging all they have created when they pursue commerce in cyberspace. What's more, Internet commerce is such a new phenomenon—and so much about it is uncertain and confusing—that it is difficult for executives at most companies, new or old, to decide the best way to use the channel. And it is even more difficult for them to estimate accurately the returns on any Internet investment they may make.

Nonetheless, managers can't afford to avoid thinking about the impact of Internet commerce on their businesses. At the very least, they need to understand the opportunities available to them and recognize how their companies may be vulnerable if rivals seize those opportunities first. To determine what opportunities and threats the Internet poses, managers should focus in a systematic way on what the Internet can allow their particular organization to do. Broadly speaking, the Internet presents four distinct types of opportunities.

First, through the Internet companies can establish a direct link to customers (or to others with whom they have important relationships, such as critical suppliers or distributors) to complete transactions or trade information more easily. Second, the technology lets companies bypass others in the value chain. For instance, a book publisher could bypass retailers or distributors and sell directly to readers. Third, companies can use the Internet to develop and deliver new products and services for new customers. And, fourth, a company could conceivably use the Internet to become the dominant player in the electronic channel of a specific industry or segment, controlling access to customers and setting new business rules.

By exploring the opportunities and threats they face in each of these four domains, executives can realistically assess what, if any, investments they should begin to make in Internet commerce and determine what risks they will need to plan for. A sound Internet-commerce strategy begins by articulating what is possible.

Establishing the Internet Channel

To deliver new services or bypass intermediaries, companies first need to build direct connections to customers. That means more than just designing a Web site to market a company's offerings. The behavior of customers who are already buying goods and services on-line clearly indicates that companies can build momentum in their digital channels by using Internet technology to deliver three forms of service to customers.

First, companies are giving customers just about the same level of service through the Internet that they can currently get directly from a salesperson. For instance, Marshall Industries, a distributor of electronic components, makes it very convenient for customers to search for and order parts on-line. Visitors to the company's Web site can hunt for a part by its number, by a description, or by its manufacturer. They can place an order for parts, pay for them electronically, track the status of previous orders, and even speed delivery time by connecting directly from Marshall Industries' Web site to the shipping company's site.

Second, companies are using new Internet technologies to personalize interactions with their customers and build customer loyalty. One way is to tailor the information and options customers see at a site to just what they want. For example, when visitors arrive at Time Warner's Pathfinder Internet site—which contains articles and graphics from more than 25 of the company's publications—they can register, identifying the topics that interest them. Then the Pathfinder site recognizes the visitors whenever they return and tailors the content delivered to their screens.

At What Point Should You Master Your Internet Channel?

Not all companies will want to conduct business over the Web yet. Ask these questions to see if you can reduce costs and increase service levels by establishing an Internet channel.

1. How much does it cost me to provide services that customers could get for themselves over the Internet?
2. How can I use the information I have about individual customers to make it easier for them to do business with me?
3. What help can I give customers by using the experience of other customers or the expertise of my employees?
4. Will I be at a significant disadvantage if my competitors provide these capabilities to customers before I do?

Similarly, Staples is using personalization to reduce the cost large companies incur when ordering its office supplies electronically. Staples is creating customized supply catalogs that can run on its customers' intranets. These catalogs contain only those items and prices negotiated in contracts with each company. The Staples system can maintain lists of previously ordered items, saving customers time when reordering. By searching and ordering electronically, Staples' customers can reduce their purchase-order processing costs—which through traditional channels can sometimes amount to more than the cost of the goods purchased. And over time, Staples could learn a great deal about its customers' preferences and use that information to offer other customized services that competitors, especially in the physical world, would find difficult to duplicate. For example, Staples could recommend new items to customers to complement what they have previously purchased or offer price discounts for items that customers have looked at in their on-line catalogs but have not yet bought.

Third, companies can provide valuable new services inexpensively. A company could, for example, draw on data from its entire customer base to make available wide-ranging knowledge of some topic. For instance, if a customer has a problem with a product, he or she might consult a site's directory of frequently asked questions to see how others have solved it. Or the customer might benefit from knowing how others have used a particular product. Amazon.com, the on-line bookstore, encourages customers to post reviews of books they have read for other visitors to see, making it possible for customers to scan reviews by peers—in addition to those from publications such as the *New York Times*—before deciding to order a book.

The combination of these three levels of service could make the Internet channel very compelling for customers. And because these services are basically just electronic exchanges, they can be delivered at very low cost. Investments in the electronic channel displace traditional sales, marketing, and service costs; moreover, the technology allows companies to offer increasingly higher levels of service without incurring incremental costs for each transaction. For example, Cisco Systems conducts 40% of its sales—$9 million per business day—over the Internet. The company expects the volume to increase from its current level of more than $2 billion per year to $5 billion by July. By selling through the Internet, the company has reduced its annual operating expenses by nearly $270 million. But Cisco's managers say the real value of the electronic channel is that it allows the company to provide buyers with a range of advantages—convenience, information, personalization, and interactivity—that competitors cannot.

The opportunity for those companies that move first to establish electronic channels is a threat to those that do not. When customers choose to do business through an Internet channel, they make an investment of their time and attention. It takes time to figure out how to use a site and become comfortable with it. If a site involves personalization, customers have to fill out profiles and, perhaps, update or otherwise adjust them over time. They may also modify their own systems to make better use of electronic connections: for instance, ten of Cisco's largest customers are installing new software in their own computers to tie their inventory and procurement systems to Cisco's systems. Finally, customers must offer sensitive information, such as credit card numbers, and trust that the seller will manage that information discretely. For these reasons, the average customer, once he or she has established a relationship with one electronic seller, is unlikely to go through the effort again with many suppliers.

This all-too-human reluctance to abandon what works is a formidable obstacle to companies that do not move aggressively enough. Followers in this new channel risk being stuck with the unenviable task of getting customers to abandon investments they have already made in a competitor—and this will be a barrier that increases over time as the relationship between customer and competitor deepens.

The emergence of the direct connection could have another consequence that managers need to anticipate. Companies that currently do not want to participate in Internet commerce may be forced to by competitors or customers. Consider how Internet commerce could affect Dell and Compaq as potential suppliers of computer equipment to General Electric. Several major divisions of GE are completing plans to put parts and equipment up for bid on the Internet. They intend to deal directly with suppliers over the Net and to receive multiple bids for every part. Based on early trials, GE estimates that it will shave $500 million to $700 million off its purchasing costs over three years and cut purchasing cycle times by as much as 50%. The company expects that in five years it will purchase the majority of everything it buys through this Web-based bidding system.

Dell sells computer equipment directly to its customers, sometimes over the Internet, but Compaq sells through distributors. That could put Compaq at a disadvantage for GE's business. Its distribution costs are higher, its pricing and information systems are designed for conducting business through distributors, and any move Compaq makes toward accepting orders over the Internet could threaten those distributors.

What's worse from Compaq's point of view, Dell could gain internal efficiencies through the Internet channel, as Cisco has discovered, and learn a great deal more about customers. Dell is currently selling almost $3 million worth of computers a day through its Web site. By the year 2000, the company expects to handle half of all its business—ranging from customer inquiries to orders to follow-up service—through the Internet. Such developments are forcing Dell's rivals in the computer industry to develop Internet channels of their own. And first movers like Dell, both established companies and start-ups, are already beginning to emerge in other industries, such as auto retailing (General Motors and Auto-By-Tel), financial services (Merrill Lynch and E*Trade), and trade publishing (Cahners and VerticalNet).

As pioneering companies in an industry begin to build electronic channels, rivals will need to reexamine their value chains. New companies have no existing value chains to protect, of course, and so can set up their businesses in ways that take advantage of the Internet. But companies that deal through others to reach end customers (such as Compaq and IBM in the computer industry) will need to weigh the importance of protecting existing relationships with the distributors and partners that account for most of their current revenue against the advantages of establishing future strategic positions and revenue streams. This is one of the most difficult issues that large, established companies face in making decisions about engaging in Internet commerce. For instance, although a book publisher might be tempted to use the Internet to sell directly to bookstores or even to readers, it runs the risk of damaging long-standing relationships with distributors.

Pirating the Value Chain

Companies may find they have little choice but to risk damaging relationships in their physical chains to compete in the electronic channel. The ubiquity of the Internet—the fact that anyone can link to anyone else—makes it potentially possible for a participant in the value chain to usurp the role of any other participant. Not only could the book publisher bypass the distributor and sell directly to readers, but Barnes & Noble and Amazon.com could decide to publish their own books—after all, they have very good information, gathered and collated electronically, about readers' interests.

Should You Pirate Your Value Chain?

When companies pirate the value chain of their industry, they are essentially eliminating layers of costs that are built into the current distribution system. Ask these questions to see if the distribution chain in your industry is likely to consolidate and if you should take the initiative to make that happen.

1. Can I realize significant margins by consolidating parts of the value chain to my customer?
2. Can I create significant value for customers by reducing the number of entities they have to deal with in the value chain?
3. What additional skills would I need to develop or acquire to take over the functions of others in my value chain?

4. Will I be at a competitive disadvantage if someone else moves first to consolidate the value chain?

Consider how various participants in the personal-computer value chain are already squaring off against one another to reach the end customer. Currently, computer manufacturers like Apple, Compaq, and IBM purchase the components that make up the computers from suppliers like Intel (which makes microprocessors), and Seagate Technology (which produces hard-disk drives). Manufacturers supply machines to distributors such as Ingram Micro and MicroAge, which in turn supply retailers like CompUSA. That is the physical value chain for much of the industry (excluding manufacturers that sell through direct mail, such as Dell and Gateway 2000). But Internet commerce is already blurring the boundaries in that chain. Ingram Micro and MicroAge are seeking to bypass the physical retailers by setting up Internet-based services that would allow anyone to become an on-line retailer of computers. MicroAge lets physical or virtual resellers choose from a selection of computer systems on-line whose availability and prices vary daily. Soon, on-line retailers will be able to relay orders directly from customers to Ingram Micro, which will acquire the computers from the manufacturer or if necessary assemble the components, ship the computers directly back to the customer, and provide subsequent support services.

At the same time, retailers like CompUSA are establishing their own brands of computers, which they intend to sell both in stores and over the Internet. They will order parts electronically from component suppliers. (The Internet makes the logistics of such a system easier to manage.) Finally, Apple and other computer makers have made the difficult choice to sell computers over the Internet, too.

Competition is even coming from outside the value chain. United Parcel Service has announced that it is setting up a service for virtual merchants. Using Internet commerce software, a merchant can create a product catalog and a storefront on the Web. UPS will then manage the operations. The merchant or its customers will be able to schedule deliveries, track packages, and coordinate complex schedules over the Web. Conceivably, an on-line PC vendor could let consumers create customized machines, made up of components drawn from several different manufacturers. UPS would then gather the parts overnight, deliver them to an assembly facility, pick up the assembled product, and deliver it to the customer.

On-line providers of information about computers, such as CNET, are already becoming resellers of software and hardware products. For instance, visitors to the CNET Web site can read reviews of software and then order a highly touted product from the CNET store without ever leaving the site. The Internet search-service Yahoo! also sells hardware and software through its site by linking seamlessly to partners' sites. Even ancillary players in the industry's value chain—including banks like Barclays and First Union, and telecommunications providers, such as AT&T—have established shopping services on their sites and could sell computers (or anything else) to their customers. In other words, once companies establish an electronic channel, they could choose to become pirates in the value chain, capturing margins from other participants up or down the chain.

Pirates will probably emerge from the ranks of those innovative companies that can recognize where core value will be most effectively delivered to customers over a network. Consider how RoweCom, an electronic subscription agent on the Internet, has captured margins from intermediaries in the value chain for periodicals by using the network to change the industry's business model. Publishers traditionally have sold periodicals to libraries through subscription agents. Agents typically consolidate orders from many libraries and forward them to publishers, charging 3% to 5% of the list price for their services. RoweCom allows libraries to order periodicals directly from publishers over the Internet and make payments electronically through Banc One. RoweCom also provides a new level of service. For instance, libraries can place orders at any time and can easily use the site to track their budgets. Most important, however, RoweCom charges $5 per transaction, not the 3% to 5% of the list price. As a result, libraries have been moving their expensive orders to RoweCom. In the past 18 months, more than 75 libraries—including some of the largest in the nation—have subscribed to RoweCom's Internet service.

Individual publishers are also linking directly to end users. For example, Academic Press has established an Internet channel to deliver content electronically to libraries. Other academic and professional publishers have also done this, but Academic Press has changed the business model for electronic-content delivery. Rather than issuing licenses to individual libraries, the company has begun selling site licenses for all the libraries in an entire country. For instance, any library in Finland can now access all of Academic Press's publications under a single countrywide license—eliminating the need for a distributor or an agent. Competing publishers will now need to reconsider their distribution chain in any nation where libraries have signed up for Academic Press's broader license.

Value chain pirates are in a position to define new business rules and introduce new business models. But pirates will also need to develop new capabilities. Those companies that stand to lose margins to pirates currently provide very real value to customers—such as merchandising skills (which Ingram Micro does not have but CompUSA does), logistics expertise (which CompUSA does not have but UPS does), and information management (which CNET can do better than Apple). To succeed, pirates must be able to provide that value, either by building the skills in house or by allying with others.

IBM discovered this to be the case when in 1996 it launched Infomart, an electronic-content delivery initiative, and World Avenue, a cyberspace mall. IBM had believed that it could use its computer network to become a new intermediary, pirating margins from physical distributors. Infomart would have challenged the physical distribution chain for publications by making it possible for customers to go to a single site to have material from several different publishers delivered to them electronically. World Avenue was to be a single site from which consumers could access a number of different electronic stores. But IBM soon recognized that being a superpublisher required more than just making content available, and on-line merchandising meant more than just being a storefront. IBM lacked the editorial and magazine-circulation skills of publishers and the merchandising and advertising skills of retailers. The computer company had the direct connection to customers, but that was not enough to make the initiatives succeed. IBM halted both initiatives the following year.

Digital Value Creation

Instead of (or perhaps in addition to) pirating value from others in the value chain, companies that establish Internet channels can choose to introduce new products and services. Not only is the Internet channel a direct connection to customers or to any participant in the value chain, it is also a platform for innovation. It is a way to produce and distribute new combinations of digital information—or to create new transaction models and services—without incurring the traditional costs of complexity that exist in the physical world. And clearly, innovation will heighten competition if companies choose to create new value through the Internet by providing something that had previously been furnished by someone else.

For instance, a broker that has established an Internet channel to offer securities transaction services might begin to provide customers with access to research reports for free, which, of course, will harm businesses that offer such reports for a fee. Each time a company, large or small, succeeds in taking away a small piece of someone else's business, it undermines the economics of that business—like termites eating away at the support beams of a house.

The Internet presents three opportunities for creating new value by taking away bits of someone else's business. First, a company can use its direct access to customers; each time a customer visits a company's Web site is an opportunity to deliver additional services or provide a path for other businesses that want to reach that customer. Snap-on Tools Corporation, a manufacturer of professional-grade tools for automobile repair businesses, adds new value for its customers by supplying them with regulatory information about such subjects as waste disposal at no fee. This strengthens Snap-on Tools' relationship with its customers, but it weakens the business of commercial publishers that provide such information for a fee. Netscape Communications Corporation, a company that develops and sells Internet software, receives significant additional revenue at very little marginal cost by selling advertising space on its site. Netscape effectively draws revenue away from sites that derive the bulk of their revenue from advertising.

Can You Create New Digital Value?

Companies that seek to create digital value using their Internet channels could do so in a number of ways. Ask these questions to see how your company could best leverage its existing digital assets or leverage the digital assets of other companies that are on the Internet.

1. Can I offer additional information or transaction services to my existing customer base?
2. Can I address the needs of new customer segments by repackaging my current information assets or by creating new business propositions using the Internet?
3. Can I use my ability to attract customers to generate new sources of revenue, such as advertising or sales of complementary products?

4. Will my current business by significantly harmed by other companies providing some of the value I currently offer on an à la carte basis?

Second, a company can mine its own digital assets to serve new customer segments. Standard & Poor's Corporation, a company that has traditionally provided financial information to institutional customers, is using the information it has stored digitally to provide financial planning services to individuals over the Internet. For a small fee, customers will be able to evaluate the risk of their individual securities portfolios, make portfolio allocation decisions based on the advice of market experts. They can even be alerted electronically to changes in analysts' recommendations that affect their portfolios. Standard & Poor's could never afford to target individuals with this service through a sales force or other traditional sales channels. But by offering the service at low cost over the Internet, the company will be able to compete with brokers and financial analysts.

Finally, a company can take advantage of its ability to conduct transactions over the Internet to take away value from others. For example, a major bank that has traditionally provided check-clearing services is planning to use the Internet to offer complete bill-payment services for universities and order-management services for retailers. The new, targeted services should help strengthen the bank's core transaction-processing business, and it will also eat away at the business of companies that currently provide these services, such as those that furnish electronic data interchange (EDI) services.

In all three cases, each addition of digital value by one company weakens the business proposition of another company in a small way. Ultimately, the risk for established businesses is not from digital tornadoes but from digital termites.

Creating a Customer Magnet

Companies that can establish direct links to their customers, pirate their industry's value chain, and take away bits of value digitally from other companies may put themselves in a position to become powerful new forces in electronic commerce. They may become the on-line versions of today's category-killer stores—such as Toys "R" Us and Wal-Mart—and become *category destinations*.

Certainly, there are economies of scale inherent in concentration on the Internet. Traditional reasons for having numerous suppliers in an industry are not valid on the Internet. First, the Internet makes physical distance between consumers and suppliers largely irrelevant: any store is equally accessible to any customer. Second, stores that establish a strong position or dominant brand on the Internet can grow rapidly, relatively unhampered by the costs and delays common when expanding in the physical world. Third, single stores can differentiate services for many customer segments, customizing offerings and tailoring the way visitors enter and move around the site to address regional or individual differences. As a result, a small number of companies can meet the diverse needs of large segments of the global market.

But more important, if customers are not willing to learn how to navigate hundreds of different sites, each with its own unique layout, then the Web will turn out to be a naturally concentrating medium. People feel comfortable returning to the stores they know, virtual or physical, because they can easily navigate the familiar aisles and find what they are looking for. They will gravitate toward sites that can meet all their needs in specific categories. And customers will head for the places many other customers frequent if they can interact with one another and derive some value from the interaction.

Consider how this might work. A customer magnet for music compact discs might offer visitors a choice of practically any CD available by connecting to all major distributors. The site might also offer a rich selection of CD reviews from public and specialized sources—everything from the most popular music magazines to the electronic bulletin boards of major music schools. It could enable customers to interact with one another, sharing experiences and opinions. It could also offer several transaction options: customers might choose to participate in for-fee membership programs or benefit from affinity or loyalty programs. The site might be structured to appear differently to customers from different countries or to those with varying levels of technical skills. It might also co-opt other sites aimed at the same customer base by offering commissions for every visitor a customer sends along. Finally, the site could create marketing programs in the physical world to ensure that its brand became synonymous with music CDs. The customer magnet would own the connection, the access, and the direct interface to the customer. Industry participants, such as the CD distributors and music magazines, would have to operate through the magnet.

The steps a company could take to become a customer magnet are remarkably similar in very different industries. A solid-waste company, too, could develop the ability to provide its customers with an electronic place for gathering information, for interacting with other customers, and for conducting transactions, and then invest in creating critical mass and momentum. In this instance, industry participants might include government agencies in different countries and various suppliers of pumps and valves.

In any case, it is conceivable that some companies will attempt to control the electronic channel by becoming the site that can provide customers with everything they could want. Customer magnets could organize themselves around a specific type of product or service, a particular segment of customers, an entire industry, or a unique business model. A given industry may have room for only five, or even fewer, such magnets. Being few in number, they will have a tremendous influence on the shape of their industry. They will not own all the assets for delivering service—such as CD distribution or solid-waste pumps—but they could control access to suppliers and subtly sway customers' choices by promoting or ignoring individual brands. Over time, a customer magnet could become the electronic gateway to an entire industry.

Should I Become a Customer Magnet?

Becoming a customer magnet involves a substantial investment in marketing and infrastructure. Ask these questions to see if you should make the investment to become a magnet or how you should work with other companies to influence the type of customer magnet that develops in your industry.

1. Can my industry be divided into logical product, customer, or business-model segments that could evolve into customer magnets?
2. What services could an industry magnet offer my customers that would make it efficient for them to select and purchase products or services?
3. What partnerships or alliances could I create to establish the critical mass needed to become an industry magnet?
4. Will the emergence of a competing industry magnet hurt my relationships with customers or my margins?

PRODUCT MAGNETS

Amazon.com has quickly established itself as a product magnet and today is synonymous with book retailing on the Web. Amazon offers customers virtually every book available, provides access to reviews, to book discussion groups, and even to authors themselves. It also offers a number of other services, such as notifying readers by E-mail when a new book is available and recommending books based on patterns perceived in customers' past purchases.

Consider the implications of Amazon's success. Today, only Barnes & Noble rivals Amazon in the electronic channel. Customers will probably need no more than four or five of these companies. As on-line revenues increase for these two electronic merchants, what role will there be in the channel for the thousands of book retailers that have physical operations? Moreover, could Amazon use its infrastructure to move into music or professional periodicals? The tendency toward concentration in the electronic channel, which is unfolding in book sales, is likely to occur in a variety of other product categories as well.

SERVICE MAGNETS

Companies like Yahoo!, Excite, and Lycos are becoming magnets in information services about the Internet. In less than two years, the field of competitors in this category has been reduced from more than 20 to fewer than 5 companies, and none of the established yellow-page companies or other paper-based search providers, such as the *Thomas Register,* is on the list. Today, new search services targeted at ever narrower subsegments—such as those for locating people or telephone numbers—find it more efficient to market themselves under the Yahoo! umbrella rather than go it alone. The cost of attracting a critical mass of customers on the Web is too high for companies that are not magnets. The fact that smaller companies are willing to offer their services through Yahoo! suggests that Yahoo! has already achieved the critical mass it needs to be a service magnet.

CUSTOMER SEGMENT MAGNETS

New companies are targeting well-defined segments of customers and becoming their premier electronic channel. Tripod, for example, bills itself as an "electronic community" that targets Generation Xers— 18 to 35 year olds. The service provides information on such issues as careers, health, and money, and facilitates commerce by linking directly to the sites of other companies directed at this segment. Visitors to Tripod's Web site can find jobs through Classifieds2000, for instance, or establish bank accounts through Security First Network Bank. In less than two years, Tripod's community has grown to more than 300,000 members.

INDUSTRY MAGNETS

Companies such as Auto-By-Tel and Microsoft CarPoint (which sell cars, trucks, and other vehicles over the Internet); IMX Mortgage Exchange; the FastParts Trading Exchange (which distributes electronic components); and InsWeb Corporation (which offers insurance) could become customer magnets for entire industries. These companies bring hundreds of suppliers together under one virtual roof, providing customers with an easy, convenient way to compare and purchase offerings.

InsWeb, for example, allows customers to compare prices for several different products, including health, life, and automobile insurance. The site also contains consumer information about insurance products, lists available agents, gives visitors access to Standard & Poor's ratings of insurance companies, and offers on-line simulation tools to help customers estimate the amount of coverage they may need for certain lines of insurance. If a customer likes a quote for, say, a ten-year term-life insurance policy from a highly rated company, he or she can click on a button to obtain an on-line application form and begin the application process.

The insurance companies that market themselves and sell policies through InsWeb will face challenges similar to those other established companies are likely to encounter when more industry magnets begin to appear in Internet channels: How can a company differentiate its products when the rules are determined by other parties? In side-by-side comparisons, how can a company emphasize its unique value? How can it differentiate itself through marketing when the magnet can standardize the information or determine which differentiating features will be emphasized? For a while, insurance providers could refuse to join InsWeb's listings. They might even sell policies through their own individual sites. But customers will prefer the convenience of shopping in one location. If InsWeb can get enough providers and build significant traffic to its site, laggard insurers will have little choice but to participate.

BUSINESS MODEL MAGNETS

Companies could become magnets by introducing new business models that take advantage of the interactive capabilities of the Internet. For instance, Onsale is an on-line auction house for consumer electronic products, computer equipment, and sporting goods. Customers can visit the site any time, day or night, to learn about various goods and make a bid. Similarly, NECX is establishing a spot market for computer parts. And Altra Energy Technologies is an Internet-based marketplace for natural gas that had revenues of more than $1 billion in 1997. Other companies are trying to establish similar marketplaces for advertising space, airline seats, ship-cargo space, and other perishable goods. In each case, an entire industry really only needs one magnet to manage the interactions between suppliers and customers.

Clearly, few companies can justify the investment that will be needed to become a customer magnet. Managers can't yet quantify the financial rewards from such an initiative, and the risks are daunting. It is difficult and expensive for companies to integrate their existing business applications with the Internet technologies they will need to conduct commerce on-line. It will also be difficult to integrate electronic processes for commerce with existing physical processes that often involve numerous functions and many business units within an organization. And companies that create customer magnets will likely need to work with competitors—and their systems and processes—to offer customers everything they could want.

But if companies decide that Internet commerce is too important to ignore, it may be possible for them to adopt less risky approaches to protect their positions in the electronic channel. For instance, more than ten of the nation's largest banks, including Banc One, Citicorp, and First Union, have formed a joint venture with IBM to create a common industry interface for retail banking over the Internet. The banks recognize that owning direct access to the customer is critical. They do not want to cede that access to an industry outsider, such as a home-banking software provider like Intuit or Microsoft, or to a single enterprising bank. Instead, the partners in the joint venture are sharing the costs of building a technological base for electronic banking, and in the process they are attempting to protect their industry's existing relationships with its customers.

Established companies might also stake out competitive positions in the electronic channel by allying with others to create cascading value chains. That is, companies that furnish complementary services to a common customer base could band together to establish an exclusive bundle of services in the electronic channel. For instance, hotels, travel agents, guidebook publishers, and car rental agencies could create an exclusive network that would provide customers with everything they need when traveling.

Finally, established companies could find ways to embed their products or services in customer magnets. For instance, Amazon has become a book provider to Yahoo!'s customers. When someone visits Yahoo!'s site to search for, say, furniture repair, a button pops up asking the visitor if he or she wants a book on the topic.

For managers in established businesses, the Internet is a tough nut to crack. It is very simple to set up a Web presence but quite difficult to create a Web-based business model. One thing is certain: the changes made possible by the Internet are strategic and fundamental. However these changes play out in individual industries, they will unquestionably affect every company's relationship with its customers and the value propositions for many companies in the foreseeable future.

Executive Summaries

The Coming of Knowledge-Based Business

Stan Davis and Jim Botkin

The next wave of economic growth is going to come from knowledge-based businesses. What will those businesses and their products look like?

A tire that notifies the driver of its air pressure and a garment that heats or cools in response to temperature changes are early versions of knowledge-based, or "smart," products already on the market. They are smart because they filter and interpret information to enable the user to act more effectively.

Consumers become learners when they use smart products, which both oblige them to learn and assist them in learning. And businesses become educators when they make products that promote the learning experience. In the years ahead, Davis and Botkin argue, people's use of knowledge-based products will be critical to their economic success. And businesses that know how to convert information into knowledge will be more successful than those that do not. The authors identify six basic elements of knowledge-based business to help companies get started.

The development of knowledge-based business reflects an even larger transformation occurring in our society. Education is no longer focused on the student years but is considered a life-long pursuit. In knowledge economies, the rapid pace of technological change means that learning must be constant and that education must be updated throughout one's working life.

Business, more than government, is instituting the changes that are required for the emerging knowledge-based economy. And over the next few decades, the private sector will come to eclipse the public sector as our predominant educational institution.

205

Strategy and the New Economics of Information

Philip B. Evans and Thomas S. Wurster

We are in the midst of a fundamental shift in the economics of information—a shift that will precipitate changes in the structure of entire industries and in the ways companies compete. This shift is made possible by the widespread adoption of Internet technologies, but it is less about technology than about the fact that a new behavior is reaching critical mass. Millions of people are communicating at home and at work in an explosion of connectivity that threatens to undermine the established value chains for businesses in many sectors of the economy.

What will happen, for instance, to dominant retailers such as Toys "R" Us and Home Depot when a search through the Internet gives consumers more choice than any store? What will be the point of cultivating a long-standing supplier relationship with General Electric when it posts its purchasing requirements on an Internet bulletin board and entertains bids from anybody inclined to respond?

The authors present a conceptual framework for approaching such questions—for understanding the relationship of information to the physical components of the value chain and how the Internet's ability to separate the two will lead to the reconfiguration of the value proposition in many industries. In any business where the physical value chain has been compromised for the sake of delivering information, there will be an opportunity to create a separate information business and a need to streamline the physical one. Executives must mentally deconstruct their businesses to see the real value of what they have. If they don't, the authors warn, someone else will.

Exploiting the Virtual Value Chain

Jeffrey F. Rayport and John J. Sviokla

Every business today competes in two worlds: a physical world of resources that managers can see and touch and a virtual world made of information. Executives must pay attention to how their companies create value in both arenas—the *marketplace* and the *marketspace*. But the processes for accomplishing this are not the same in the two worlds. Managers who understand how to master both can create and extract value in the most efficient and effective manner.

The stages involved in creating value in the physical world are often referred to as links in a value chain. The value chain is a model that describes a series of value-adding activities connecting a company's supply side with its demand side. By analyzing the stages of a value chain, managers have been able to redesign their internal and external processes to improve efficiency and effectiveness. However, the value chain model treats information as a supporting element of the value-adding process, not as a source of value itself.

To create value with information, managers must look to the marketspace. The value-adding processes that companies must employ to turn raw information into new marketspace services and products are unique to the information world. In other words, the value-adding steps are *virtual* in that they are performed through and with information. Creating value in any stage of a virtual value chain involves a sequence of five activities: gathering, organizing, selecting, synthesizing, and distributing information. Just as someone takes raw material and refines it into something useful, so a manager today collects raw information and adds value through these five steps.

The Dawn of the E-Lance Economy

Thomas W. Malone and Robert J. Laubacher

Will the large industrial corporation dominate the twenty-first century as it did the twentieth?

Maybe not. Drawing on their research at MIT's Initiative on Inventing the Organizations of the 21st Century, Thomas Malone and Robert Laubacher postulate a world in which business is not controlled through a stable chain of management in a large, permanent company. Rather, it is carried out autonomously by independent contractors connected through personal computers and electronic networks.

These electronically connected freelancers—*e-lancers*—would join together into fluid and temporary networks to produce and sell goods and services. When the job is done—after a day, a month, a year—the network would dissolve and its members would again become independent agents.

Far from being a wild hypothesis, the e-lance economy is, in many ways, already upon us. We see it in the rise of outsourcing and telecommuting, in the increasing importance within corporations of ad hoc project teams, and in the evolution of the Internet.

Most of the necessary building blocks of this type of business organization—efficient networks, data interchange standards, groupware, electronic currency, venture capital micromarkets—are either in place or under development. What is lagging behind is our imagination. But, the authors contend, it is important to consider sooner rather than later the profound implications of how such an e-lance economy might work. They examine the opportunities, and the problems, that may arise and anticipate how the role of managers may change fundamentally—or possibly even disappear altogether.

The Real Virtual Factory

David M. Upton and Andrew McAfee

By now, the monolithic factory was supposed to have given way to the virtual factory: a community linked by an electronic network that would enable numerous partners to operate as one. But for most companies, that promise has been elusive. The traditional technologies—electronic data interchange, proprietary groupware, and wide-area networks—are proving inadequate.

Traditional systems cannot meet the three basic requirements of a large-scale virtual factory. First, an internet-work must be able to accommodate members whose IT sophistication varies enormously. Second, it must, while maintaining tight security, cope with partners in both transient and long-term relationships. Finally, it must provide a high level of functionality, including letting partners operate programs on one another's computers.

The confluence of several trends, however, now makes it possible to build a more flexible and cost-effective manufacturing community. These are the emergence of widely accepted and open computing standards, ever cheaper computing power, increasingly abundant bandwidth, the development of essentially unbreakable computer security, and accumulated expertise.

McDonnell Douglas Aerospace and a spin-off named AeroTech have created a real virtual factory. AeroTech acts as an information broker for the community. It signs up new partners, tracks network memberships, oversees security, and serves as a converter that permits partners with different formats to communicate. A flexible, low-cost network, it is a model for a new era in manufacturing. In this new era, those that choose to go it alone or that cling to closed, proprietary systems will find it tough to survive.

Developing Products on Internet Time

Marco Iansiti and Alan MacCormack

The rise of the World Wide Web has provided one of the most challenging environments for product development in recent history. The market needs that a product is meant to satisfy and the technologies required to satisfy them can change radically—even as the product is under development. In response to such factors, companies have had to modify the traditional product-development process, in which design implementation begins only once a product's concept has been determined in its entirety. In place of the traditional approach, they have pioneered a *flexible* product-development process that allows designers to continue to define and shape products even after implementation has begun. This innovation enables Internet companies to incorporate rapidly evolving customer requirements and changing technologies into their designs until the last possible moment before a product is introduced to the market.

Flexible product development has been most fully realized in the Internet environment because of the turbulence found there, but the foundations for it exist in a wide range of industries where the need for responsiveness is paramount. When technology, product features, and competitive conditions are predictable or evolve slowly, a traditional development process works well. But when new competitors and technologies appear overnight, when standards and regulations are in flux, and when a company's entire customer base can easily switch to other suppliers, businesses don't need a development process that resists change—they need one that embraces it.

Trust and the Virtual Organization

Charles Handy

The technological possibilities of the virtual organization are seductive. But its managerial and personal implications require rethinking old notions of control. As it becomes possible for more work to be done outside the traditional office, trust will become more important to organizations. Managers need to move beyond fear of losing efficiency, which makes some cling to expensive and deadening "audit mania."

Handy proposes seven rules of trust. Trust is not blind: It needs fairly small groupings in which people can know each other well. Trust needs boundaries: Define a goal, then leave the worker to get on with it. Trust demands learning and openness to change. Trust is tough: When it turns out to be misplaced, people have to go. Trust needs bonding: The goals of small units must gel with the larger group's. Trust needs touch: Workers must sometimes meet in person. Trust requires leaders.

Virtual organizations call for new forms of belonging. A desk of one's own has been a security blanket for generations; a sense of place is important to people. What happens when that disappears? If workers get membership rights in an organization, a sense of belonging to a *community* can substitute for the sense of belonging to a *place*.

Virtuality's Three I's (information, ideas, intelligence) can improve quality of life. The question Handy asks is, Will they be for everyone? He believes the potential exists for the Three I's to benefit not just organizations but also those with whom they do business and society as a whole.

If businesses let virtuality turn them into mere brokers or boxes of contracts, then they will have failed society. Their search for wealth in the end will have destroyed wealth.

Predators and Prey: A New Ecology of Competition

James F. Moore

Much has been written about networks, strategic alliances, and virtual organizations. Yet these currently popular frameworks provide little systematic assistance when it comes to out-innovating the competition. That's because most managers still view the problem in the old way: companies go head-to-head in an industry, battling for market share.

James Moore sets up a new metaphor for competition drawn from the study of biology and social systems. He suggests that a company be viewed not as a member of a single industry but as a part of a *business ecosystem* that crosses a variety of industries. In a business ecosystem, companies "co-evolve" around a new innovation, working cooperatively and competitively to support new products and satisfy customer needs. Apple Computer, for example, leads an ecosystem that covers personal computers, consumer electronics, information, and communications.

In any larger business environment, several ecosystems may vie for survival and dominance, such as the IBM and Apple ecosystems in personal computers or Wal-Mart and Kmart in discount retailing. In fact, it's largely competition among business ecosystems, not individual companies, that's fueling today's industrial transformation. Managers can't afford to ignore the birth of new ecosystems or the competition among those that already exist.

Whether that means investing in the right new technology, signing on suppliers to expand a growing business, developing crucial elements of value to maintain leadership, or incorporating new innovations to fend off obsolescence, executives must understand the evolutionary stages all business ecosystems go through and, more important, how to direct those changes.

Real-Time Marketing

Regis McKenna

It's no secret that managing a brand in today's chaotic marketplace is a daunting task. Consumers are bombarded with messages from broadcast and narrow-cast television, radio, on-line computer networks, the Internet, faxes, telemarketing, and niche magazines. But by harnessing new and emerging technologies, companies can start real-time dialogues with their customers and provide interactive services with valuable side effects.

Netherlands-based Philips NV, for example, used a research team to brainstorm with children and adults to develop a new product; in the end, its enthusiastic young product developers became potential loyal customers. Using today's technology, companies can involve broader numbers of customers in new product development and thus speed up the time it takes to get the market to accept a new product. Although most companies strive to reduce time to market, it's time to acceptance that determines success.

Marketing managers must take responsibility for systems that link companies with customers, suppliers, and distributors. They must give consumers access and learn to think of feedback as part of product development. They need to provide customers with support and information. Finally, they need to become personally competent in information technology and to expand the role of marketing within the organization.

Senior managers might consider shifting portions of marketing units into product design. Marketers might get involved in guiding the efforts to shape brand-building systems. It's even possible that marketing will no longer be one group but will become every employee's responsibility. One thing is certain: Marketing will change, and managers must be prepared to change with it.

The Coming Battle for Customer Information

John Hagel III and Jeffrey F. Rayport

Companies collect information about customers to target valuable prospects more effectively, tailor their offerings to individual needs, improve customer satisfaction, and identify opportunities for new products or services. But managers' efforts to capture such information may soon be thwarted. The authors believe that consumers are going to take ownership of information about themselves and start demanding value in exchange for it. As a result, negotiating with customers for information will become costly and complex.

How will that happen? Consumers are realizing that they get very little in exchange for the information they divulge so freely through their commercial transactions and survey responses. Now new technologies such as smart cards, World Wide Web browsers, and personal financial management software are allowing consumers to view comprehensive profiles of their commercial activities—and to choose whether or not to release that information to companies. Their decision will hinge, in large part, on what vendors offer them in return for the data.

Consumers will be unlikely to bargain with vendors on their own, however. The authors anticipate that companies they call *infomediaries* will broker information to businesses on consumers' behalf. In essence, infomediaries will be the catalyst for people to start demanding value in exchange for information about themselves. And most other companies will need to rethink how they obtain information and what they do with it if they want to find new customers and serve them better.

The Real Value of On-Line Communities

Arthur Armstrong and John Hagel III

The notion of community has been at the heart of the Internet since its early days, when scientists used it to share data, collaborate on research, and exchange messages. But how can businesses best use its community-building capabilities? Not merely by putting their products or services on-line, the authors contend. Real value will come from providing people with the ability to interact with one another—from satisfying their multiple social needs as well as their commercial needs. Companies that create strong on-line communities will command customer loyalty to a degree hitherto undreamed of and, consequently, will generate strong economic returns.

The authors present four different types of community: communities of transaction, interest, fantasy, and relationship. Examples of each type already can be found on the Internet or through on-line services, but the successful community of the future will incorporate all four—or as many as possible. As for economic value, the authors see four ways for a company to generate returns: through usage fees, content fees, transactions and advertising, and synergies with other parts of its business.

In the near future, new business definitions may emerge around the notion of owning a specific customer segment across the full range of its interests and needs; owning specific products and services may no longer be so important. The authors urge businesses marketing to consumers to make the small investment required to "buy an option" on electronic communities in order to understand both their potential value and the radical changes they may cause.

Making Business Sense of the Internet

Shikhar Ghosh

For managers in large, well-established businesses, the Internet is a tough nut to crack. It is very simple to set up a Web presence and very difficult to create a Web-based business model. Established businesses that over decades have carefully built brands and physical distribution relationships risk damaging all they have created when they pursue commerce through the Net. Still, managers can't avoid the impact of electronic commerce on their businesses. They need to understand the opportunities available to them and recognize how their companies may be vulnerable if rivals seize those opportunities first.

Broadly speaking, the Internet presents four distinct types of opportunities. First, it links companies directly to customers, suppliers, and other interested parties. Second, it lets companies bypass other players in an industry's value chain. Third, it is a tool for developing and delivering new products and services to new customers. Fourth, it will enable certain companies to dominate the electronic channel of an entire industry or segment, control access to customers, and set business rules.

As he elaborates on these four points, the author gives established companies a systematic way to sort through the risks and rewards of doing business in cyberspace.

About the Contributors

Arthur Armstrong is director of development for McKinsey & Company's Business Technology Office, based in Stamford, Connecticut. He has served a broad range of clients in the telecommunications, media, and consumer goods industries on issues of strategy, organization, and performance. More recently he has advised clients in the financial services, media, and healthcare industries on their e-commerce strategy. He is the coauthor, with John Hagel III, of the book *Net Gain* (HBS Press).

Jim Botkin is an internationally-known business writer and public speaker. He is cofounder and president of InterClass, the International Corporate Learning Association, a consortium of 15 *Fortune* 500 companies exploring the knowledge business and knowledge communities. Dr. Botkin earned his M.B.A. and doctorate from the Harvard Business School. In addition to writing *The Monster Under the Bed* with Stan Davis, he is the author of *No Limits in Learning: A Report to the Club of Rome*, published in a dozen languages, as well as the forthcoming *Smart Business: Leveraging the Power and Potential of Knowledge Communities*.

Stan Davis is an independent author and speaker based in Boston. He is known as a visionary business thinker who advises leading companies and fast-growing enterprises around the world. Dr. Davis spends one day a week as senior research fellow at the Ernst & Young Center for Business Innovation in Cambridge, Massachusetts. He has written eight influential books, including *Blur, 2020 Vision, The Monster* *under the Bed* (with Jim Botkin), and the best-selling *Future Perfect*, which was the recipient of Tom Peter's "Book of the Decade" Award.

Philip B. Evans is a senior vice president in The Boston Consulting Group's Boston office, and worldwide coleader of BCG's Media and Convergence Practice, which focuses on the strategic implications of the economics of information. His client work is primarily focused on strategy in the media, information, and financial services industries. He was educated at Cambridge University and the Harvard Business School, and was also a Harkness Fellow in the Economics Department at Harvard. He writes on business strategy, and is currently writing a book (with Tom Wurster) for the Harvard Business School Press on the new economics of information.

Shikhar Ghosh is chairman and cofounder of Open Market, Inc., an Internet commerce and information publishing software company. Prior to leading Open Market, Ghosh was the CEO of Appex Corporation from 1988 to 1994. He was also a partner with the Boston Consulting Group, where he worked on assignments developing business strategy for *Fortune* 500 companies, including major long-distance, media, and communications companies. The Massachusetts Electronic Commerce Association recently named Ghosh one of the Top Ten Most Influential People in the Massachusetts electronic commerce community. He was recognized as one of 1996's "Best Entrepreneurs" by *Business Week*. He has an M.B.A. from Harvard Business School and holds an undergraduate degree from the University of Bombay, India.

John Hagel III is a principal at the Silicon Valley office of McKinsey & Company, Inc., and leader of McKinsey's Global Electronic Commerce Practice. His work is primarily with clients in the electronics, telecommunications, and media industries, with a focus on strategic management and performance improvement. Prior to joining McKinsey, he served as senior vice president for strategic planning at Atari; as president of Sequoia Group, a systems house selling turnkey computer systems to physicians; and as a consultant with the Boston Consulting Group. Mr. Hagel is the author of legal, as well as business books and articles, including *Net Gain* (with Arthur G. Armstrong) and the forthcoming *Net Worth* (both from HBS Press).

Charles Handy was for many years a professor at the London Business School. He is now an independent writer and broadcaster and describes himself as a social philosopher. Prior to joining the London

Business School, Handy worked at Shell International as a marketing executive, economist, and management educator. His main concern is the implication for society and for individuals of the dramatic changes that technology and economics are bringing both to the workplace and to our lives. His books on the organization and the future, including *The Age of Unreason* (HBS Press), *The Age of Paradox* (HBS Press), *Gods of Management, Understanding Organizations,* and *Beyond Certainty* (HBS Press), have sold over a million copies worldwide. His most recent books are *The Hungry Spirit* and *Waiting for the Mountain to Move.*

Marco Iansiti is a professor of technology and operations management at Harvard Business School. His research focuses on the management of technology and product development. He has worked as a consultant to several major *Fortune* 500 companies and he is a board member of the Corporate Design Foundation. His work has appeared in a variety of journals, including *Harvard Business Review, California Management Review, Research Policy, Industrial and Corporate Change, Production and Operations Management,* and *IEEE Transactions on Engineering Management.* He is the author of *Technology Integration* (HBS Press).

Robert J. Laubacher is a research associate with the Initiative on Inventing the Organizations of the Twenty-First Century at MIT's Sloan School of Management. The Initiative's scenarios project, which he heads, attempts to envision the range of alternative organizational forms that may emerge over the next twenty years. Mr. Laubacher has also undertaken research on the social aspects of highly-flexible, project-based work organizations. Prior to joining the Twenty-First Century Initiative, he worked as a strategy consultant and was researcher for *The Prize,* a Pulitzer Prize–winning history of the international oil industry. He was also executive producer of the independent feature film, *Home Before Dark.*

Alan MacCormack is an assistant professor at the Harvard Business School in the area of Technology and Operations Management. His research explores the management of technology and product development in rapidly changing environments. Prior to arriving at Harvard, Professor MacCormack worked as a management consultant for Ernst & Young and Booz•Allen & Hamilton, where he focused on manufacturing and operations issues for clients in the automotive and aerospace industries. Professor MacCormack received his D.B.A from the Harvard Business School and his M.S. degree from the MIT Sloan

School of Management. His work has appeared in a number of books and journals, including the *Harvard Business Review* and *Sloan Management Review*.

Thomas W. Malone is the Patrick J. McGovern Professor of Information Systems at the MIT Sloan School of Management. He is the founder and director of the MIT Center for Coordination Science and one of two founding codirectors of the MIT Initiative on Inventing the Organizations of the Twenty-First Century. Professor Malone's research focuses on how computer and communications technology can help people work together in groups and organizations, and on how new organizations can be designed to take advantage of the possibilities provided by information technology. Before joining the MIT faculty, Professor Malone was a research scientist at the Xerox Palo Alto Research Center (PARC). He has been a cofounder of three software companies and has consulted and served as a board member for a number of other organizations. He has published over 50 research papers and book chapters and has been frequently quoted in publications such as *Fortune, Scientific American,* and the *Wall Street Journal.*

Andrew McAfee joined the faculty of the Harvard Business School in Technology and Operations Management in 1998. His research focuses on understanding the impact of information technology on companies and their performance, and on strategies to maximize the benefits of IT. He was the recipient of a U.S. Department of Energy Integrated Manufacturing Fellowship for his doctoral research, which focused on enterprise information systems. His other research interest is a collaboration with Professor David Upton on designing and implementing improvement strategies for operations. McAfee, who is currently completing his D.B.A. at Harvard, graduated with dual M.S. degrees in mechanical Engineering and Management from MIT as a Leaders for Manufacturing Fellow.

Regis McKenna is chairman of The McKenna Group, an international consulting firm specializing in the application of information and telecommunications technologies to business strategies. McKenna consults, writes, and lectures on the social and market effects of technological innovation as applied to marketing theories and practices. McKenna worked with hundreds of entrepreneurial start-ups during their formation years including America Online, Apple, Electronic Arts, Genentech, Intel, Silicon Graphics, and 3Com. He is the author of *Relationship Marketing, Real Time* (HBS Press), and *The Regis Touch.*

James F. Moore is an author, strategy consultant, and investor. He is the founder and chairman of GeoPartners Research Inc., a strategy consulting and investment firm that serves many of the world's major high-technology companies. Moore is also engaged in *pro bono* work in health care, and social and economic development, in association with members of the Harvard School of Public Health and other organizations. His book *The Death of Competition: Leadership and Strategy in the Age of Business Ecosystems* is a best-seller and has become a classic of business strategy for the new economy. His pioneering article *Predators and Prey: A New Ecology of Competition*, reprinted in this volume, won the prestigious McKinsey Award for Management Article of the Year in 1993.

Jeffrey F. Rayport is an associate professor of business administration in the Service Management Unit at the Harvard Business School. His research is on the impact of new information technologies on service management and marketing strategies for business, with a focus on digital commerce in information-based and knowledge-intensive industries. As a consultant, Dr. Rayport has worked with corporations and professional practices in North and South America, Europe, Japan, and the Pacific Rim. His consulting work helps companies develop breakthrough service strategies in network-based or digital sectors of the economy.

John J. Sviokla is a partner with Diamond Technology Partners, a strategy consulting firm headquartered in Chicago, Illinois. Prior to joining Diamond, he was a professor at Harvard Business School. His research and consulting work has focused on electronic commerce and knowledge management; in particular, how managers can use the power of technology to create value for customers and extract value through superior financial performance. Dr. Sviokla has edited books and authored many cases and journal articles, including "Managing in the Marketspace" (coauthored with Jeffrey F. Rayport) for the *Harvard Business Review* and "Virtual Value and the Birth of Virtual Markets" in *Sense and Respond* (HBS Press, 1998). He is a frequent speaker, educator, and consultant to large and small companies around the world.

Don Tapscott is president of New Paradigm Learning Corporation and chairman of the Alliance for Converging Technologies. He is known as one of the world's leading cyber-gurus and was described by the *Washington Technology Report* as one of the most influential media authorities since Marshall McLuhan. A consultant and speaker on information technology in business, Tapscott consults to some of the world's largest corporations and his clients include the top executives of many *Fortune* 100 companies and other leading enterprises around the world. He is the author of several journal articles and books, including *Growing Up Digital: The Rise of the Net Generation, The Digital Economy: Promise and Peril in the Age of Networked Intelligence, Who Knows: Safeguarding Your Privacy in a Networked World,* and *Paradigm Shift: The New Promise of Information Technology.* Tapscott holds a B.Sc. in Psychology and Statistics and an M.Ed. specializing in Research Methodology.

David M. Upton is an associate professor at the Harvard Business School. He is faculty chair of Harvard's executive course on Operations Strategy and Improvement and has taught in the International Senior Managers program and the China-based Managing Global Opportunities program. His current research focuses on the issue of improvement of flexibility in manufacturing companies. Dr. Upton has published many journal articles on manufacturing, most recently in *Management Science, Harvard Business Review, California Management Review,* and the *Journal of Manufacturing Systems.* He is the author of the book *Strategic Operation: Building Competitive Advantage through Operating Capabilities,* written with Robert Hayes and Gary Pisano. He graduated with honours in engineering from King's College, Cambridge University and earned a master's degree in manufacturing from the same institution. He completed his Ph.D. in industrial engineering at Purdue in computer integrated manufacturing (CIM) systems.

Thomas S. Wurster is a vice president in The Boston Consulting Group's Los Angeles office and worldwide coleader of BCG's Media and Convergence Practice. He has extensive experience consulting to leading media and consumer companies, and to a wide variety of other clients in the areas of information, entertainment, telecommunications, and computing. He is a graduate of Cornell University, where he earned an A.B. in economics and mathematics with distinction and was elected to Phi Beta Kappa. He received his M.B.A. with honors from the University of Chicago and earned his Ph.D. in economics from Yale University. Mr. Wurster writes on media and strategy and is currently writing a book (with Philip Evans) for the Harvard Business School Press on the new economics of information.

Index